# Innovative Research in Library and Information Science

Book is Final Only ISBN Remain

# INNOVATIVE RESEARCH IN LIBRARY AND INFORMATION SCIENCE

*Editor*

**Mrs. Pankaj K. Bhardwaj**

**Ess Ess Publications**
New Delhi

# INNOVATIVE RESEARCH IN LIBRARY AND INFORMATION SCIENCE



**ISBN : 978-93-87698-01-7**

**First Published 2018**

Published by:
**Ess Ess Publications**
4831/24, Ansari Road,
Darya Ganj,
New Delhi-110 002.
INDIA
Phones: 23260807, 41563444
Fax: 41563334
E-mail: info@essessreference.com
www.essessreference.com

Cover Design by *Patch Creative Unit*

Printed and bound in India

*Dedicated to*

***My Parents***

**SH. JAI PARKASH SHARMA**

**SMT. KAILASH DEVI**

*AND*

***My Mama Ji & Mami Ji***

**SH. KRISHAN K. BHARDWAJ**

**SMT. ARCHANA BHARDWAJ**

# Contents

## PART II



## PART III

# Preface

In the earlier times, the libraries were having only printed books and some other printed material in their collection. At that time there was a small number of library users and they had limited needs. But now a days because of knowledge explosion and printing machine it has become a challenging job to maintain books in a library. It has become necessary to keep pace with time and to provide the necessary and relevant information and required material to the users without wasting time.

Today, in this progressive world, traditional libraries are being converted into automated libraries, digital libraries virtual libraries etc. Now almost all the libraries are working online. Now a days, many researches are being done in the every field of library and information science in the entire world. This book is related to research in all the fields of library and information science such as innovative technologies and services in libraries, digital libraries, library automation, cloud computing, library classification and knowledge management etc. By reading this book one can have knowledge about the use of recent innovative technologies in library and its services. In this book we have tried to provide all the relevant information about the library services in this electronic era, and it has been done by getting articles from various knowledgeable working librarians as well as teachers in different organizations, university from nook and corner of India to depict the working experience of the various libraries also. This book is divided into four parts according to their relevance.

Part one consists of Digital Libraries, Information Communication Technology and Web based Library Services, Innovative Technology and services in Libraries, use of RFID Technology in Library Management, Secure Access system of RFID.

Part Two Provides information about the knowledge management technologies, E-Learning and Virtual Learning to Smart Class, Public Library System and Services in North India, Information Literacy among PG Students and Bibliotherapy.

Part Three is having chapters on Historical perspective of Library Automation and Networking, Role of ICT's in changing Library Services in Universities, changing and Challenging Role of Academic Librarians in Digital Environment, Online and open Access resources in the field of Agriculture Science and Technology, Study of Digital Reference Services in Agriculture Libraries.

In the Fourth Part, Discuss about Library Classification its need and what is the purpose of cloud computing in Library Management and recent Trends in Library and Information Science Services, E-Resources Management in college Library, Academic Plagiarism: A Besetting Sin and Document reproduction.

I cannot move forward without paying my deep regards to Dr. Sanjay Kaushik (Deputy Librarian K.U. Kurukshetra) Who has always guided me in the field of Library and Information Science with deep sense of gratitude I must say that I cannot minimize the depth of respect to my "GURUJI" Dr. Sanjay Kaushik Ji. I will always remain indebted to him.

After joining in the field of Library and Information Science I came in contact with Dr. Mehtab Alam Ansari

(Associate Professor in A.M.U. Aligarh) it is just because of his worthy guidance that I have been able to write this book.

When a work is to be completed it requires the co-operation of many people. I am grateful to my husband Sh. Bhupender Bhardwaj without whose emotional co-operation I would not have been able to accomplish this work of mine. My special thanks to my son Harsh and Daughter Kanchan. I cannot forget the co-operation of my brother in law Mr. Umesh Bhardwaj, his wife Mrs. Poonam Bhardwaj and their lovely kids Aanchal & Jai. All family members provided me a healthy atmosphere at home.

I am very thankful to Mrs. Poonam Bhola Associate Professor, RDS, PG, College, Rewari for giving her valuable time and full co-operations in completing my work.

Undoubtedly, I am greatful to all paper contributors of this book.

Last but not the least my thanks are due to Ess Ess Publication for their untiring efforts in bringing out this book well in time.

**— Pankaj K. Bhardwaj**
*Librarian, RDS Public Girls College*
*Rewari, Haryana - 123401 (India)*

# Forward

The book entitled "Innovative Research in Library and Information Science" edited by Mrs. Pankaj K. Bhardwaj, contains a variety of chapters. Editing a book which has a range of themes authored by numerous persons is not a simple task. Editor take all the pains from contacting to different authors, sending reminders and finally judging the utility of contents of the chapters received from different background of the contributors.

As one may understand, all the above-mentioned tasks exhibits number of difficulties which need to be addressed by the editor of a book, Mrs. Pankaj Bhardwaj, however, has been able to remove them with courage and conviction.

We should never forget that writing a book on the theme mentioned above is not an easy job as the landscape of research in library and information science has been changing due to rapid developments in the field of Information and Communication Technology (ICT). Perhaps, due to this constantly changing scenario, Mrs. Pankaj has tried to collect chapters on a range of topics, an attempt, thus, to justify her work.

The world is changing fast and so also the demands of various segments of the society. Therefore, this book is written keeping in view a wide range of library and information science professionals, such as student of library and information science, faculty members, library staff and others.

We all know that challenges of family life are many and we often witness an expansion in the contour of these challenges with the passage of time. Furthermore, people living in extended family come across peculiar issues and challenges. However, Mrs.Pankaj Bhardwaj had continued to achieve one of her academic goals without neglecting her family responsibilities. Hence, the editor of this book deserves special kudos.

I wish author as well as readers of this book *a good luck*.

**Dr. Mehtab Alam**
*Associate Professor,*
*Department of Library Science,*
*Aligarh Muslim University, Aligarh*

# Introduction

The invited papers/chapters are edited according to the stringent editorial review process and included in this book.

The first chapter in this book having entitled as "Digital Libraries: Promises and Practices" written by Mr. Arulpragasam introduced digital libraries as a system providing users with coherent access to a very large, organized repository of information and knowledge about it, characteristics of digital libraries, various models, copyright issues, data protection and security, various Indian initiatives in digital library, how to build digital collections, preservation is explained and concluded that, the future of library and information services is closely linked to the electronic age, and the new technologies will create, collect, store, process and retrieve information and deliver across the globe.

Mr Jitendra Kumar Dubey in his chapter "Use of RFID Technology in Libraries: A New Approach to Library Management" presented an overview of RFID such as basic concepts, structure and components of RFID. The author also highlighted the functions, major standards, advantages and disadvantages of RFID technology, enumerated the difference between Barcode and RFID system. The review of the literature on RFID technology used in the libraries has narrated both worlds as well as Indian scenario. In the conclusion he said RFID speeds up book borrowing, inventorying and saves the time of the library staff to do more user-oriented services. RFID technology needs a lot of modifications to reduce the problem in implementation. Also work should be done to reduce the cost of tags to make it more approachable to school and college libraries.

Mrs Dhanawanti Sunil Bamane stressed the need of Information Communication Technology in her chapter entitled as "Information Communication Technology and Web-based Library Services", defined what is ICT, how it is helpful and what is the role of Information Communication Technology in the library, benefits of ICT, what are the web-based library services available in this digital era and concluded that, ICT has made remarkable impact on academic libraries and library services. It is learnt that use of ICT in the library has taken the prominent place in the education and research institutes.

Mr Anil Kumar Jharotia in his chapter on "Innovative Technologies and Services in Libraries: An Overview" presents a range of relevant and useful innovative technologies and services to implement in the libraries. The author focused on the technology's applicability for the library and not on the potential budgetary impacts of said technologies i.e., Big Data, RFID technology, QR code technology, social media. Use of social networking sites, mobile devices and mobile apps in library and information centres are provided in detail. At the end, he said that, in the near future, more and more people will be able to experience digital collections in the palm of their hand through a Smartphone with Apps.

Ms Pankaj K. Bhardwaj in her chapter "Use of RFID Technologies in Library Management" examines historical perspective of RFID, which plays a very vital role in reducing theft with less human efforts. Objectives and components of RFID, advantages and disadvantages of RFID, The fast transaction with RFID technology will make it easy to handle the circulation of books. It is said in the conclusion that, it has been proved that this technology reduces labour, costs and provides efficient results, which leads to dependable security and access control.

Pradeep Kumar Gupta and Abha Gupta in their chapter "RFID Based Secure Access System" highlighted an overview of RFID, such as basic concepts, structure and components of RFID. They also described the functions, advantages and disadvantages RFID system. In the conclusion they said about RFID speedly work in libraries, save the time of users and library professionals without any trouble in library tasks.

Mr Mohd Shikoh and Mr Mohd Imran Khan in their chapter "Public Library System and Services in North India: a new narrative of Sustainable Knowledge Management" enlightened the historical perspectives of public library system in India, highlighted the collection and administration various old public libraries such as Delhi Public Library, Khuda Bakhsh Oriental Public Library at Patna, Amir-Ud-Daulah Public Library, Lucknow, Rampur Raza Library, Rampur are discussed in detail. Finally, concluded with the future of public libraries in northern India.

Dr Pankaj Kumar Singh and Nibedita Choudhury in their chapter "Knowledge Management Technologies: A Great Survey" describes the Knowledge Management, its importance in undertaking to make a general survey on knowledge management technologies, how Knowledge Management can be utilized to the maximum benefit of mankind. At the end of the conclusion, it discussed various Knowledge Management Technologies.

Mr Nagda L D writes a chapter on "Knowledge Management" wherein it provides introduction, concepts, objectives and tools of Knowledge Management in Academic Libraries, role of library professionals in

Knowledge Management, skills needed by the Library and Information Science professionals, what is the need of Knowledge Management in libraries, Principles and components of Knowledge Management and various stages of Knowledge Management developments, barriers, significance is provided in this chapter. Concluded by saying Information professionals have to transform their roles as knowledge professionals. The role of librarians should not be limited to information keepers, but they must acquire the skills to be updated in order to intelligently and objectively face the efficient and effective knowledge management in academic libraries.

Ms. Reena Anand in her chapter on "Internet Literacy Among P.G Students: A Case Study" undertaken with a view to know the extent to which internet literacy is being put to use by students of Post Graduate course, and to what extent the students felt it helped them in furthering their cause and found that the usage pattern of internet searching, satisfaction levels of the available information services along with their authenticity, evaluation and implementation among Post Graduate students. It gives a snapshot of the Internet Literacy among Post Graduate students. Further, it shows that most of the users use the Internet services daily for accessing information quickly. It was found that a maximum number of users were satisfied with the use of the Internet and the information available on the net. Most of the users preferred Google.com search engine as their main source of information and concluded that the users have a positive attitude towards the Internet.

Dr Kunwar Surendra Bahadur written a chapter on "Bibliotherapy: An Introduction" basic definition of the term bibliotherapy and historical perspective is highlighted. Further, the author informs how bibliotherapy overcomes the personal problem of a reader. Both reader's advisory and bibliotherapy transaction involve librarians recommending books for patrons to read. At the end it provided effective bibliotherapy services for children's, guidelines for librarians, further recommended Public Libraries should strive, as their resources permit, to provide bibliotherapy to individuals and developmental bibliotherapy to groups.

"Brief Historical Background of Library Automation" written by Dr Mehtab Alam Ansari introduced to Library Automation, how Information Technology helped in the transformation of the library. The growth of networks followed by birth of the Internet and World Wide Web discussed in detail. What are the recent developments in library automation software is highlighted in this chapter.

Nisha in her chapter "E-Learning and Virtual Learning to Smart Class" presents importance of E-Learning and Virtual Learning. She described the need importance, characteristics and advantages of E-Learning and Virtual Learning.

Ms Naurin Ashraf highlighted the concept, definition of Library automation, followed by prominent aspects of library automation, historical background of library automation, renowned library networks available in India, need, purpose and factors responsible for library automation and networking is discussed in detail, furthermore components of library automation, stages, advantages and disadvantages, of library automation and networking described. Concluded with recent trends in library automation and Indian scenario of Library Automation and Networking in his chapter on "Library Automation and Networking: An Indian Scenario".

Dr S. M. Abbas in his chapter "The Role of ICTs in Changing Library Services in Universities" stressed the need for Information Communication Technology. ICTs have revolutionized the working style of most organizations nationally and internationally in the digital era. University libraries have no longer lagging behind in adopting ICTs advances for their management, services and information products. Because of this adoption, the services of university libraries have changed drastically from traditional to electronic. Furthermore, he said how these ICT's have changed the services of the university library is explained in detail. And concluded that, Internet has played a very significant role in providing universal access to information.

Dr Jayaprakash G HUGAR in his chapter on "Changing and Challenging Skills (Role) of Academic Librarian in Digital Environment" introduces the concept and definition of digital library, difference of traditional librarian and digital librarian, need of digital librarian, digital library requirements, how to do collection development in the digital library, types of digital resources, use of open source software's, what are the library services, role of the librarian in digital environment, skills required for information professionals and their scope, challenges faced by the digital librarian, followed by benefits of digital library services to the library as well as users, future of library professionals in digital era, how library website delivers the information to its users is highlighted. Besides, he also enumerated that, as information professionals, we must allow modification and familiarize ourselves to the introduction of innovative methods and systems in the future also.

"Online and Open Access Resources in the field of Agriculture Science and Technology" written by Dr Nirendra Kumar Pachauri and Dr P.K. Dixit introduced readers to the agricultural sector in India, how it is necessary to adopt innovative technologies to get more yield. What are the open access electronic resources available in the field of Agriculture is highlighted. Furthermore, they expressed that all these electronic resources, e-journals, institutional repositories and e-collection are playing a significant role in the research and development in the field of Agriculture and allied sciences.

Mr Narendra Kumar Patidar and Pradeep Kumar Gupta in their chapter "A study on Digital Reference Services in Agricultural Libraries" attempted to describe the paradigm of reference and information services in the digital library environment. Furthermore, highlights the different types of digital reference services, including various components such as email and web forms, Ask services, online chat reference, video conferencing, digital robots, and cooperative digital reference. At the end advantages and disadvantages of digital reference, services are described in detail.

"Library Classification: Need and Purpose" written by Mr Balaji A.Kamble introduced the Meaning and definition of library classification, main components of a library and its different types of collection, why classification is needed in the library, what is the purpose and how users can get help from it is discussed. Concluded with classification is one such activity which we believe every living being is bestowed inherently by nature and is being used by one and all in everyday activity.

Ms Uma Rani in her Chapter called "Cloud Computing in Libraries" focused on an introduction to cloud computing, characteristics, its model and how it is used in library services, and supplemented that, there is barrier to this service like its security and privacy. What is the cloud-based library services are available, advantages and disadvantages are examined. It is concluded that Cloud computing is latest and popular technology that act as an effective role in every department and organization in these Information Technology eras.

Mrs Urmila Rajendra Kadam in her chapter "Cloud Computing For Library Management" discussed what is cloud computing, its characteristics, types of cloud computing, how we can use this cloud computing in the library and information centre management, details of cloud computing facility providing companies are highlighted. Advantages and disadvantages of cloud computing with the examples are discussed. At the end, she insisted all the library professionals make cloud-based services as a reliable medium to disseminate library services to their users.

Mrs Jitamoni Bhattacharya and Miss.Niharika Sharma discussed the recent trends in cloud computing applied to library and information centre in their chapter on "Cloud Computing: A Recent Trend in Library and Information Science Services". Further, what are the models available, types of cloud computing, advantages and disadvantages of using cloud computing is emphasized. In the conclusion part authors opinioned that though cloud computing is still at a very nascent stage in the field of library and information science, but by looking at its popularity and increasing demand, it is very clear that in the coming years, it will be the primary platform satisfying all the requirements at an easy in library and information centers.

"E-Resource Management in College Library" by Mr Y. B. Koradur examined how electronic information resources are utilized by academic library users and specific trends that can be seen among the faculties and students. Definitions of electronic resources, what type of electronic resources available for the library users, how to manage these electronic resources in a college library, some of the important methods used for the e-resource management in the library is provided. And concluded his chapter by saying, with the help of emerging trends in electronic resources, now the college libraries are more digitally resourceful & also have started collecting information in the electronic modes.

Ms Meenakshi Gupta in her chapter on "Academic Plagiarism: A Besetting Sin" described, in academia, plagiarism by students, professors and researchers are considered academic dishonesty or academic fraud which leads to academic censure world's different institutions of higher learning defined plagiarism in different senses. Furthermore, she defined what is plagiarism followed by various definitions, types of plagiarism, main forms of plagiarism committed by students are discussed in brief in this chapter.

Dr Bramha Prakash Srivastava in his chapter on "Document Reproduction (Reprography And Micrography)" provided definition of reprography, what is the importance of reprography, what are the different types of reprography methods available highlighted, and concluded that the reprography service helps library to preserve rare and special material and collections from being stolen or mishandled and then maintain availability of the resources in the library.

**— Mrs. Pankaj K. Bhardwaj**

# PART-I

# 1

# Digital Libraries: Promises and Practices

**P. Arulpragasam**
*Librarian, Seva Sadan's College of Education*
*Ulhasnagar, Mumbai*

## INTRODUCTION

Working group of the U.S. information infrastructure technology and application (IITA) has defined "Digital libraries are systems providing users with coherent access to a very large, organized repository of information and knowledge".

The digital libraries may be defined as new way of carrying out the functions of libraries encompassing new types of information resources, new approaches to acquisition (especially with move towards accessing to different library collections and their sharing) new methods of storage and preservation, new approaches to classification and cataloguing intensive use of electronic systems and networks; and dramatic shifts in intellectual, organizational electronic practices. It is also known as distributed text-based computerized information system and services. It may have several provisions to access documents; those are of high value, mostly from outside organization. In a simple language, we can even defined digital libraries as libraries which have a number of machine-readable publication and facilities for remote access to several databases.

The era of digital libraries perhaps began with emergence of electronic journals. They are now becoming very popular, especially because of fast emerging networks. The networks help us to access such electronic journals from different servers. Electronic journals are easy distributed, less expensive and easy to search. It occupies less space, possibility of instant access, availability of information in the multimedia environment. It can stay for many years.

## WHAT IS A DIGITAL LIBRARY?

There is much confusion exists and the library community has used several different phrases over the years to denote this concept-electronic library, virtual library, library without walls-and it never was quite clear what each of these different phrases meant. "Digital library" is simply the most current and most widely accepted term and is now used almost exclusively at conferences, online and in the literature.

Nurnberg, et al, in the year 1995 notified as,

- from an information retrieval point of view, it is a large database
- for people who work on hypertext technology, it is one particular application of hypertext methods
- for those working in wide-area information delivery, it is an application of the Web
- and for library science, it is another step in the continuing automation of libraries that began over 25 years ago

Obviously a digital library is all of these things.

These different approaches will all add to the development of digital libraries.

Why this confusion arises that there are many things on the Internet that people are calling "digital libraries," which—from a librarian's point of view are not.

For example:

- for computer scientists and software developers, collections of computer algorithms or software programs are digital libraries.
- for database vendors or commercial document suppliers, their databases and electronic document delivery services and digital libraries.
- for large corporations, a digital library is the document management systems that control their business documents in electronic form.
- for a publisher, it may be an online version of a catalogue.
- and for at least one very large software company, a digital library is the collection of whatever it can buy the rights to, and then charge people for using.

A fairly spectacular example of what many people consider to be a digital library today is the World Wide Web. The Web is a gathering of thousands and thousands of documents. Many would call this huge collection a digital library because they can find information, just as they banking in a "digital bank" or buy any product in the web based market.

According to Clifford Lynch, one of the leading scholars in the area of digital library research states that,

*"One sometimes hears the Internet characterized as the world's library for the digital age. This description does not stand up under even casual examination. The Internet—and particularly its collection of multimedia resources known as the World Wide Web—was not designed to support the organized publication and retrieval of*

*information as libraries are. It has evolved into what might be thought of as a chaotic repository for the collective output of the world's digital "printing presses."* In short, the Net is not a digital library".

Thus in the light of above various examples of what are called digital libraries, As a starting point, we should assume that digital libraries are libraries with the same purposes, functions, and goals as traditional libraries— collection development and management, subject analysis, index creation, provision of access, reference work, and preservation. A narrow focus on digital formats alone hides the extensive behind-the-scenes work that libraries do to develop and organize collections and to help users find information.

Waters, 1998 defined as "*Digital libraries are organizations that provide the resources, including the specialized staff, to select, structure, offer intellectual access to, interpret, distribute, preserve the integrity of, and ensure the persistence over time of collections of digital works so that they are readily and economically available for use by a defined community or set of communities*".

With the assumption that digital libraries are libraries will not be is a single, completely digital system that provides instant access to all information, for all sectors of society, from anywhere in the world. This is simply unrealistic. This concept comes from the early days when people were unaware of the complexities of building digital libraries. Instead, they will most likely be a collection of disparate resources and disparate systems, catering to specific communities and user groups, created for specific purposes. They also will include, perhaps indefinitely, paper-based collections. Further, interoperability across digital libraries-of technical architectures, metadata, and document formats-will also only likely be possible within relatively bounded systems developed for those specific purposes and communities.

For library professionals this definition of a digital library and these characteristics are the most logical because it expands and extends the traditional library, preserves the valuable work that they do, while integrating new technologies, new processes, and new media.

## CHARACTERISTICS OF DIGITAL LIBRARIES

Digital libraries require undoubtedly digital technologies. The digital library is a heterogeneous library which contains hard copy to online systems. The full fledged digital library is one in which all the information is available in the digital form. This may however be difficult to achieve. Until recently, it consisted of mostly electronic documents, which are of reference type.

Now a day's most of documents are primary in nature. Further, queries received and processed re again of reference type nature. The digital records from both local and foreign databases maybe used respectively for several purposes. Thus, a considerable saving in effort, time and resources is possible.

Now the electronic media has revolutionized. The libraries are now information data banks, knowledge bases, text base. Right from morning to late night depend upon electronic media. Information is being converted into computer readable databases gradually to meet the present need of the society. The participating information generating agencies are now creating their publication direct on computers and they prefer to provide these products in multimedia environment.

A digital library if networked with the other library networks, World Wide Web or internet cans access world over by anybody at any point. It is a user friendly interface and provides intuitive means of presenting information, scanning the volumes inside the library itself and data gathered from sources on the World Wide Web can be downloaded for taking it home. This breakthrough opens up information to professionals and the private users worldwide from all the sectors like business, education, research etc. such virtual libraries give a feeling of conventional libraries to its users while they make use of them sitting in their home on their own computing system and connect to any known and unknown library in any part of the world through world wide web on internet.

The e-journal we see today is a transformation of this internet version, which is generally a pdf image and exact look-alike of the print with the text as a searchable file. while pdf is the preferred format for e-journals by a number of leading publisher and the libraries, a large number of publisher and third party aggeregators,,offer e-journals in a Varity of other formats.

Bibliographic databases, journals, and document delivery are the three information resource components of information access and delivery mechanisms.

With the emergence of e-journals, these three components likely to submerge, intergrating all three components through a common interface technology. The e-journal revolution and all scientific journals are accessible today free.

## ACCESS MODELS

Seamless access is a possibility through linking information resources like databases and e-journal / books distributed at several sites.

1. Remote Access (through internet )
2. On site - at the library
3. Access through Databases ( Link Model)

**IPR and Copyright Issues :** These are related to marketplace issues. Quality information whether it be text, statistics or multimedia, cost time, effort and money to create. Producers seek to recoup their investments.

**Data Protection and Security :** Some data, including financial transactions, national security and commercially sensitive data needs to keep secure. In addition, we may all rightly be sensitive about the data about us that is stored in a Varity of different databases.

**Bibliographical Control and Future of Archives :** libraries have a long been concerned to maintain an archival record of information. Electronic documents pose many problems for their archival maintenance. Electronic documents may be dynamic and changing. It can have access points but it is very difficult to decide what constitutes a document. What media should be adopted for archival maintenance is still a problem to be solved. Moreover, it is a matter of anxiety for how long a certain medium will survive.

## DIGITAL LIBRARY INITIATIVES IN INDIA

Digital library system is an emerging reality. Let us prepare for step forward and make our information access system fully capable of functioning as technological gateways. There are many digital library initiatives and projects and have formed various national schemes for jointly exploring key issues.

In Indian scenario the concept of establishing digital libraries is growing up. The modern computerised libraries where all library operation is being carried out by the specialised library application software and suitable hardware and software for creating and using library databases. These libraries are also having traditional collections but they are procuring digital resources in the form of e-journal subscriptions, bibliographical and Full Text Databases in CD/ DVD – ROM format, Online Databases of specialised subjects. These e-resources can be accessed over the Internet on IP based identification of users.

**The Indian Institute of Science :** IISc, Bangalore, is the focal point of this activity in India. The project is an International cooperative attempt to digitize a million seminal books in fields that happen to be in the public domain or are copyrighted but out of print, making them freely available on the web to anyone at any time anywhere in the world. This helps bridging the barriers in terms of time, geographical location and economic strata of the users.

The project aims at digitizing a million books by 2005 in India alone. When completed, it will be an important contribution in the field of digitisation in India. As part of this project, India launched the ' Digital Library of India Portal' in September 2002. While inaugurating the Portal, Dr. A.P.J. Abdul Kalam, then Hon'ble President of India in his inaugural address said "India has taken the initiative at the right time".

**National Mission for Manuscripts :** As a part of the digitization efforts, the Department of Culture, Ministry of Tourism and Culture, Government of India, also launched the National Mission for Manuscripts in February 2003. The main objectives of the mission are to facilitate conservation and preservation of manuscripts through training, awareness, and financial support to document, catalogue, and promote access to Indian manuscripts. The basic aim of the NMM is to encourage scholarship and research in the study of Indian languages and manuscriptology and to build a National Manuscript Library.

**The digital Library of India project** is hosted by the Regional Mega Scanning centre, Indian Institute of Information Technology, Hyderabad in co-operation with IISc, CMU, NSF, ERNET and MCIT for the Govt. of India and 21 participating centres. It has developed substantial collection of books, journals, newspapers and manuscript.

**Traditional Knowledge Digital Library (TKDL)** NISCAIR and the Department of Indian Systems of

Medicine and Homeopathy (ISM&H) have entered into an agreement for establishing a Traditional Knowledge Digital Library (TKDL) on Ayurveda. NISAIR is the implementing agency for this project. Its responsibility include providing user friendly software, setting up of TKDL hardware and software platform data entry, digitizing images of Slokas, making Directory on Traditional Knowledge Resource Classification (TKRC), popularizing the database and hosting the database in web/ portal

## NATIONAL SCIENCE DIGITAL LIBRARY

National Science (Digital) Library is a comprehensive collection of Science & Technology publications in the country offering services on a national scale. It subscribes to almost all S & T periodicals and has over 1,80,000 bound volumes of books and periodicals. National Science Library has also an Electronic Library Division with a rich collection of more than 5,000 foreign journals, conference proceedings etc and a large number of databases including CA, CAB, SCI, Current Contents, Indian Standards and US Patents. It has been planned to digitize the NSL holdings and to facilitate storing of digitised information in the emerging electronic library environment, eventually converting NSL into National Science Digital Library (NSDL), which would serve as a model for other libraries throughout the country.

**Digital Library Initiative at National Library of India, Kolkata :** National Library, Kolkata has initiated a mega project of digitisation of rare manuscripts, books, artifacts, paintings etc. in digital form. The digitised documents are saved in CD-ROM / DVD. For digitisation a very modern digital lab has been established and the work of digitisation has been given to a commercial firm, which is doing the job with the assistance from the in-house staff. This project is under progress and it this project is being funded by the Ministry of Culture, Govt. of India. In this way the rare library resources are being preserved and conserved by the National Library, Kolkata.

**Nalanda Digital Library Initiatives** by NIT, Calicut Library Nalanda, the Digital Library initiated in 1999 at National Institute of Technology Calicut, is one of the largest digital libraries in the country. NALANDA serves members of the campus in meeting their academic & research needs by providing timely & up-to-date information with value added services in all the areas of Science/Engineering/Technology. Apart from the Digital Library Reading Room, members can access the NALANDA from the entire campus. Following facilities are available. Online Journals eBooks in Engineering and Science eBooks in Arts and Humanities Electronic Theses and Dissertations Journal Back Volumes Collection Conference Proceedings Database & Handbooks Application Notes and Data Sheets Special Collections NITC Resources E-Learning Courses Computer Based CD ROM Tutorials Create Profile Login

ETDs Initiative in India (Electronic Theses ad Dissertations)

- Sodhgagotri Project initiated by INFLIBNET and
- Vidya Nidhi Projects are well known ETD initiatives.

The Library and Information Science Department of Mysore University has taken up the ambitious vidya nidhi project, which aims to create an online database of all doctoral theses and dissertations published by Indian Universities. Having successfully completed the pilot project sponsored by the Union Science and Technology Ministry's National Information System for Science and Technology (NISSAT), the university has begun work in the national task of digitizing theses in English and multiple Indian languages published every year by Indian Universities and autonomous educational institutions. Vidyanidhi is a portal of doctoral research in India. Implemented by Department of Library Science, University of Mysore. Supported by NISSAT, DSIR, Government of India, Ford Foundation and Microsoft India. It began as a pilot project in 2000 with support from government, the Ford Foundation and Microsoft India archive of dissertations, as well as a set of resources for doctoral research in India. Vidyanidhi also has strategic support from the UGC (University Grants Commission). The Vidyanidhi Digital Library has two layers: a metadata database and the full text of theses. More number of full text and bibliographic records of theses submitted to the universities in India have been hosted in Vidyanidhi.

**UGC - INFLIBNET** (Information & It became an independent Inter-University Centre is a major National Programme initiated by the UGC in 1991 with its Head Quarters at Gujarat University Campus, Ahmedabad.now situated its own building in Gandhinagar. INFLIBNET is involved in modernizing university libraries in India and connecting them through network for the optimum utilisation of information. INFLIBNET is promoting scholarly communication among academicians and researchers in India. It provides access to selected scholarly electronic journals and databases in different disciplines. The Centre also extends access to e-resources to all Govt. / Govt-aided colleges under a project entitled "National Library and Information Infrastructure for Scholarly Content (N-LIST)" funded by the MHRD. An Institutional Repository (IR) is a digital collection or archives of a university's intellectual output. Universities and other institutions are producing digital information base of their Ph.D. theses& dissertations, articles, reports, conference proceedings, lecture notes, presentational, audio-video records using open source software and making them available to their end users. The IR and ETD initiatives are quite remarkable and includes,

(i) **Shodhganga** : a reservoir of Indian Theses and Dissertations

(ii) **Shodhgangotri :** a repository of approved synopsis submitted to the universities for registration under Ph.D. programme

(iii) **OJAS@INFLIBNET** : An open access journal publishing platform

(iv) Shibboleth-based access management system

(v) Open source software R & D

(vi) **InfoPort :** A comprehensive gateway to all Indian electronic scholarly content

(vii) **e-PG Pathshala :** e-Content for PG Courses, and

(viii) Measuring Research Output of Indian Universities.

## DIGITAL LIBRARY OF ONLINE COURSEWARE

**NPTEL** The National Programme on Technology Enhanced Learning is an open courseware initiative by seven Indian Institutes of Technology (IITs) and the Indian Institute of Science (IISc). This initiative is funded by the Ministry of Human Resource Development (MHRD). The main objective of this programme is to enhance the quality of engineering education in the country by developing more than 200 curricula-based video and web courses.

**e-Gyankosh** Indira Gandhi National Open University (IGNOU) is a mega open university that offers distance and open education to millions of learners in India and other countries. It produces self-instructional study materials for various programmes and also hosts a number of educational broadcasting channels. IGNOU has initiated the establishment of a National Digital Repository of learning resources eGyankosh. This repository envisages to store, index, preserve, distribute and share the digital learning resources of open and distance learning (ODL) institutions in the country: The repository supports seamless aggregation and integration of learning resources in different formats such as self-instructional study materials, audio-video programmes, and archives of radio and television-based live interactive sessions.

## LIBRARY CONSORTIUM

Accesses to e-resources to Indian institutions are also available through Library Consortia. Some of the major example of library consortia in India which provides access to peer reviewed journals to their member institutions is as follows.

**UGC-INFONET :** The UGC-INFONET Digital Library Consortium was launched by A. P. J. Abdul Kalam, the then President of India, in December 2003. The consortium provides differential access to eresources to 206 universities and 150 institutions covered under associate membership prgramme. These e-resources covers almost all subject disciplines including arts, humanities, social sciences, physical sciences, chemical sciences, life sciences, computer sciences, mathematics, statistics, etc. It provides current as well as archival access to more than 8,500 core and peer reviewed electronic journals and ten bibliographic databases from 28 publishers, scholarly societies and aggregators, including university presses in different disciplines.

**INDEST-AICTE Consortium :** The Indian National Digital Library in Engineering Sciences and Technology (INDEST) Consortium was set-up by the Ministry of Human Resource Development (MHRD) in year 2003 to provide access to selected electronic journals and databases to technical institutions including IISc, IITs, NITs, IIMs and a few other centrally-funded Government institutions. It provides access to the entire peer reviewed journals and bbilographical database to its member institutions.

**NISCAIR Online Periodicals Repository :** (NOPR) to preserve its research journals, working papers, preprints, technical reports, conference papers and data sets in various digital formats. All publications can be access full-text in PDF format. National Science Digital Library (NSDL) was then established to provide comprehensive S&T information to students of science, engineering and technology. NSDL provides curriculum based access to e-books and lecture notes, presentation for the undergraduate students of science.

**DRDO E-journal Consortium :** Defense Research and Development Organization (DRDO), Ministry of Defense is the largest government funded research and development organization in India. The DRDO e-journal consortium was established on January 2009 to provide access to e-resources to S & T community of DRDO. The Consortium is governed by a Monitoring Committee having the representatives from different subject clusters and headquarters. It provides access to 628 full text e-journals to 50 DRDO Labs. JCCC service was added to facilitate access to contents of all the journal titles subscribed by DRDO labs.

**N-LIST :** The Project entitled "National Library and Information Services Infrastructure for Scholarly Content (N-LIST)", being jointly executed by the UGC-INFONET Digital Library Consortium, INFLIBNET Centre and the INDEST-AICTE Consortium, IIT Delhi, provides for access to scholarly content to colleges, universities as well as centrally-funded technical institutions through its four distinct components. The basic aims of the NLIST are , for

(i) cross-subscription to e-resources subscribed by the two Consortia, i.e. subscription to INDEST-AICTE resources for universities and UGCINFONET resources for technical institutions, and

(ii) access to selected e-resources to colleges. The N-LIST project provides access and download the e-resources to students, researchers and faculty from colleges and others through proxy server(s) installed at the INFLIBNET Centre.

**C-DAC Projects :** Centre for Development of Advanced Computing is the premier R&D organization of the Department of Electronics and Information Technology (DEITY), Ministry of Communications & Information Technology (MCIT) for carrying out R&D in IT, Electronics and associated areas. It conducts the following,

- Mega Centre for Digital Library
- Mobile Digital Library : Dware Dware Gyan Sampada
- Digital Library at President's House
- Digital Library at Nagari Pracharini Sabha Varanasi
- Digital Library at Uttaranchal
- GyanNidhi : Multilingual Parallel Corpus in Indian Languages
- Digital Library at Gujrat Vidyapeeth, Ahmedabad
- Digitization of Libraries

## ISSUES AND CHALLENGES IN CREATING DIGITAL LIBRARIES

Creating effective digital libraries poses serious challenges. The integration of digital media into traditional collections will not be straightforward like previous new media (e.g., video and audio tapes) because of the unique nature of digital information—it is less fixed, easily copied and remotely accessible by multiple users simultaneously. Some the more serious issues facing the development of digital libraries are outlined below.

## TECHNICAL ARCHITECTURE

The first issue is that of the technical architecture that underlies any digital library system. Libraries will need to enhance and upgrade current technical architectures to accommodate digital materials. The architecture will include components such as:

- high-speed local networks and fast connections to the Internet
- relational databases that support a variety of digital formats
- full text search engines to index and provide access to resources
- a variety of servers, such as Web servers and FTP servers
- electronic document management functions that will aid in the overall management of digital resources

One important thing to point out about technical architectures for digital libraries is that they won't be monolithic systems like the OPAC's with which librarians are most familiar. Instead, they will be a collection of disparate systems and resources connected through a network and integrated within one interface, most likely a Web interface or one of its descendants. For example, the resources supported by the architecture could include

- bibliographic databases that point to both paper and digital materials
- indexes and finding tools
- collections of pointers to Internet resources
- directories
- primary materials in various digital formats
- photographs
- numerical data sets
- and electronic journals

Though these resources may reside on different systems and in different databases, they would appear as though there were one single system to the users of a particular community.

Within a coordinated digital library scheme some common standards will be needed to allow digital libraries to interoperate and share resources.

## BUILDING DIGITAL COLLECTIONS

One of the largest issues in creating digital libraries will be the building of digital collections. There are essentially three methods of building digital collections

- **digitization**, converting paper and other media in existing collections to digital form .
- **acquisition of original digital works** created by publishers and scholars. For example electronic books, journals, and databases.
- **access to external materials** not held in-house by providing pointers to Web sites, other library collections, or publishers' servers.

Acquiring digital works and doing in-house digitization are expensive. By collective digital collection building would enhances resource sharing and increases the richness of collections to which users have access across.

## DIGITIZATION

Any fixed or analogue media such as books, journal articles, photos, paintings, etc, are converted into electronic form through scanning, sampling, or in fact even re-keying. An obvious obstacle to digitization is that it is very expensive. It is estimated that n the JSTOR project cost of digitizing a single page at $2 to $6 dollars US. Naturally one has to check with the digitations criteria for conversion of collections.

## METADATA

Metadata is another issue central to the development of digital libraries. Metadata is the data that describes the content and attributes of any particular item in a digital library. As cataloguing records that describe documents metadata is important in digital libraries because it is the key to resource discovery and use of any document. Anyone who has used Alta Vista, Excite, or any of the other search engines on the Internet knows that simple full-text searches don't scale in a large network. One can get thousands of hits, but most of them will be irrelevant. While there are formal library standards for metadata, namely AACR, such records are very time-consuming to create and require specially trained personnel. Human cataloguing is just too labour extensive for the already large and rapidly expanding information environment.

To simplify the most prominent Dublin Core, an effort to try and determine the "core" elements needed to describe materials. The first workshop took place at OCLC headquarters in Dublin, Ohio, hence the name "Dublin Core." The Dublin Core workshops defined a set of fifteen metadata elements in much simpler than those used in traditional library cataloguing. In the absence of metadata information access and use in a digital library is a huge problem.

## NAMING, IDENTIFIERS, AND PERSISTENCE

The fifth issue is related to metadata. It is the problem of *naming* in a digital library. Names are strings that uniquely identify digital objects and are part of any document's metadata. Names are as important in a digital library as an ISBN number is in a traditional library. They are needed to uniquely identify digital objects for purposes such as:

- citations
- information retrieval
- to make links among objects
- and for the purposes of managing copyright

Any system of naming must be developed and be permanent, lasting indefinitely.

## COPYRIGHT AND RIGHTS MANAGEMENT

Copyright is a major delicate issue in the digital library. Digital objects are less fixed, easily copied and remotely accessible by multiple users simultaneously. To overcome the libraries will have to develop mechanisms for managing copyright, mechanisms that allow them to provide information without violating copyright and rights management.

Some rights management functions could include for example,

- usage tracking
- identifying and authenticating users
- providing the copyright status of each digital object and the restrictions on its use or the fees associated with it
- handling transactions with users by allowing only so many copies to be accessed, or by charging them for a copy or by passing the request on to a publisher

## PRESERVATION

Another important issue is preservation, keeping digital information available in time without end. In the preservation of digital materials the real issue is technical obsolescence. Technical obsolescence in the digital age is like the deterioration of paper in the paper age. The preservation of digital information will mean constantly coming up with new technical solutions.

When considering digital materials, there are three types of "preservation" one can refer to,

- **The preservation of the storage medium :** Tapes, hard drives, and floppy discs have a very short life span when considered in terms of obsolescence. The data on them can be refreshed, keeping the bits valid, but refreshing is only effective as long as the media are still current. The media used to store digital materials become obsolete in anywhere from two to five years before they are replaced by better technology. Over the long term, materials stored on older media could be lost because there will no longer have the hardware or software to read them. Thus, libraries will have to keep moving digital information from storage medium to storage medium.

- **The preservation of access to content :** This form of preservation involves preserving access to the content of documents, regardless of their format. While files can be moved from one physical storage medium to another, what happens when the formats e.g., Adobe Acrobat PDF containing the information become obsolete? This is a problem perhaps bigger than that of obsolete storage technologies. One solution is to do data migration that is translating data from one format to another preserving the ability of users to retrieve and display the information content. But data migration is costly and there are as no standards for data migration and distortion or information loss is inevitably introduced every time data is migrated from format to format.
- **the preservation of fixed-media materials through digital technology :** This slant on the issue involves the use of digital technology as a replacement for current preservation media, such as microforms. Again yet no common standards for the use of digital media as a preservation medium.

## CONCLUSION

Digital libraries can be housed in a very small room and can house a large amount of data. The future of library and information services is closely linked to the electronic age, and the new technologies will create, collect, store, process and retrieve information and deliver across the globe.

With the availability of advanced information and communication technologies (ICTs) and information infrastructure, India becomes an active contributor in digital library movement by digitizing and providing free access of traditional knowledge, century-old publications and rare documents, theses and dissertation and journals available in Indian libraries. The Digital Library of India is one major initiative that is striving to create a truly digital library. Online availability of electronic theses through centrally-maintained digital repositories called ShodhGanga does not only provide easy access and archiving of Indian doctoral theses, it also helps in raising the standard and quality of the research. Open courseware and cross archive search services are also being developed by different organizations, including the apex higher education agencies. India has spearheaded the digital library movement in developing countries. As with most other technical developments in libraries over the years, we will have to move forward in small, manageable, evolutionary steps, rather than in a rapid revolutionary manner.

## REFERENCES

Ambati, V., N.Balakrishnan, Reddy, R., Pratha, L., Jawahar, C.V. (2006) The Digital Library of India Project: Process, Policies and Architecture. In: Second International Conference on Digital Libraries(ICDL).

Arora, J., & Bhattacharya, P. (2002). Digital library development in India: A case study of the development at the Central Library of IIT Delhi. In: Proceedings of the National Conference on Information Management in e-Libraries (IMeL 2002), IIT Kharagpur, Kharagpur.

Bhattacharya, P. (2004). Advances in digital library initiatives: a developing country perspective. The International Information & Library Review, 36 (3):165–175.

Das, Anup Kumar. (2008). Open Access to Knowledge and Information: Scholarly Literature and Digital Library

Initiatives,- the South Asian Scenario. (Eds: BimalKanti Sen and Jocelyne Josiah), UNESCO, New Delhi, 137.

Ghosh, Maitrayee (2009). E-theses and Indian academia: A case study of nine ETD digital libraries and formulation of policies for a national service. The International Information & Library Review, 41: 21-33.

Jeevan, V.K.J. (2004). Digital library development: identifying sources of content for developing countries with special reference to India. The International Information & Library Review, 36: 185–197.

Madalli, Devika P. (2003). Digital Libraries and Digital Library Initiatives, Digital Libraries: Theory and Practice, DRTC, Bangalore. National Task Force on Information Technology and National Development, Government of India. (1999). IT action plan (Part III): Long term national IT policy. Chapter 5: Content creation industry. Retrieved July 25, 2006 from *http://it-taskforce.nic.in/actplan3/chap5.htm*

Nazim, Mohammad and Devi, Maya (2008). Open access journals and institutional repositories: practical need and present trends in India. Annals of Library and Information Studies, 55.

P.K. Jain, P. K. and Babbar, Parveen. (2006). Digital libraries initiatives in India, the International Information & Library Review, 38:161–169. Registry of Open Access Repositories, available at: http://roar. eprints.org/

Sujatha, Gurram (2008). Digital library initiatives in India: a proposal for open distance learning. Proceedings of the IATUL Conferences. Availalbe at: *http://docs.lib.purdue.edu/iatul/2008/papers/25*

Gary Cleveland (2000). Digital Libraries: Definitions, Issues and Challenges. IFLA: UDT Core Programme. Retrieved from : *www.ifla.org.*

*www.nptel.iitm.ac.in*

*www.egyankosh.ac.in*

*www.inflibnt.ac.in/econ*

*www.nlist.inflibnet.ac.in*

*http://www.nlindia.org*

*http://cdac.in/index.aspx?id=mc_hc_digi_lib*

*www.dsl.drdo.gov.in/ejournals*

*www. Paniit.iitd.ac.in/indest*

*http://dli.iiit.ac.in*

# 2

# Use of RFID Technology in Libraries : A New Approach to Library Management

***Jitendra Kumar Dubey***
*(MA, Mphil, PhD., UGC-NET)*
*Librarian, Hindustan College of Science & Technology, Farah, Mathura (U.P.)*

**ABSTRACT**

To increasing the quality of library services and improving efficiency of operations, new technologies are always helpful. At present time, when all kinds of libraries are facing financial hardships the overwhelming reason for considering new technologies are the potential for cost saving in operations and management of materials flow. Radio Frequency Identification (RFID) is the latest technology to be used in library and information centers for theft detection system, make strong security and automatic identification surveillance. RFID provides easier and faster circulation work, security of reading materials, shelf check out, check in and stock verification. In this paper, the author provides basic concepts, structure and components of RFID. Author also reflects functions, major standards, advantages & dis-advantages of RFID technology. The review of literature on RFID technology used in the libraries is narrated both world as well as Indian scenario.

**Keywords** : RFID Technology, Tags, Standards, Security features, Self check in, Self check out etc.

## INTRODUCTION

Today, Libraries are moving towards latest technological environment due to the fulfilling users need and organizing learning resources. RFID system is the latest technology for implementation in libraries.

Radio Frequency Identification (RFID) was invented 1948, but its implementations started in 1970. The first U.S. patent for an active RFID Tag with rewritable memory was obtained by Mario E. Cardullo on January 23, 1973. In 1973 Charles Walton, a Californian industrialist, received a patent for a passive transponder that was used to unlock a door without a key. Then Walton licensed the technology to a lock making company called Schlage and RFID technology is another form of automated identification system, which is similar to bar codes. In India, RFID technology was developed in the 1940 for defence applications. First time it was used for commercial purpose in 1980 for cattle tracking application. The first library suppliers started to market their in the mid 1990's.

In this technology wireless radio communications is used to uniquely identify objects or people and one of the fastest growing automatic data collection technologies. RFID can be used as a data carrier, with information being written and updated to the tag on the fly. RFID systems carry data on tags and retrieve data by machine readable means to satisfy particular application needs.

RFID is a combination of radio-frequency and microchip. RFI chips are very small in size and can be added every kind of document and can be read and updated from a distance. RFID is the latest technology to be used as theft detection system, fast circulation.

## CONCEPT OF RFID SYSTEM

The concept of RFID can be simplified to that an electronic barcode and can be used to identify, track, sort or detect library holdings at the circulation desk and in the daily stock maintenance process. RFID based system have been implemented for efficient document tracking purpose throughout the libraries that combine, easier and faster charging and discharging of documents, security of materials, inventorying, stock verification and shelf handling.

## BARCODE TECHNOLOGY VS. RFID TECHNOLOGY

RFID is an identification technology. It does the same job as barcode but offer potentially a lot more along with smart cards and magnetic strip technology and a host of others, this is a method of automating our need of data.

Barcode is a fundamental technology for library operations. It provides the coupling between the information system and the physical flow of library materials. In application at the circulation desk, barcode technology has been proven to the robust, reliable and efficient.

The main differences between Barcode and RFID are:

| S. No. | RFID | Barcode |
|---|---|---|
| 1 | More Durable | Limited lifetime due to printing |
| 2 | Can be read and write | Read only |
| 3 | RFID tags can be read at much greater distance | The range to read a barcode is much less |
| 4 | Multiple items can be read simultaneously | Single item scan only |

| | | |
|---|---|---|
| 5 | No line of sight is required to either active RFID or passive RFID | Needs direct line of sight to the printed barcode |
| 6 | RFID readers can interrogate or read RFID tags much faster | Reading of barcode take more time |
| 7 | RFID tags are typically more thick, since the electronic components are better protected in a plastic cover and can be implanted book itself | Line of sight requirement also limit the thickness of barcodes as well as the usability of barcodes because since the line of sight is required the printed barcode must be exposed on the outside of the book. |
| 8 | Stock verification process made easier as no need of taking the books out from shelf. You can read multiple books from the shelf at a time | Stock verification takes more time because of each book has to take out from shelf and then scanned with the scanner |

## COMPONENTS OF RFID

Generally, a RFID system mainly consists of four components i.e. the tag, the reader, Antenna ( RFID Gates) and server but a RFID system for library contain of eight components i.e. RFID tags, a shelf check-out and check in stations, staff check-out station, a self-return of book drop with an automatic check-in feature, a tagging station, a set of security gates. A shelf scanner for inventory and administrative station

**1. Tags :** Tags are the heart of an RFID System, because they store the information that describes the object to which it is installed. Specific object information is stored in the memory of tags and is accessed via the radio signal of RFID readers. Data is transferred between a tag and a reader via low power radio waves. A transceiver sends a signal to the RFID tag to retrieve information. The transceiver then reads the signal, converts it to a digital format, and transmits it to a designed application such as an inventory management system.

**Fig. 1. RFID Tag**

RFID tags can be categorized by the capability to read and write data. This leads to following three classes:

**1. Read Only :** These tags were used in the beginning of the RF technology. The memory of such tags is not more than 96 bits. These tags are used only for the item identification more similar to EM tags.

**2. Write Once Read Many (WORM) :** This type of tag is manufactured with no data written in to the memory. Data can then either be written by manufacturer or by the user – one time. Following this no further writes are allowed and the tag can only be read. Tags of this type usually act as simple identifiers.

**3. Read and Write (R/W) :** This is the most flexible type of tag, where users have access to read and write data into the tags memory. They are typically used as data recorder and therefore contain more memory space than what is needed for just a simple id number.

*i.* ***Read-Write (with on board sensors)*** **:** These tags contain on board sensors for recording parameters like temperature, pressure and motion, which can be recorded by writing in to the tags memory. As sensor readings must be taken in the absence of a reader, the tags are either semi-passive or active.

*ii.* ***Read-Write (with Integrated Transmitters)*** **:** These are like miniature radio devices which can communicate with other tags and devices without the presence of the reader. This means that they are completely active with their own battery power source.

RFID tags are basically active or semi active and passive in nature.

**Active Tags** are battery powered devices that have an active transmitter. Unlike passive tags, active tags generate RF energy and apply to the antenna. This autonomy from the reader means they can communicate at the distance of over several KMs.

**Passive Tags** are activated through the radio frequency. The performances of such tags are less than the active tags. But due to cost effectiveness these tags are most used by the librarians in worldwide.

## RFID TAGS FREQUENCIES

Frequency and ranges of the tag varies from tag to tag. It depends on the size and quality of the tag. The standard ranges are as under:

| | | | |
|---|---|---|---|
| Low Frequency (LF) | 125-134.2 KHz | Up to 18 inches | Passive Tags |
| High Frequency (HF) | 13.56MHz | Up to 18 inches | Passive Tags |
| Ultra High Frequency (UHF) | 869-915MHz | Up to 20 feet | Active Tags |
| Microwave Frequency (MWF) | 2450MHz | Up to 06 feet | Active Tags |

KHz is for Kilo Hertz, MHz is for Mega Hertz

Most of the libraries are using HF (High Frequency) Tags due to their performance and cost effectiveness.

### 1. Selection of Tags

Choosing the right tag for particular RFID

applications is an important task and while selecting tags following factors should take into account:

- Size of the document where tag has to fit
- How close the tags be to each other
- Durability
- Reusability of the tag
- Resistance to harsh environment
- Exposure to different temperature ranges
- Communication distance
- Influence of the materials such as metals and liquids

**2. Readers (Sensors)**

An RFID reader is a device that is used to interrogate an RFID Tag. The reader has an antenna that emits radio waves; the tag responds by sending back its data. A number of factors like frequency used for identification, the antenna gain, the orientation and polarization of the reader antenna and the transponder antenna, as well as the placement of the tag on the object can affect RFID system's read range.

Depending on mobility, RFID readers are classified into two different types: Fixed RFID and Mobile RFID. Readers in RFID library are used in the following ways:

- **Conversion station :** where library data is written to the tag
- **Staff work station at circulation :** used to change and discharge library materials
- **Self check-out station :** used to check out library materials without staff assistance
- **Self check-in station :** used to check in library materials without staff assistance
- **Exit sensors :** to verify that all material leaving in the library has been checked out

- **Book Drop Reader :** used to automatically discharge library materials and reactive security.
- **Sorter and conveyor :** automated system for returning material to proper area of library.
- **Hand-held reader :** Used to inventorying and verifying that material is shelved correctly.

**Fig. 2. RFID Management System in Libraries**

**3. Antenna**

Antenna is the most important device of the RFID system. Antenna is responsible for generating the radio-frequency in passive tags. The reliability of the RFID system is depending upon the performance of the antenna used.

**4. Server**

It is the communication gateway among the various components of the RFID System. Server is the soul of the system; therefore, it must be of latest configuration with all security software. Other equipment are also used in the RFID system like RFID label printer, slip printer etc.

## RFID STANDARDS

The electromagnetic spectrum on which RFID resides is regulated by local govt. bodies. The International Organizations for Standardizations and EPC global have been very active in developing RFID standards. There are two ISO standards designed for library RFID systems; ISO: 18000 mode-2 and ISO: 15693.

The current standard ISO: 15693 was not designed for the item-level tracking done in libraries. Yet most library RFID tags follow this standard. ISO: 15693 was designed for supply chain applications. It defines the physical characteristics, air interface and communication protocol for RFID cards. The emerging standard for library RFID solutions is to employ a frequency of 13.56MHz.

## BENEFITS OF RFID SYSTEMS

**1. Fast Circulation :** The use of RFID reduces the amount of time required to perform circulation operations. The most significant time savings attribute is that information can be read from RFID tags much faster than from barcodes and that several items in a stack can be read at the same time. There can be as much as a 50 percent increase in output.

**2. Self Check-Out / Check-in :** Self-check systems have become very popular with both library user and staff. RFID self check systems allow user to check-in or check-out several books rather than just one at a time. Self check systems reduce the number of staff needed at the circulation desk. The unit has a simpler interface, which can make it easier for user to serve themselves. Circulation staff be free to perform other public service work.

**3. High Reliability :** Security is another aspect of

library operations that may be improved with RFID based security systems. No additional device is needed to install for security if we are using RFID system, A single tag can be used for identifying items and securing them. As users leave the library, the tags are read to ensure that the item has been checked out. The theft detection rate of RFID is high as compare to other such device.

**4. High-Speed Inventorying :** A unique advantage of RFID system is their ability to scan books on the shelves without removing them out from the shelf. A hand-held inventory reader can be moved rapidly across a shelf of books to read all of the unique identification information. Using wireless technology, it is possible not only to update the inventory, but also to identify items which are out of proper order.

**5. Automated Materials Handling :** Another application of RFID technology is automated materials handling. With the help of this application library material can be divided into different categories, As a result it reduces the amount of staff time required to ready material for re-shelving.

**6. Long Life of RFID Tag :** Finally, RFID tags last longer than barcodes because these are placed inside the document and thus chances of tear off or spoiling of tags is less as compare barcodes.

## LIMITATIONS OF RFID SYSTEMS

There are some limitations also in the RFID. Some of these are as follows:

1. Tags and readers are still too expensive.
2. Licensing and maintenance costs for using hardware and software are high and integration option limited.
3. The RFID tags are typical affixed to the inside back cover of the book, which can be easily removed and threaten the security gates.

4. Lack of standards and protocols
5. Blocking the RF wave is easily done by anybody through ordinary aluminum foil/Mylay
6. It is also possible to compromise the RFID system by placing two books against one another so that tags overlays another that may cancel out of signal.
7. Item with odd shapes and metal components, such as CDs, DVDs, , are stretching the creativity of vendors of RFID systems for libraries.
8. RFID System alternatively reduces staff and patron interaction, so that proper interaction can not be maintained among them.

## GUIDELINES FOR IMPLEMENTATION OF RFID IN LIBRARIES

Because libraries are implementing RFID systems, it is important to develop best practices guidelines to utilize the technology in the best way. The following guidelines for library may be concerned:

- The library should be open about its use of RFID technology including providing publicity available.
- Documents stating the rationale for using RFID, objective of its use and associated policies and procedure and how to with questions.
- Only authorize personnel should have access to the RFID system.
- No personal information should be stored on the RFID tag.
- Information describing the tagged item should be encrypted on tag even if data is limited to a serial number.
- No static information should be contained on the tag that can be read by unauthorized readers.
- All communications between tag and reader should be encrypted via a unique encryption key.

- All RFID readers in the library should be clearly marked.

## STATUS OF IMPLEMENTATION OF RFID SYSTEM IN INDIAN LIBRARIES

The situation of implementation of RFID system in Indian libraries is not good due to costly project. All types of libraries are not able to afford the cost of RFID system. Some government institutions like IIM's and IIT's, NISCAIR, CSIR, NASSDOC, DESIDOC,SENDOC and Some Central/ State University Libraries have deployed RFID system in their libraries for automated charging and discharging of reading materials and library theft detection etc. but college libraries, public libraries, private institutions libraries have not sufficient fund for implementation this system. So, Government of India and State government agencies should take initiatives in this direction

## CONCLUSION

It is clear that RFID system is a comprehensive system to meet both the security and materials tracking needs of a library. RFID in the library is not a threat if best practices, guidelines followed. It speeds up book borrowing, inventorying and frees staff to do more user – services tasks. While library RFID systems have a great deal in common with one another, including the use of high frequency, passive read write tags, lack of standard and compatibility of tags produced by different vendors are some of the major problems in implementation of RFID in libraries. Current standard ISO 15693 apply to container level tagging used in supply chain applications and do not address problem of tracking hot listing. The newer tags are capable of resolving many of the privacy problems of today's tag. However, no library RFID products are currently available using the new standard. It is concluded that RFID technology needs lot of modifications to reduce problem in implementation. Also work should be done to reduce the cost of tags to make it more approachable.

## REFERENCES

1. Boss, Richard W. (2004), RFID Technology for Libraries, *http://www.ala.org*
2. Coyl, K. (2005), Management of RFID in Libraries. Journal of Academic Librarianship,Vol.3No.5, PP486-489.
3. Chachra, Vinod and Mcpherson, Daniel (2003), Personal Privacy and Use of RFID Technology in Libraries, *http://www.vtls.com*
4. Hussain, A. (2007), RFID in Libraries, IASLIC Bulletin. Vil.52 No.1, pp 49-56.
5. Ispen, E. (2004), Librarians focus on RFID, available at *http://www.rfidjournal.com/article/view/829.*
6. Kumar, R. (2008), Role of RFID in Academic libraries, Proceeding of the 6th International CALIBER, 28-19 February, University of Allahabad, Allahabad, pp120-126.
7. Yu, S.C. (2008), Implementation of an innovative RFID application in Libraries, Library Hi Tech, Vol26 No.3, pp.398-410.
8. *http://www.rfid-library.com*
9. RFID for Libraries http://www.biblio-tech.com.
10. Shahid, Syed Md, (2005), Use of RFID Technology in Libraries: A New Approach to Circulation, Tracking, Inventorying and Security of Library materials, *http://www.webpages.uidaho.edu.*
11. http://*www.libsys.co.in*
12. RFID Systems: Its Application in Libraries. Indian Journal of Information, Library and Society (IJILIS), Cuttack. V.22, No. 1-2, January – June, p75-81.
13. Klaus, Finkenzeller. RFID Handbook, 2nd ed.- translated by Rachel Warrington. John Wiley, 2003.
14. *http://www.iso.ch*
15. *http://www.hightechaid.com/standards/RFID_Standards_Sc31.htm*

# 3

# Information Communication Technology & Web Based Library Services

***Dhanawanti Sunil Bamane***
*Librarian, Jaysingpur College, Jaysingpur*

## INTRODUCTION

The information technology challenges the various field in the society. The invention of computer made historical changes in every sphere of human life. Every walk of life, information technology is used with great speed ICTs are a powerful to extending educational opportunities in education especially in higher education in country like India, where the population is scattered, rural and traditional. IT is the acquisition, processing, storage and dissemination of vocal pictorial, textual and numerical information by a micro electronics- based combination of computing and telecommunication. Communication technology implies the knowledge, skills and understanding needed to exchange information verbally or non-verbally. The explosion of information through the WWW and human interaction through wireless devices and mobile telephony is increasing day by day.

**DEFINITION**

Information Communication Technology is-

"diverse set of technological tools and resources used to communicate and to create, disseminate, store and manage information".

"Information Communication Technology means the Technology which send the proper information from the proper place to the another place on to the proper time using the means of communication."

The means like telephone, telegraph, broadcasting, television, faxing. Projector, computer, tape recorder, VCR, C.D. Player and mobile are the spectacular ones to connect man to man in the world of information technology.

ICT consists of three words i.e. information, communication and technology.

I = Information = it is the behavior initiating stimulus between a sender and receiver. Information is in the form of symbols arranged in an order and they are coded for representation of data.

C= Communication= it is meaningful conversation between two or more peoples is called as a communication.

T=Technology=new digital technology means technology. It is a set of technological tools and resources to create, disseminate bring value addition and manage information communication.

Information and communication technologies (ICTs) which include radio and television, as well as newer digital technologies such as computers and the Internet

— have been proven as potentially powerful tools for educational change and reform. When used appropriately, different ICTs can help expand access to education, strengthen the relevance of education to the increasingly digital workplace, and raise educational quality by helping make teaching and learning into an active process connected to real life

## ROLE OF ICT'S IN LIBRARIES

With the application of ICTs in libraries, access to information has become more dynamic for the scholars who need to gain specialized knowledge. Modern ICT tools has changed traditional teaching methods and made distance learning education more effective and efficient by providing multimedia data repositories which can serve as continuously changing up-to-date information. ICTs facilitate closer cooperation among libraries and distant learning communities. The librarian can provide various services by making use of ICT in the library. Using ICT librarians are making available the information required by readers. It is possible to make database and classify different types of information with the help of ICT. The librarian is expected to be well versed in using this technology with changing time. By using electronic media, the librarian should explore various resources, while preserving the valuable reading material. Using library network benefits like resource sharing can be given to the library members. The readers will also have an access to the main librarian. The librarian can perform the important task of Bibliographic Control with the aid of resource sharing and library network. It is the task of the librarian to explore the new ICT techniques, enabling the techno savvy generation to acquire information and ultimately knowledge.

Information technology is being increasing used in all fields of life. It works on three different levels. Initially database of information is prepared. Then the information is operated with the help of a software, and then it is finally made available to the readers. Librarians should assist their readers in enhancing the skills of locating the source of information. They should also assist the readers in the methods of retrieving information, managing the information, evaluating the information sources etc. They should also create an awareness about Right to Information. In this manner the librarian can help in raising the quality of education.

## BENEFITS OF ICT IN LIBRARY

1. The world book list is made available on internet.
2. Readers are provided with information of books and other materials with union catalogue system.
3. Service regarding information is also extended with online system.
4. ITC helps to provide easy and precise service of information.
5. It brings into use the new technique of scanning , security system i.e. RFID system ,3M- tatal tape , bar-coding etc.
6. Photography for rare collection.
7. The concept of virtual classroom is received.

## WEB BASED LIBRARY SERVICES

### OPAC

After computerization of the library ,by the means of OPAC that is the readers comes to know about the collection in the library. This system enables to save the space required for catalogue cards. Hence minimum space is used.

### WEB OPAC

It is stand alone version of OPAC which can be used within network of library or through internet also for searching library collection. WebOPAC is the Online

Public Access Catalogue which allows users avail the services of the library.

## DIGITAL LIBRARY

In the field of Digital library, scanned printer matter, photos, digital audio video data etc. material can be used. Also, information sources like online database, CD ROM/ DVD ebooks, multimedia, encyclopedia can be made available to readers with the help of digital library ,the aim of paperless library has been achieved.

## LIBRARY NETWORKING

It is possible to provide any type of information and to make reading material available to the readers with the help of library networking. Important things like reading material and information are how easy to access. It has also became easier to curtail manpower and still effectively manage resources sharing, acquisition and circulation. Library networking has made Bibliographic control as easy task.

## LIBRARY WEBSITE

Most of libraries provide their information on website. Various kinds of services can be offered through website like link to databases, subject gateways. It is also used to promote and market the library services

## E-REFERENCE SERVICES

Some services such as SDI (Selective dissemination of information) or Current Awareness Services (CAS) and virtual reference desks, announcements of new acquisitions and other reader advisory services can be made easier through the internet.

## ERESOURCES

Eresources are the reading material or information that has been converted into electronic or digital format. Such digitized information can be explored by the means of ebooks, ejournals or enews.

## INSTITUTIONAL REPOSITORIES

Institutional repositories are publications that originate locally from within the university community such as theses, dissertations, reports, conference papers and seminar papers.

## SOCIAL MEDIA NETWORKS

Social media networks have become a powerful tool to encompass multitudes of readers. Libraries ar using media like twitter, facebook, whatsapp, etc. to disseminate the knowledge and information about libraries and reading material among readers.

## DIGITAL REFERENCE SERVICES

Some services such as SDI (Selective dissemination of information) or Current Awareness Services (CAS) and virtual reference desks, announcements of new arrivals can be made easier through the internet. Users can have online interaction with the reference staff. This is also called as virtual reference.

## ELECTRONIC DOCUMENT DELIVERY

Name it self suggests that document is delivered using electronic device. Libraries send documents through electronic networks that can deliver documents in various formats like PDF, word, jpg straight to users' desktops.

## CONCLUSION

Present day library can't fulfill the needs of users without a proper internet connection due to its various applications. The cost of printed information resources is increasing every year. It is not possible to every library to acquire theses resources. Library services provided in traditional libraries are getting new face and provided with comfort, ease and speed with the help of ICT. ICT has made remarkable impact on academic libraries and library services. The traditional print library and traditional library services will not disappear. But, as librarians, we must accept and adapt to the introduction of new techniques and systems. . College libraries can use today a wide variety of technology options that exist now. Fruitful results can, however, be obtained only when we make the best use of the technologies. Use of ICT in the library has taken the prominent place in the education and research. Libraries are also given due importance to substantiate the teaching; learning and research activities of the institutes.

## REFERENCES

1. Godia, Kundan (2007). Electronic Services in Library and Information Science. New Delhi: Adhyayan Publishers & Distributors.
2. Kumar, P.S.G. - Information Technology Basics, B.R.Publication, Delhi
3. Gupta, R. K. & Usha, Pawan. Eds. Library and Information Services. Jaipur: R.B.S.A. Publishers.
4. Mittal, Savita. Digital Library Resources 2005 New Delhi Ess Ess Publication.
5. Cleveland, Gary. Digital Libraries : Definitions, Issues and Challenges. http://www.ifla.org/udt/op (12/6/1998). 8 pp.
6. Saxena, Archana., 2009: *Electronic Publishing: Impact of ICT on Academic Libraries*, Retrieved from https://www. *crl.du.ac.in/ical09/papers/index_files/ical-117_142_311_2_RV.pdf*
7. Remeikis, L. A. (Winter, 1996). Knowledge Management — Roles for Information Professionals. Business and Finance Division Bulletin. SLA, 41-43.
8. *http://www.google.com*
9. What are digital Libraries. *http://www.clir.org/pubs/issues/issuesorg.html#dlf*

# 4

# Innovative Technologies and Services in Libraries: An Overview

***Anil Kumar Jharotia***
*Librarian, Tecnia Institute of Advanced Studies,*
*GGSIP University, Delhi*

## INTRODUCTION

Librarians should lead the way in technology use among fellow residents and gain more time for the most important activity: helping patrons. Since the main mission of most libraries is to offer equality of access to information for every citizen, then why not be a trendsetter in digital use and implement innovative technologies and services in libraries.

This chapter presents a range of relevant and useful innovative technologies and services to implement in the libraries. We focus on the technology's applicability for the library and not on the potential budgetary impacts of said technologies i.e., Big Data, RFID technology, QR code technology, Social Media use in library service etc.

## SOCIAL MEDIA

The growing use of social media such as Linkedin, Facebook, Twitter, Google+ etc. by users in the 21$^{st}$ century social media play a vital role in libraries and providing new challenges for libraries to keep up to with the growing needs of their users. This paper describes the role of social media in libraries. In this digital era, data can be accessed from anywhere, at any time without borders. Social media involves social relations amongst people who have some type of relationship or affiliation. It encompasses Blogs, Facebook, Social marks, Podcasting, Mash-up, YouTube, RSS, Flickr, Tag Cloud, Folksonomy, Wikis, MySpace, Twitter, among others. It may be conceptualized as socio-technical arrangements incorporating technologies that support such activities. Social media ethical concerns include identity, privacy, surveillance, friending, and user exploitation. At present, the ethical issues associated with social media spaces are not being tackled. Most crucially for our study, the ethical values embodied by the technologies themselves are not called into question. Social media ethics are informed by normative theories that aim to develop a set of best practices governing human conduct. Normative theories view ethics as a human concern.

Today libraries are using latest trends to make their services popular & user friendly especially in western countries. These trends are now also catching up with Indian library professionals. Everybody is now talking about Lib 2.0 applications. One of them is Social Media.

## LIBRARIANS' ROLE ON SOCIAL MEDIA

Time is rapidly running out for librarians to confront the ethical issues inherent to social media of the benefit of the information users. Social mediums are controlled by third parties; they represent a space whose owners create the parameters for what is possible. Even on MySpace, where users can use html to customize most profile features, including adding new graphics and videos, there are limits to how much control they can truly exert. While most libraries do not have the budget for services advertisements, many librarians are beginning to recognize the power of these social media and are working hard to integrate them into their outreach efforts by creating profiles that allow them to interact with their patrons in the new space.

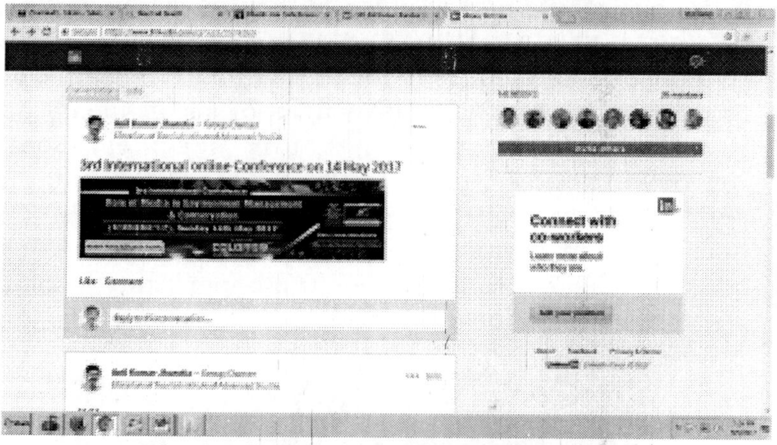


**Fig. 1. Librarian can share information of conference on LinkedIn**

**Fig. 2. 'Library Dot Com' group on Facebook for Library Professionals**

The librarian can make groups on social media and marketing library events on social media to aware library professionals about library seminar, conference, workshops.

## SOCIAL NETWORKING SITES (SNS) AND LIBRARIES

Social Networking sites are usually used for keeping in touch friends and families by posting their updates, photos, blogs, chatting and also for enjoyment and relaxation. But the schools and libraries can work together to integrate positive uses of social media into their classroom, programs, and services. Social Networking Sites (SNSs) provide an online space for people to share their opinions with others and to participate in a variety of activities. Social networking sites are also offering libraries the opportunity to reach out to its clients for the libraries.

**Fig. 3. Social Networking Sites (SNS)**

## USE OF SOCIAL NETWORKING SITES FOR MARKETING

The Social Networking Sites (SNS) are an online platform that allows users to create a public profile and interact with other users on the website. Social networking sites usually have a new user input a list of people with whom they share a connection and then allow the people on the list to confirm or deny the connection. After connections are established, the new user can search the networks of his connections to make more connections. A social networking site may also be known as a social website or a social networking website.

Librarians and social media users can publicity and marketing of educational events like conference, seminars, workshops etc. through social media in the digital era. For example users can publicity and marketing of Conference, Seminar on social sites like Linkedin, Facebook, Lislinks, Twitter and YouTube etc.

**Fig. 4. Conference marketing on LinkedIn**

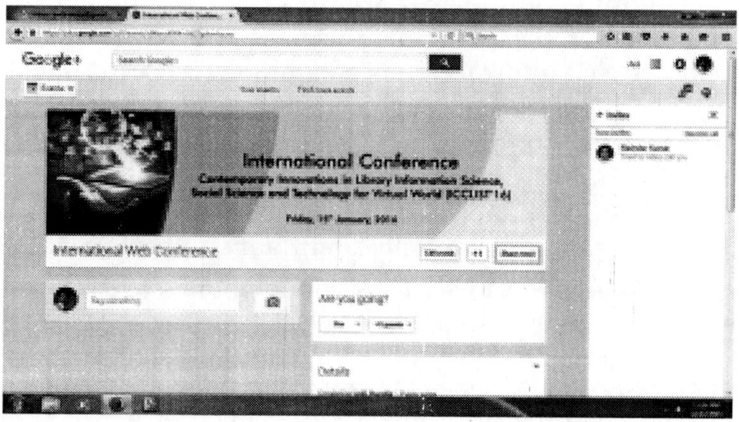


**Fig. 5. International Conference marketing on Google+**

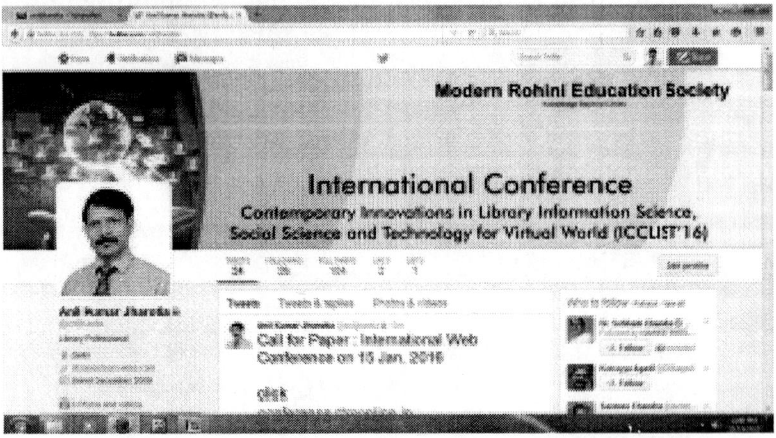


**Fig. 6. International Conference marketing on Twitter**

## MOBILE DEVICES IN LIBRARY AND INFORMATION SERVICES

Mobile technology has become boon to the libraries. A library may reach the remote users effectively by adopting of mobile apps and mobile technology in its services. Mobile phones are inevitable tools for information communication. Human beings in a society use mobile phone to communicate thoughts, facts, conversations, in general, information. The dissemination of processed information is a common factor in a civilized society. Mobile technology is fast becoming the preferred method for connecting to the internet, especially for people on the go. Library professionals must keep pace with this trend and integrate themselves into the mobile realm if they wish to deliver enhanced user services.

**Mobile Phones :** The mobile phones are not only a phone portal to mobile outreach. Library and information professionals who used more traditional cell phones can consider text reference for their mobile outreach programs. With Google Voice and library-based options such as MyInfoQuest and Mosio's Text a Library and information professionals can set up a text reference service that can help in handle ready reference questions or even more complicated questions quickly and easily.

**Electronic textbooks :** E-readers and tablets have new features that allow students to highlight and add annotations to the text, just as they would with paper texts. They give students the capability to link to additional information.

**E-readers :** Due to the popularity of Amazon's Kindle and Barnes & Noble's Nook. The latest generation takes content delivery to new levels, allowing for wireless browsing, purchasing, and delivery of content through these devices.

**MP3 players :** An iPod, iPhone or other MP3 player mobile devices can use in library for audio and/or video tours. With an iPod or MP3 player, users can explore the library at their convenience, concentrating on the parts of the collection most relevant to their needs.

**Tablets :** Tablets or Tablet PCs can be used in various activities for example searching databases, downloading articles, and perusing the catalog either through apps or tablet-formatted websites. The overall utility of tablets also makes them an ideal device for accessing a variety of documents, including e-books, e-journals and e-databases etc. Their ability to play audiovisual materials and their web connectivity could signal a new form of academic text that is both immersive and interactive.

Tablets can also use on-the-spot reference services. The user can access the library's resources conveniently through tablets while away from the reference desk. The design of the recent generation of tablets with Flash web technology can provide accessing some websites, especially video sites.

Libraries Can Provide The Following Specific Services On Mobile Devices:

- **Academic affairs administration :** provides the

latest news and notices from a university. Users can select a menu and see results that are designed specifically for mobile viewing email notices of new books and journal articles, set up preferences for catalogue searching, etc.

- **e-Contents :** offers access to a variety of databases and digital resources such as e-Books, e-Journals,Web databases, dissertations, and article databases. Users can get fast relevant answers whenever needed with e-Contents Search, search designed just for mobile user.
- **Library guide :** gives users the best of library guide information such as library use guide, question answering service, and library statistics delivering rich content in a way that works best for users. If users have questions and want to contact the library professionals for help, they can get a fast response from the library via the mobile device and find the appropriate information needed.
- **Mobile-based Library Lending Service :** Libraries can formulate regulations for using mobiles for circulation of reading materials and maintenance of users account. Mobile phones make ILL/ document delivery services faster and cut-down the time to request/visit different libraries and complement the geographically remote users. Library can provides the following services such as lending extension/inquiry, return information/ inquiry, interlibrary loan requests, SDI service application, email service of academic journals, database use education application, etc. The library is a personal library space where users can find information and resources of their choosing. Users can read alerts, check records, renew resources, request items, track interlibrary loans and document delivery requests, set up future application and work in mobile library services.

**Fig. 7. Mobile based Services**

- **News and Events :** Information on job openings, varieties of scholarly competition, library events such as orientations program, stock verification, book recall, lectures on special topic, news in relation to scholarly work, awards and so on can be given using mobile devices in order to update the user's knowledge short messages regarding the library events and news can be sent to the users personally.
- **Notice :** provide the latest news, notices and reach users wherever they might be via SMS and MMS from libraries. Users can get notified instantly with notice alerts: alerts on overdue books, outstanding fines, reminders to return library items, library event information, etc.
- **In-house search :** accesses a variety of library-owned resources and databases. Users can just enter search terms and see results that are designed specifically for mobile viewing. This service includes OPAC (online public access catalogue), integrated search, and original document search.
- **SMS Alert Service :** Existing e-mail alert services like bringing new books to the notice of users for suggestion, intimation of arrival of indented documents by users, informing availability of reserved documents for collection, appraising about

which/when books are overdue, library circulars, e-journals subscribed, change in timings, information about important events, etc., can be upgraded by sending through SMS alert services. SMS messages can be sent to group of users simultaneously through many free applications, and intermediary websites/clients. To send SMS to collect the requested books, Acknowledging the user about renewal of a book, OPAC service, Users may request the opening and closing hours of the library.

- **Suggest a purchase :** Library professionals can receive the suggestions from the users sent via mobile phones. In such cases users need not to visit the libraries and write the requirements in a register.
- **Location of the library :** Users might be provided with virtual tours of the library sections and their services.
- **Audio Tour :** Libraries even can provide audio tour of a library.
- **Video Lecture :** Librarians can provide education video lecture's clips to user on demand through smart phone.
- **Image Services :** The Image Services in a library might offer a number of high quality, fee based photographic and document imaging services including digitized photographs, diagrams, maps, photos of places of national importance.
- **Research consultation and instruction :** It is a kind of customer care service. Research scholars may have an interaction with the library staff to get the consultation and get suggestions via mobile phones.
- **Catalogue search :** Libraries can provide their catalogue on the mobile devices.

- **Journal finder :** Library Journal Finder provides access to full text journal, magazine, and newspaper content as well as links to titles held in print.
- **Reference service :** Library users can ask library professionals anything through the live chat and texting with mobiles. The reference services can be provided with the help of sending and receiving SMS. Immediate feedback is also possible from the user's side.
- **Wi-fi - Internet Access :** Mobile phones are available with 4G facility. Libraries can offer wi-fi facility to access electronic information sources to users.

## MOBILE APPS

App is the abbreviated form of the word "application". An application is a software program. It is designed to perform a specific function directly for the users. A mobile app is a computer program designed to run on smart phones, tablet computers and other mobile devices. Mobile applications are move away from the integrated software system. Each app provides limited and isolated functionality such as social networks, education, games, online commerce, calculator, map set.

**Fig. 8. Mobile Apps**

Some useful mobile Apps Google Maps, Duolingo, Science 360, Drop box, Ted, Coursera, Math tricks, Earth viewer, Medscape, NASA, My open courses are very useful for students can use these Apps in smart phones and search required information through these Apps. It is innovative technology which students can use in digital era.

## FUTURE POTENTIALS OF MOBILE APPLICATION IN THE LIBRARIES

The mobile apps have changed the way one connects and interacts with the world and mobile library services can meet people's needs for information in a fast-paced society. The objective of this paper is to shows the major library and information services provided by using mobile apps and technology to satisfy the information needs of variant users. Mobile learning is the ability to obtain or provide educational content on personal pocket devices such as PDAs, smart phones and mobile phones.

More and more changes are expected within four to five years in the field of mobile technology and its application to the libraries, the day is not far when we will use phone to read barcodes or RFIDs in the library and OPACs will develop GIS sensitivity and be able to communicate with users through their mobiles for holds, fines, late notices, alerts, etc.

Social Networking Sites (SNS) are used for marketing of educational events, the way of advertising and publicity of events, its product and services via various modern technologies.

## QUICK RESPONSE (QR) CODES: INNOVATIVE TECHNOLOGY

Quick Response codes or QR codes are two-dimensional barcodes that can be scanned by mobile phone with embedded camera. In the automatic identification fields QR code has been widely. These codes can be used to provide fast access to URL, an SMS message, a phone number, a V-card, or any text and QR codes can hold much more information than a regular barcode. The information encoded in a QR code images. In this paper focused on QR innovative Technology which use in modern libraries

**Fig. 9. Sample of QR Codes**

Quick Response code is a matrix barcode readable by smartphones and mobile phones with cameras. They are sometimes referred to as 2d codes, 2d barcodes, or mobile codes. On most phones purchased in the United States, one must download a free app (application) in order to read the QR code, although some phones have one preinstalled. Now QR Codes uses in many ways like Books, Advertisement and Identity Cards which are latest technology.

## QR CODES IN THE LIBRARY

Quick Response (QR) Codes are use in the Library:

- On the Library catalogue, individual records of books and journal titles available on the shelves include a QR Code. By reading the code, you can save the Title, Author and Class mark of the book you are viewing on the catalogue to help you find it on the shelves (link to catalogue to view example)
- Library Floor plans have a QR Code that links users directly to an MP3 Audio Tour on that Subject Floor. (Downloads are in MP3 format and the file size is around 7.5 Mb)

**Fig. 10. QR Code use in University Library**

## QR CODE ON PAN AND IDENTITY CARDS

We can define an identity document as the document and it will help to make the proper verification of the personal identity of a person. The ID is also known as ID or the portion of identification or the paper of any person. It is a small standard size card and usually called the identity card that can be easily kept in a pocket or inside wallet. A card can show data of the identification about any person including names (first name, surname), age, address, a portrait photograph to have color of body,

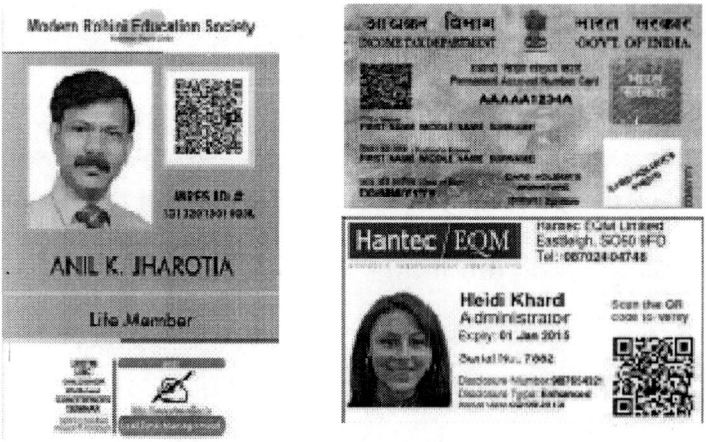


**Fig. 11. QR Code on PAN & I-Card**

hair and eyes. These types identification are used commonly in place of school for the student, companies for the employees. Therefore it can be said that student ID card is the card of identification which is used for holding specific characteristic of students.

## HOW TO GENERATE QR CODE AND READ USING SMART PHONE?

Many of smartphones already have installed inbuilt QR code. Those Smart phones are not installed QR Code. They can follow following procedure: Start internet connection. Open the Google Play Store link to *www.google.com* and type the QR Code generator and QR code decoder and click on go button.

**Fig. 12. QR Apps reads QR Code**

We will find many types of software free and easily operational QR Code software will be used. eg. QR code generator (YKART,Excelsior Studios) and Scan Life, Neo Reader for read.

Now mostly libraries use QR Codes on in house production because it is quick response technique. Librarians can install "QR Apps" on Smartphone and easily access the QR Codes in libraries.

## CONCLUSION

Quick Response (QR) Code is latest technology which used in Advertisement, Identify Cards and Books in place of Barcodes. Libraries are poised to benefit from the momentum created by the uptake of QR codes in the corporate world and popular culture. However, for this to succeed, we need to take care to implement QR codes where they really make our users' lives easier. Blanketing a library with QR codes that provide little value could backfire, leaving users less apt to try other QR codes. This could result in a lost opportunity for libraries and campuses to leverage a really useful technology. We can use QR technology in library for update the latest technology.

Libraries use social media to fulfill a range of objectives, with most focused on promotion (visibility for and usage of the library service and resources). Librarian can share seminar, conference, workshop's information on social media to aware library professionals and it is very good platform to marketing library events on social media like Facebook, Google+, Twitter and Linkedin.

The mobile applications and technology has changed the way one connects and interacts with the world and mobile library services can meet people's needs for information in a fast-paced society. Libraries are moving forward in providing access to digital collections via mobile devices. In the near future, more and more people will be able to experience digital collections in the palm of their hand through a smart phone with Apps.

## REFERENCES

1. Adarsh Bala . (2010). Use of Mobile Technology in Enhancing Library Services. International Journal of Library Science, , (J10), 56-63. Retrieved from *http://www.ceser.com/cpjour/index.php?journal=ijls=article&op=view&path%5B%5D=18*
2. Barile, Lori. (2011). Mobile technologies for libraries: A list of mobile applications and resources for development. College & Research Libraries News, 72 ( 4), 222-228 . Retrieved from http://crln.acrl.org/content/72/4/222.full
3. Choi, Wontae. (2007). Current status of mobile library service. Industrial information programs in Korea: an overview. Inter

lending & Document Supply, 35(2): 60 – 65. Retrieved from *www.researchgate.net/.../235318748_Industrial_information_programs_in...*

4. Choi, Wontae. (2009). Development and Application of Mobile Technology in South Korean Libraries . Libri, 59, 14 –22.
5. Dresselhaus, Angela & Shrode, Flora. (2012 ). Mobile Technologies & Academics: Do Students Use Mobile Technologies in Their Academic Lives and are Librarians Ready to Meet this Challenge? Information Technology and Libraries, *31, ( 2 ).* Retrieved from *http://ejournals.bc.edu/ojs/index.php/ital/article/view/2166/pdf_1#*
6. Jharotia, Anil Kumar (2012). M-Learning is the future of e-learning: A new dimension in library services *Conference proceeding of National conference on beyond librarianship: Search for new frontier* held at G.B.U on 21-22 Sept. 2012. Vol-1 pp.203-210.
7. Jharotia, Anil Kumar (2016). Use of Social Networking Sites (SNS) for Marketing of Educational Events, *National Conference: Freedom of Expression,* 12 March 2016, TIAS, pp.80-84.
8. Jharotia, Anil Kumar (2017). Mobile Apps for Users: An Innovative Technology, *International Conference - Global Business and Innovative Management: Challenges & Issue,* TIAS, 15 April 2017, pp.171-181.
9. Jharotia, Anil Kumar (2016). Use of Quick Response (QR) Code in Libraries: A Study retrieved from *http://www.rtmonline.in/proceeding/icclist16-proceeding.pdf*
8. Jharotia, Anil Kumar (2017). The Role of Social Media in Libraries, *International Conference on Role of Media in Environment Management and* Conservation, MRES, 14 May 2017, pp.56-60.
10. M.V. Sunil, N.S. Harinarayan and Kumbar Mallinath, (2014). User Perception towards QR Code for Libraries: A Study retrieved from *http://eprints.uni-mysore.ac.in/16686/*

## WEB REFERENCES

1. *http://www.libsuccess.org/index.php?title=QR_Codes*
2. *http://library.murdoch.edu.au/Borrowing-and-access/Library-apps/What-is-a-QR-code/*
3. *http://library.ryerson.ca/qr/*

4. *http://www.libsuccess.org/QR_Codes*
5. *http://ijssst.info/Vol-15/No-5/data/5198a076.pdf*
6. *http://scholarsarchive.byu.edu/cgi/viewcontent.cgi?article=2548&context=facpub*
7. *http://eduscapes.com/sessions/qrcodes/*
8. *https://www.google.co.in/?gfe_rd=cr&ei=UccxVqg06cjwB8rDi1A&gws_rd=ssl#q=QR+code+use+in+library+and+information+centre*
9. *http://www.gonzaga.edu/academics/libraries/foley-library/FAQs-and-Information/QR_Codes.asp*
10. *http://www.academia.edu/15753859/QR_Code_Implication_For_Library_and_Information_Centre_Usage*
11. *http://www.ijarcsse.com/docs/papers/Volume_4/11_November2014/V4I11-0369.pdf*
12. *http://schools.natlib.govt.nz/blogs/libraries-and-learning/11-12/qr-codes-school-library*
13. *http://www.practicalecommerce.com/articles/2854-20-QR-Code-Tools-and-Uses*
14. *https://princh.com/8-technologies-to-implement-at-the-library-of-the-future/*
15. *http://www.rtmonline.in/index.php?linkName=download.php*
16. *http://www.librarydotcom.webs.com*
17. *http://crln.acrl.org/content/71/10/526.full*
18. *http://vabulous.com/wp-content/uploads/2011/06/social-media-marketing.jpg*
19. *http://kirkmktgblog.com/wp-content/uploads/2011/11/social-media-seo-tips-and-tricks.jpg*
20. *http://leonspencer.com/wp-content/uploads/2010/09/social-media-implementation_02.jpg*
21. *http://socialnetworkinglibrarian.com/2010/12/21/social-media-and-library-trends-for 2011/*
22. *http://www.ajms.co.in/sites/ajms/index.php/ajms/article/view/366*
23. *http://whatis.techtarget.com/definition/social-media*
24. *https://en.wikipedia.org/wiki/Social_media*
25. *http://ijiset.com/vol2/v2s3/IJISET_V2_I3_114.pdf*
26. *http://collaborativelibrarianship.org/index.php/jocl/article/viewFile/299/259*

27. *http://digitalcommons.unl.edu/cgi/viewcontent.cgi?article=1897&context=libphilprac*

28. *http://conferences.alia.org.au/alia2012/Papers/18_Crystall.Choi.pdf*

29. *http://irjlis.com/wp-content/uploads/2014/06/10-IR174.pdf*

30. *http://www.asis.org/asist2012/proceedings/Submissions/85.pdf*

31. *http://librarydotcom.webs.com/*

32. *http://www.i-socialmarketing.org/assets/social_marketing_definition.pdf*

# 5

# Use of RFID Technologies in Library Management

***Pankaj K. Bhardwaj***
*Librarian R.D.S. Public Girls College*
*Rewari-123401(Haryana) India*

## ABSTRACT

RFID System are becoming a very popular now days. RFID play a very vital role in reducing theft with less human efforts. In those days RFID systems have become an essential part of day to day life. RFID in libraries are a developing technology and is being implemented in small and medium sized libraries. This paper proposes "RFID Technology In Libraries" that would allow fast transaction flow and will make it easy to handle the circulation of books from the library without much interference of manual book keeping which benefits by adding properties of traceability and security. The RFID based library system helps the fast circulation of books and other activities of library.

**Keywords** : RFID/Radio Frequency Identification, WORM/ Right Ones Read Many.

## INTRODUCATION

RFID invented in 1969 and patented in 1973. RFID first used in Harsh industrial environment i8n 1980's.

RFID is a technology that facilitates non line of sight identification of items. Basic components of a comprehensive RFID system for library kind of environment are tags, readers and library management system. Radio frequency identification systems have been in use in libraries for book identification, for self-checkout, for anti-theft control, for inventory control and for the arranging and conveying of library books. These applications can lead to significant saving in labour costs, with improve use services, lower books theft and provide a constant record update of new collections of books. Implementing RFID system in libraries will aid task such as circulation, re-salving and theft recognization and it has several other important advantages.

## RFID TECHNOLOGY IN LIBRARIES

Using RFID technology in libraries saves library staff by automatizing their burden. An establishment that user RFID technology in libraries saves a book reader valuable time that he would have been spend waiting for his turn n queue for borrowing or returning a book. Taking care of books and making them available to the book readers are important tasks. Most of the library staff's time is spent in recording information of incoming and outgoing books. Circulation of books can be fully automatized with the help of self-checkout and check in systems. This system associates installation of special software. A user using this system to borrow books is presented with opportunities on a computer screen. This user has to identify himself with a code, which is preferably a personal identification number or any form of individual identy code. Books selected by the user are identified by the system's built in RFID reader. And the surveillance bit in the book's tag is deactivate by the system. When a book is returned, the check-in/out system activated the surveillance bit.

## OBJECTIVE OF RFID

1. To know the latest trends use to ICT.
2. To know the different library automation short wave models.
3. Useful of library automation software in college and university libraries.
4. To know about the different services provide by the library automation software.
5. To know the different types of library automation software and its developers.

## COMPONENTS FO RFID SYSTEM

**1. Tags :** RFID tags are the heart of the system, which can be fixed inside a book's back cover or directly onto CD's and videos. This tag is equipped with programmable chip and an antenna. Each paper thin tag involves and engraved antenna and microchip with a capacity of at least 64 bits. These are three types of tags "read only" WORM and "read/write". Tags are read only if the identification is encoded at the time of manufacture and not rewritable. WORM (Write once read many) tags are programmed by the using organization, but without the ability of rewrite them later "Red/Write Tags". Which are chosen by most libraries, can have information changed or added. In libraries using RFID is common to have part of the read/write tag secured against rewriting e.g. the identification number of the item.

**Fig. 1. Tag**

**2. Readers :** A receiver device called as reader identifies the signal as soon it enters into its radio range and decode the number for comprehension; reader. interrogates the tags and offers maximum reading performance enabling instant data capture when passed alongside the items in a continuance movement. The device used within the building are usually called "readers" while the ones used at building exists are usually called" sensors".

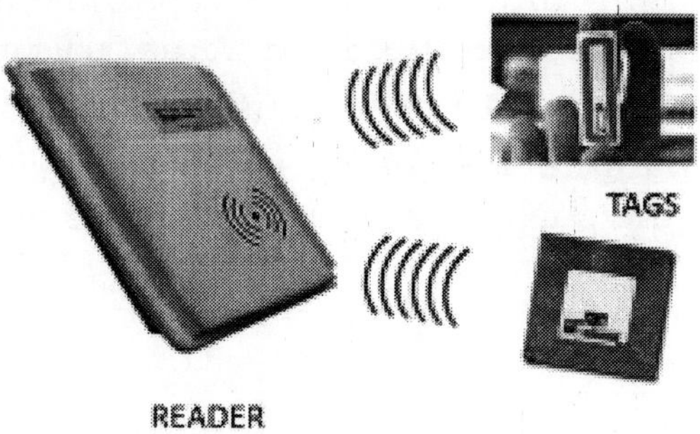


**Fig. 2. Reader**

**3. Antenna :** An antenna is connected to the reader to help to process identification of the items and activate/ deactivate the tag anti-theft function simultaneously. Additional antenna canbe added the increase the number of item processed in case of large transection.

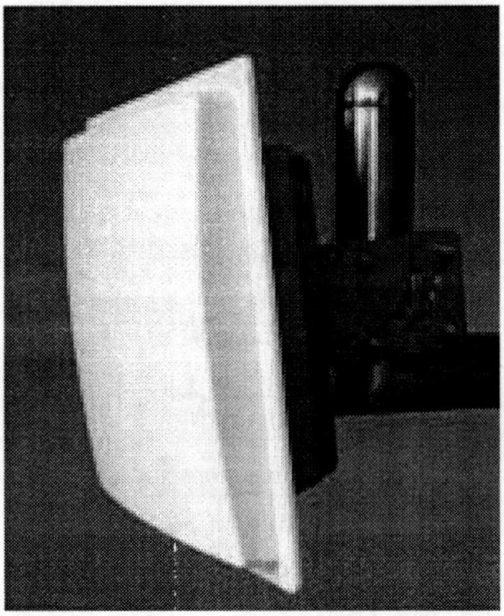

**Fig. 3. Antenna**

**4. Server :** The server is the heart of RFID system. It is the communication gateway among the various components. It receives the information from one or more of the readers and exchange information with the circulation database. Its software include the SIP/SIP2 (Session initiation protocol) API's (Application Programming Interface) NC/P or SLNP necessary to interface it with the integrated library software.

**5. RFID label Printer :** used to print the labels.

**6. Handheld Reader :** It can be moved along the items on the shelves without touching them. It used in stock-verification, used in search for book mishelved, search for individual book on request.

**Fig. 4. Handheld Reader**

**7. Shelf Check Unit :** User identification is done with an RFID ID card. User can put item onto the reader surface in front of the self-check unit to be registered under particular user's name. multiple items can be checked put at the same time.

**Fig. 5. Selfcheck Unit**

**8. External Book Return/Book Drop Station :** Libraries can offer a distinct service, such as ability to return the books when library is closed. It is a machine with a slot with a chip RFID reader integrated in to a wall. User identifies him or her than put the books in to a slot. Upon completion of return, user gets a receipt showing how many and which books are returned.

**Fig. 6. Book Drop Station**

**9. Staff and Conservation Station :** Staff station consists of antenna, electronic module and power supply. There are additional software windows integrated in to library management systems.

## TECHNICAL PROBLEMS IN RFID SYSTEM:

1. A problem with RFID Standards.
2. RFID system makes use of electromagnetic spectrum, so it can be easily discontinues.
3. RFID leader gives the different result when the signals from to or more readers overlap and tag unable to respond to coincidental queries.
4. RFID tag collision occurs.

## ADVANTAGES OF RFID SYSTEM

**1. Rapid Charging/ Discharging :** The use of RFID reduces the amount of time required to perform circulation operations. The most important time saving are characteristic to the facts that information can be read from RFID tags much faster than from barcodes and that several items in a stock can be read at the same time. While at the beginning unreliable, the anti-collision formula that allows an entire stack to be charged or discharged now appears to be working well.

**2. Simplified Patron self-charging/discharging :** Form patron using self-charging, there is a marked improvement because they do not have to carefully place materials within a designated diagram and they can charge several items at the same time. Patron self-discharging shift that work from staff to patrons. Staff is relived further when readers are installed in book drops.

**3. The Perfect Tracker :** An another feature of this technology in time saving and security aspect is that the RFID tags replace both the EM security strips or RF tags of older theft detection systems and the barcodes of the automated library system i.e. the system is a comprehensive RFID system that compounds RFID security and the tracking of materials throughout the library; or it's a hybrid system that uses EM for security and RFID for tracking, but handles both together with a single piece of equipment. In either case, there can be as much as a 50% increase in throughout.

**4. Highly Reliable :** Several RFID library systems claim an almost 100% detection rate using RFID tags and there are very few false alarms than with older technologies once a RFID system is properly turned.

**5. High Speed Inventorying :** A unique advantage of RFID systems is their ability to scan book on the shelves without confusing them out or removing them. A hand held inventory reader can be moved speedily across a shelf of books to read all of the unique identification information. Using wireless technology, it is possible no only to update the inventory, but also to identify items, which are out of proper order. This feature of technology is very helpful in stock-verification, where much time was wasted in manual entries.

**6. Automated Identification of Materials :** Another application of RFID technology is automated identification of materials. This includes conveyor and sorting systems that can move library materials and arrange them by category in to separates bins or on to separate carls. This significantly reduces the amount of time required for reshelving the reading material.

**7. Better Than Bar-Code :** RFID tags are for better than bar-codes, as these are not required to be scanned through some reader or recorder as required in bar-code. Finally, the RFID tags last longer than bar codes because nothing comes into contact with them. Most RFID vendors claim a minimum of 1,00,000 transactions before a tag may be need to be replaced.

## DISADVANTAGES OF RFID SYSTEMS

**1. High Cost :** Major disadvantage of RFID technology is its high cost. The readers and sensors used to read the information are costing between Rs.1,00,000/- to 1,50,000/- a server cost as much as Rs. 5,00,000/- to 6,00,000/- and the tags cost Rs. 30/- to Rs. 45/- each.

**2. Easy To Deceive The Technology :** It is possible to disappoint and RFID system by wrapping protected material in two or three layers of ordinary household foil to block the radio signal. Clearly, bringing household foil in to a library using RFID would represent planned theft. It is also possible to create a fault in an RFID system by placing two items against one another so that one tag overlays another. That may cancel out the signals. Although this is require knowledge of the technology and careful arrangement.

**3. Removal of Tags :** The RFID tags are typically affixed to the inside back cover of the book an d are exposed for removal. This is a rare case but that does not mean that there won't be problems when patrons become more familiar with the role of the tags. If a library wishes, it can insert the RFID tags in the spines of all except thin books, however not all RFID tags are flexible enough. A-library can also imprint the RFID tags with its logo and make them appear to be book plates, or it can put a printed cover label over each tag.

**4. Exit Sensor Problems :** The performance of the exit sensors is disputable. They must read tags at up to twice the distance of the other readers. If the library install a smaller antenna at check point than there can be problems for sensor to check every patron, because it will not work properly. The performance of exit sensors is better when the antenna on the tags are larger.

**5. Fear of Interface Patron Privacy :** There is a perception among some that RFID is a threat to patron privacy. That perception is based on two misconceptions: (1) that are tags contain patron information and (2) that they can be read after someone has taken materials to home or office.

## LIMITATION OF RFID

**Reader difference :** One problem encounter with RFID in the signal from one reader can interface with the signal from another where coverage overlaps the causes to different problems:

**1. Tag Difference :** Multiple tags are energized by the RFID tag reader coincidently and reflect their respective signal back to the reader at the same time.

**2. Removal of Pasted tag :** The tag pasted on the item can be easily removed which many disastrously effect the services and create problem for the library staff.

## CONCULSION

Although the RFID technology is quite expensive, still it has admitted excellent result for all the organization. The technology is set to become more popular in India with more development in the coming time in various sectors. It has been proved that this technology reduces labour, costs and provides efficient results, which leads to dependable security and access control. The only barrier in the journey is its high cost, but it is expected that in coming days the cost will come down further and very early we will see mass adoption of this technology in various libraries and in India and in the world.

## REFERENCES

1. International Journal of Innovative Research in Advanced Engineering (IJIRAE) ISSN: 2349-2163. Issue 1, Volume 2 (January 2015) Topic: RFID Based Library Management System by S. Vimalraj and Others.
2. International Journal of Advanced Computer Science and Applications (IJACSA) Volume 1, No 1, July 2010 Radio Frequency Identification Based Library Management by Grover Priyanka and Ahuja Ansul.
3. Application of RFID Technology in Libraries and Role of Librarian Written by Pandey Prabhat and Mahajan KD.
4. Application of RFID Technology in Libraries by Sumi Suman and Jatinder Kumar.
5. The Analysis of RFID System Implementation by Diffusion of Innovation Theory by Iuan Yuan Lu and others.
6. Use of RFID System in libraries and its important by Biswas Ripan Ranjan.
7. RFID Technology in libraries "An overview by Srivastva Neha and Upadhyay Sunil K.
8. Images by Google.

# 6

# RFID Based Secure Access System

**_Pradeep Kumar Gupta_**
*Research Scholar, Dept. of Library and Information Science,*
*Mandsaur University, Mandsaur (M.P.)*

**_Dr. Ashwini Yadav_**
*Asst. Professor & Head, Dept. of Library and Information Science,*
*Mandsaur University, Mandsaur (M.P.)*

**_Mrs. Abha Gupta_**
*Librarian, Mandsaur Institute of Ayurvedic Education & Research*
*Mandsaur University, Mandsaur (M.P.)*

## ABSTRACT

The System was based on Radio Frequency Identification (RFID) Technology and consists of a passive RFID tag. The passive micro transponder tag collects power from the 125 KHz magnetic field generated by the base station, gathers information about the Tag ID and sends this information to the base station. The base station receives, decodes and checks the information available in its Database and Manchester code was used to send those information. The system performed as desired with a 10cm diameter antenna attached to the transponder. The Base Station is built by using the popular 8051 family Microcontroller. It gets the tag ID and if the tag ID is stored in its memory then the microcontroller will allow the person inside. RFID Reader Module, are also called as interrogators. They convert radio waves returned from the RFID tag into a Form that can be passed on to Controllers, which can make use of it.

## INTRODUCTION

RFID is an automatic identification method, relying on storing and remotely retrieving data using device called RFID tags or transponders.

An RFID tag is an objects that can be applied to or incorporated into a product, animal or person for the purpose of identification using radio waves. Some tags can be read from several meters away and beyond the line of sight of the reader.

Most RFID tags contain at least two parts. One is an integrated circuit for storing and processing information, modulating and demodulating a (RF) signal, and other specialized functions. The second is an antenna for receiving and transmitting the signal. A technology called chips RFID allows for discrete identification of tags without without an integrated circuit, thereby allowing tags to be printed directly onto assets at a lower cost than traditional tags.

Today, a significant thrust in RFID use is in enterprise supply chain management, improving the efficiency of inventory tracking and management. However, a threat is looming that the current growth and adoption in enterprise supply chain market will not be sustainable. A fair cost-sharing mechanism, rational motives and justified returns from RFID technology investments are the key ingredients to achieve long-term and sustainable RFID technology adoption.

RFID tags come in three general varieties:- Passive, Active or Semi-Passive(also know as battery passive). Passive tags require no internal power source, thus being pure passive devices(they are only active when a reader is nearby to power them), whereas semi-passive and active tags require a power source, usually a small battery.

## A BRIEF REVIEW

### Block Diagram

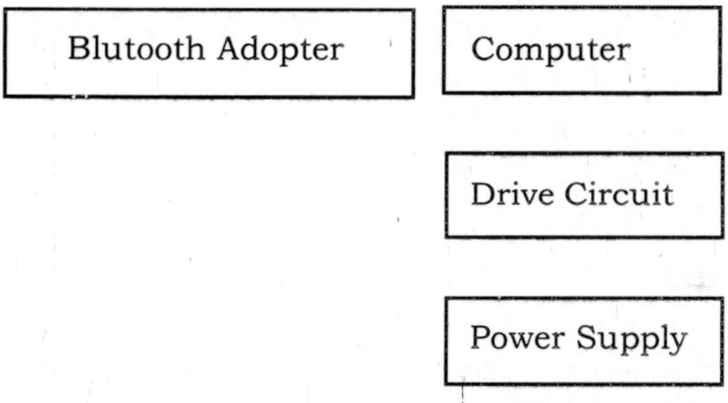


**RFID Module :** RFID Reader Module, are also called as interrogators. They convert radio waves returned from the RFID tag into a form that can be passed on to Controllers, which can make use of it. RFID tags and reader have to be turned to the same frequency in order to communicate. RFID systems use many different frequencies, but the most common and widely used & supported by our reader is 125 KHz.

**RS 232 Standards :** RS-232 is a standard for transferring data in serial data in serial format. Information is sent in small packets of data called data frames. A data frame consists of the following sequence: a start bit. The actual data word, an optional parity bit and ends with one or two stop bits. The data word can be 7 or 8 bit long. RS-232 offers asynchronous communication with the combination of start and stop bit of being used to synchronize each data frame. The parity bit is used by the receiver to determine if an old number of bits were corrupted during transmission there are two types of parity, odd and even. For example, if even parity is used the transmitter makes the parity bit a 1 anytime there is an odd number of 1's in the data word. This makes a total even number of its in the data frame. If an odd number of bit arrive at the receiver then the data frame was corrupted.

The standard not only specifies the order of bits but also specifies the voltage level used to send data. Bipolar signaling is used in the RS-232 protocol to support long cabling with minimum noise. A logic 0 is represented by a positive voltage between +3VDC and +15VDC and a logic 1 is represented by negative voltage between -3VDC and -15VDC.

The IBM PC Serial port contains a number of handshaking lines that are used to indicate the willingness of the receiver to receive data and sender to send data. These are not strictly needed and so I will not cover them here.

## APPLICATION

Current and proposed uses of RFID span a wide spectrum of application areas and a fully comprehensive overview would certainly surpass the limits of this paper. It is, however, easy to see that the nature of a given use of RFID can be put in either one of three groups:

- Items instance or item class identification,
- Location identification,
- Data transfer from or to the RFID tag.

**1. Instance or class identification :** If RFID tags are only used for the purpose of item type or instance identification, usually, a data-base is maintained in the background to provide or receive the additional needed. Augmented with this support, destination or way of handling can be determined for the given item, an already proven concept in a number of logistics solutions (several shipping and postal services, such as UPS, FedEx, USPS and Finland post [8]). Also examples in manufacturing demonstrate the benefits of RFID, such as with identifying individual car bodies in customized automotive production(BMW's car body identification in their din golfing factory [5]).

In the agriculture, farm animals can be identified using RFID tags, and a retrieval service for lost pets also relies on RFID implants as the means of identification ('Home Again' pet retrieval service [13]). Also, RFID tags are widely on in security systems which grant access to facilities etc.

**2. Location identification** : If a given reader is assigned to a known location, it is possible to track the current place of a given uniquely identifiable item. Numerous logistics companies and some postal services have already integrated such RFID based features into their tracking services (several shipping and postal services, such as UPS, FedEx, USPS and Finland post [8]; automatic vehicle location systems in public transport control in Vejle, Denmark [10]; location of rolling stock at the Swiss Federal Railways), and similarly, the physical location of work pieces is being kept track of in several manufacturing facilities , too (e.g.: in Dell's facility in Xiamen, china[12]). The RFID tags to be read for localization can be either attached to containers or items, or they can identify the transporting vehicle itself. Aside from the benefits of providing exact information (as opposed to the risk of incomplete, delayed or corrupted data if entries are made manually), reading RFID tags does not require a long halt in the transportation process, making thus delivery more efficient. Also, farm animals can be efficiently localized using RFID tags while a similar tracking principle is applied in some prisons as well. Other location-specific application examples are envisaged using direction-selective readers. These aim to find exact location of a tag in a wide area, such as golf balls on a golf course[9].

**3. Transfer of further data :** In the third application group, not only an identity is extracted from the tag but also auxiliary data read or written. Data read the tag usually contains information which would be difficult im-practical or impossible to obtain from a remote or pre-recorded database, or measurement results. Some products may provide instructions for proper handling this way (envisaged are cases where tags in food packaging would instruct an oven about the optimal cooking time[2, or tags in clothing would select the right program for a washing machine[17]), while in a number of already implemented uses, tags provide medical measurement data e.g., about eye-ball pressure(sensor and transmitter integrated into artificial lens implant [6]). Writing data to a tag usually adds information about the process in of the given item(or delivery progress in transportation), and in a few cases, a new identity is assigned to the tag by rewriting .

**ADVANTAGE**

- Barcode readers require a direct line of sight to the printed barcode; RFID readers do not require a direct line of sight to either active RFID tags or passive tags.
- RFID tags can be read at much greater distances; an RFID reader can pull information from a tag at distance up to 300 feet. The range o read a barcode is much less, typically no more than fifteen feet.
- RFID readers can interrogate, or read , RFID tags much faster; read rates of forty or more tags per second are possible. Reading barcodes is much more time-consuming; due to the fact that a direct line of sight is required , if the items are not properly oriented to the reader it may take seconds to read an individual tag. Barcode reader usually takes a half-second or more to successfully complete a read.
- Line of sight requirements also limit the ruggedness of barcode as well as the reusability of barcodes. RFID tags are typically more rugged, since electronic components are better protected in a

plastic cover. RFID tags can also be implanted within the product itself, guaranteeing greater ruggedness and reusability.

- Barcodes have no read/write capability; that is, you cannot add to the information written on a printed barcode. RFID tags however, can be read/write devices; the RFID reader can communicate with the tag, and alter as much of the information as the tag design will allow.

## DISADVANTAGE

- RFId tags are typically more expensive than barcodes, in some cases much more so.
- **Problems with RFID standards :** RFID has been implemented in different ways by different manufacturers; global standards are still being worked on. It should be noted that some RFID devices are never meant to leave their network (as in the case of RFID tags used for inventory control within a company). This can cause problems for companies. Consumers may also have problems with RFID standards. For example, ExxonMobil's Speed Pass system is a proprietary RFID system; if another company wanted to use the convenient Speed Pass(say, at the drive-in window of your favorite fast food restaurant) they would have to pay to access it-an unlikely scenario.
- **RFID systems can be easily disrupted :** Since RFID systems make use of the electromagnetic spectrum they are relatively easy to jam using energy at the right frequency. Although this would only be an inconvenience for consumers in stores it could be disastrous in other environments where RFID is increasingly used, like hospitals or in the military in the field. Also, active RFID tags can be repeatedly interrogated to wear the battery down, disrupting the system.

## FUTURE ASPECTS (THE NEXT FOUR YEARS & BEYOND)

The Proceeding examples demonstrate how users of RFID System Leave digital footprints in a variety of setting .In some cases, thease footprints are used to build up a digital identity of the users and provide appropriate feedback through the system : price differentiation, direct marketing, measure employee productivity, etcetera. In some sectors such as employment and leisure, we found little direct evidence of user opposition to RFID. Opposition, where it occurs, is often led by campaign groups. Although a more comprehensive survey would need to be undertaken to draw definite conclusion, these first accounts suggest that, relative to the scale of implementation, few identity management issues occur. In general, both user and maintainer of the RFID settings perceive RFID merely as an electronic key or wallet. The reason for this can be twofold. First of all, in all the cases it is clear who maintains the data and needs to comply with the guidelines on the data protection. Second, many systems currently only cover a small area of a specific setting and run parallel to legacy systems. The RFID systems therefore only disclose small fragments of their user's identity, limiting the maintainers possibilities for control.

In the near future this could be different. Once RFID systems work exclusively with RFID it will become easier to aggregate and analyze the data on the level of the whole user population. Further, once different RFID systems will become connected to each other, technologies such as GSM, GPS or internet, a much richer image of its users will appear. The scenario unfolding then is currently known as 'The internet of things'. In this chapter we elaborate on these technological developments to explore how these could affect the relation between users and maintainer of RFID Setting and the role of government in the coming four years.

## CONCLUSION

In the Result we can say that RFID security access circuit is better for the purpose of security system .the point which are given in the future enhancement is also very impressive.

## REFERENCE

[1] Karen Coyle, "Management of RFID in Libraries", *Preprint version of article* published in the Journal of Academic Librarianship, v. 31, n. 5, pp. 486-489

[2] www.wikipedia.org - Library [last accessed on 20/2/2009]

[3] Psion Teklogix handheld reader manual – www.psionteklogix.com [last accessed on 20/2/2009].

[4] Mercury 4 RFID reader manual – www.thingmagic.com [last accessed on 20/2/2009]

[5] WWW.ADILAM.COM.

[6] WWW.WEKPEDIA.COM

[7] WWW.EFY.COM

[8] WWW.HOWSTUFFWORK.COM

[9] RFID MODULE MANULE

# Part II

# 7

# Public Library System and Services in North India : A New Narrative of Sustainable Knowledge Management

**Mohd Shikoh**
*Research Scholar, Department of Library & Information Science, Aligarh Muslim University, Aligarh, India*

**Mohd Imran Khan**
*Research Scholar, Department of English, Aligarh Muslim University, Aligarh, India*

## INTRODUCTION

Public Library System in India was first introduced by His Highness Sayaji Rao Gaekwad III, Maharaja of Baroda; he was a great visionary, who spearheaded the development of Public Library System in India during the decade of 1910. He carefully established a compulsory program of community education, initially in one district of Gujarat in 1893, and thereafter extended it to the entire

State by 1907. His Highness also made elementary education compulsory to all boys and girls in the State. He also realized that there was an emergent need of universal education which would pave the way for a network of public libraries accessible to public for free. The motive was to keep literacy rates soaring and making men and women in the remote areas to access the sources of knowledge without paying anything.

The Maharaja demanded that "libraries ought not constrain their advantages to the couple of English knowing perusers, yet should make sure that their great work penetrates through to the numerous", and that "the vernacular libraries ought to be energized" so every subject of the State "may enlist himself as a student in the people groups' college the library". With this honorable thought he set up free open libraries in the State starting from 1910. For this reason he built up a different Library Department with Mr. W. A. Borden as the primary full time Director of State Libraries. The following stage was to set up a Central Library at Baroda with a core gathering of 88,764 volumes which incorporated the Maharaja's private accumulation of around 20,000 books. A full time Curator of Libraries with staff quality of 50 specialists were delegated to oversee it methodically.

It is interesting to learn that even a century back the Maharaja procured a Photostat camera and a camera projector purchased by the State funds. The projector was used to see the silent movies and so forth. He additionally propelled production of a quarterly diary called Library Miscellany in English, Gujarati and Marathi with Shri J. S. Kodalkar as its first manager, began Library Relationship from Taluk level, sorted out 'Mitra Mandal' in the town and town libraries and composed consistent library meetings. Versatile library benefit was sorted out to oblige the book require at remote towns. The Maharaja likewise settled an Oriental Establishment and Library with 6,846 printed books and 1,420 original copies in Sanskrit, Gujarati and different dialects. He was the first to start the production of Gaekwad's Oriental series in the year 1915.

This was the first ever public library system in the nation. The successors of Gaekwad III had no enthusiasm for the public libraries programs. Because of absence of regal support, the public library arrangement of Baroda collapsed. It was revived after the execution of the Gujarat Public Libraries Act in 2001, which signifies that there was still an emergent need of harnessing public library system and services in the country so as to conserve the information sustained by our precedents in that order and transform it to coming generations as knowledge.

## PUBLIC LIBRARIES IN INDIAN LEGISLATURE

India attained freedom in 1947 and became a Republic in 1950. To facilitate administrations, it now has a National Capital Region of Delhi, 28 States and 6 Union Territories after Independence. Even before Independence, Kolhapur Princely State, in the Western India passed Public Libraries Act in 1945. So far, only half of the States of the Indian Union have successfully passed the library legislation, However, in the coming few years, there is greater possibility for a library law being enacted in the remaining States. Out of these the enactment of Public Library Law at Puducherry State is in the forefront.

## PUBLIC LIBRARIES IN INDIAN STATES

Public library is largely regarded as the People's University. It has tremendous developments in India from the early period to till date at various stages. Most of the Indian states now have free public library services to develop the people of India at different levels. In India, there are 54,856 public libraries (Survey Report ORG-MARG) starting from English Colony Library at Chennai in 1661. There is no authentic survey over their growth and decay. Most of these public libraries were managed by voluntary organizations, and did not continue long due to lack of adequate financial support from the public. Presumably, almost 50% of such public libraries started by voluntary organization would close down after a period. Only those public libraries which are supported by public library legislation or State Government, through continuous grant-in-aid, are functioning. Before 1950, there were about 6000 public libraries in Andhra Pradesh State organization by NGOs. Now this figure has reduced to 3000 or less. The scenario may be identical in other states also.

## DELHI PUBLIC LIBRARY, DELHI

**Delhi Public Library, Delhi**

The Delhi Public Library is a national repository library in the National Capital Territory of Delhi. The library has 35 branches over the territory. The Library was set up on 27 October 1951 as a pilot venture supported by UNESCO and the Government of India. The library venture goes back to the year 1944 when Shri Ramkrishna Dalmia gave the greater part of the sum required to develop a library working at the demand of

Gen. Sir Claude Auchinleck. In February 1950 the Indian government and UNESCO consented to start the undertaking, and the library was formally opened on 27 October 1951, by then Prime clergyman Jawaharlal Nehru. The library structures were gained in the vicinity of 1951 and 1953, with operations formally exchanged from UNESCO to the Indian Government in 1955. The library provides training facilities to students, library professionals, researchers and social workers from its initial days.

The Delhi Public Library is an autonomous organization under the Ministry of Culture, built up with specialized help from UNESCO and was introduced by Prime Minister, Pt. Jawaharlal Nehru, on 27th October, 1951. DPL is the busiest Public Library in South-East Asia.

The Delhi Public Library has a system of a Central and Zonal Library, 3 Branch Libraries, 24 Sub-Branch Libraries, 2 Community Libraries, 10 Resettlement Colonies Libraries, 73 Mobile Service Points and 24 Deposit Stations spread all finished Delhi. Moreover, it runs a Braille library for the outwardly weakened, Prison library for the detainees of Tihar Jail and gives portable library administrations to zones without library offices. All fundamental branches libraries have a different youngsters' segment. The Library collections are valuable fortune of the Delhi Public Library (DPL). The gathering comprises of rich and extensive variety of books, diaries and other perusing materials in Hindi, English, Urdu, Punjabi and other Indian Languages. With a consistently extending enrollment, the Delhi Public Library has a gathering of more than 18 million books. The collections have a book for each member whatever their perusing interests are.

The collections including gramophone/records/ tapes in the library add up to 9,431.The Delhi Public Library lends gramophone records/sound/video tapes for its subscribers for no extra costs or charges. These records/tapes include traditional instrument and light music, bhajans, ghazals, film melodies and so forth. Those having interest in Delhi Public Library (DPL) can make use of them through Head telephones/Computer Accessories.

## KHUDA BAKHSH ORIENTAL PUBLIC LIBRARY, PATNA

**Khuda Bakhsh Oriental Public Library, Patna**

Located on the banks of the Ganges, in the capital city of Bihar, Patna, it was opened in October, 1891 by the famous visionary of Bihar, Khan Bahadur Khuda Bakhsh with 4,000 compositions, out of which he acquired 1,400 from his father. Khuda Bakhsh gave his entire personal collection to the common people of Patna through this library. Recognizing the tremendous records and scholarly excellence of its rich and esteemed accumulation, the Government of India declared this library, an Institution of National Importance by an act of Parliament in 1969. The Library, autonomous establishment is completely subsidized by the Ministry of Culture. This self-sufficient establishment is being administered by a Board with the Governor of Bihar as its ex-officio Chairman and Director is conveying the obligation of everyday administration of Library issues.

The Library is a unique storehouse of the India's rich heritage, conserved as creations, made on paper, palm-leaf, deer-skin, texture and sundry materials. Meanwhile it has a forefront face, holding up about printed books in Arabic, Persian, Urdu, English and Hindi, other than a couple in German, French, Punjabi, Japanese and Russian. The Library joins the twin features of a point of convergence of research in Oriental examinations and an open library considering the prerequisites of understudies, youth and senior nationals. It is as of now framing into a propelled library, with more than 2,000 Manuscripts open in mechanized association to peruser inside the library. The Library is outfitted with LAN and email workplaces with Internet organize. The Library has two scrutinizing rooms, one for examiners and analysts, and the other for accommodating perusers. The Library welcomes scientists, authorities and perusers from wherever all through the world and considers their need. Reference advantage is connected through fax, phone and through the email in addition. Organizations are in like manner rendered to scientists at home and abroad through supply of microfilm, Xerox, photograph, et cetera which is an extraordinary part of this Library.

Curzon Reading Room named after Lord Curzon is open for all. A broad number of every day papers, magazines in English, Urdu and Hindi, reference books and books for centered exams are open in this Reading Room. The Library is constantly aiming at undertakings to procure and protect records and book and conserve valuable data using every possible means and manners. Scholarly Workshops, Symposia, Talks, Lectures and Seminars are being dealt with to make investigate build commonality with learning both in light of National and International levels. The library progresses ask about activities specifically extends, for instance, Islamic Studies, Arabic, Persian and Urdu Literature, Comparative Religion, Tibb or Unani remedy, Tasawwuf of Mysticism, History of the Islamic land, Medieval Indian History and Culture and the National improvement.

Towards the dispersal of learning on a yet greater scale, the Library has been disseminating its rarities. An obvious section of Research and Publication is wearing down essential material. The Library has its own one of a kind quarterly research journal, which has been disseminated routinely since 1977, the year it was introduced.

## AMIR-UD-DAULAH PUBLIC LIBRARY, LUCKNOW

**Amir-Ud-Daulah Public Library, Lucknow**

The Amir-Ud-Daulah Public Library was established in the year 1882 as part of the Provincial Museum founded which was established in 1868, although it was opened initially as a conservative repository, it was opened for students in 1887. Housed in the first floor of Lal Baradari, the present Museum building was reserved for Library in 1907. The library was shifted to Chattar Manzil in 1910, which housed the Central Drug Research Institute for decades after Indian independence. It was finally opened to public and named as Amir-ud-Daulah Public Library, Lucknow. During the year 1926, on 6$^{th}$

March, it was shifted to its present location in a building specially dedicated to it, and gifted to Government of Uttar Pradesh by the Taluqdars of Awadh named after Amiruddaula Raja Mohmmad Amir Hasan Khan of Mahmoodabad, a former president of the B.I. Association, Lucknow. The Taluqdar's Association transferred land in front of the Library for construction of a park in order to commemorate India's independence, 1947.

The Amir-Ud-Daulah Public Library reminds us of the great patronage of Taluqdars of Oudh, who dedicated the library in the loving & grateful memory of the Amir-ud-Daulah Said-Ul-Mulk, the Honourable Raja Sir Mohammad Amir Hasan Khan Khan Bahadur K.C. I.E. Mumtaj Jang of Mahmudabad, President British Indian Association Oudh. The Foundation stone for the renovation and up gradation was laid by H.E. Sir Harcourt Butlor, K.C.S.I., C.I.E., and Governor of U.P. of Agra & Oudh on Saturday 22nd January 1921. This public library serves the knowledge seekers of Lucknow to the most it could offer and attracts readership from students to officials and from home makers to business people.

Lucknow happens to be a city of culture and rich heritage and has a great deal of information accompanied with knowledge to be offered, it was realized that just one library couldn't suffice the reading needs of citizens therein. The British Council established Public Library post independence and it was received very warmly as it catered to the general public living in central Lucknow. It ran a course of nostalgia across the vicinity it was housed in, the legendary Mayfair building in Hazratganj, due to reasons not known, in the year 2001, the library shut its doors and was closed permanently, it was a sad year for the city's bibliophiles. Despite veteran members of the great library seeking intervention of the then Prime Minister Atal Bihari Vajpayee to keep the library intact, nothing could be done. Several members of the 'Friends of British Library' wrote letters to the then secretary general of UNESCO, and several Indian origin MPs in Britain, but to no avail, nothing could avert the decision of its closure. It speaks in volumes about the reading interest of general public of the city and hence the government has been taking care of the Amir-Ud-Daulah public library in the best ways possible, keeping in view the knowledge seekers sharing common heritage.

## RAMPUR RAZA LIBRARY, RAMPUR

**Rampur Raza Library, Rampur**

The Rampur Raza Library is considered one of the most important libraries of South Asia. Besides works relating to different religions, traditions, it is a treasure house of Indo-Islamic culture and serves as a pedestal for learning and arts. Raza Library in Rampur was established by Nawab Faizullah Khan in 1774 AD, since the Nawabs of Rampur were great patrons of cuture, hence the learned clergymen, poets, painters, calligraphers and musicians enjoyed their great patronage. Following Indian independence and annexation of the state in the union of India, the library was brought under the management of the trust, which was established on 6th April, 1951. The library was brought under the administration of a Trust till the Government of India assumed control over the library on 1 July 1975 under the Act of Parliament, which pronounced it as an institution of national importance. Professor Saiyid Nurul Hasan, former Minister of Education, Government of India, brought this library under an Act of Parliament on 1st. July, 1975.

Currently, the Library involves the position of a self-governing foundation of national significance under Department of Culture, Government of India and is completely supported by Central Government. The Library has now accomplished an International status of education and research. It is having 17000 manuscripts in Arabic, Persian, Pashto, Sanskrit, Urdu, Hindi and Turkish languages. Moreover, it possesses a good collection of paintings and palm leaves in various Indian languages. A collection of around 60,000 printed books in various Indian and foreign languages are also available. It houses exceptionally uncommon and significant gathering of original copies, authentic archives, examples of Islamic calligraphy, micro depictions, galactic instruments and uncommon represented works in Arabic and Persian dialects other than 80,000 printed books.

## LIBRARIES AS KNOWLEDGE CENTERS

There have been growing discussions on the role of the public library in recent years. The discussions have been ranging from defining of the role of the public library to more recent policy changes to incorporate the public library as a knowledge centre in the society that endeavors to make learning a habit. It has been learnt that unless public libraries are prepared to accept that they have actually arrived at a critical moment in the advancements of their services, and devise the new knowledge economy embarking globalization of knowledge, they might face declining usage and uncertain funding.

Public libraries must realize the challenges of future in order to prepare them for participation in knowledge economy, subsequently moving quickly to supply the existing clientele and the potential clientele with the skills and opportunities. This would ultimately result into the application of new technology which would provide the infrastructure for the gateways for framing new knowledge economy.

Public libraries have always been the learning centres for the populations that they serve. There is no emergent need for public libraries to abdicate the role which they play in society because of the technology advancements which have effectively brought different access points to knowledge, considerable self-help and functional learning.

Public Libraries must look into the products they offer to their readers and to the very potential brought about by new technologies in order to expand their services. The notion of public libraries becoming knowledge centers is one that needs to be dealt patiently by library management and their principal funding bodies. This would result in enhancing the competence of readers and significantly improving the learning experiences which continue to attribute the overall learning of the populations they cater.

## KNOWLEDGE SUSTAINABILITY

Learning is a perpetual process and people engage themselves in it every day, by learning to cook, fixing the car, pruning the roses, finding their way to unvisited places, finding out the best concerts, cinema and art exhibitions to exploit themselves with. They also endeavour to learn crafts, hobbies and special interest projects, which make the entire learning process effective and enduring.

People learn everyday and the public library is where many of them find the materials to enable them to learn new skills that they probably do not even think of as lifelong learning. A special role which has belonged to public libraries since their inception is to impart knowledge voluntarily. If people are unable to use the new technologies that are being developed to access the information they need to survive and to make their lives more enriched, then the new knowledge economy will be open only to those with the financial capability to exploit it. The vision is that the models discussed in this paper incite public library managers to explore opportunities for their service to participate in the knowledge society, and for their public libraries to envision a model that will be relevant to their community.

Politicians across the world have acquainted themselves with the role played by public libraries in assisting the nations for taking the advantage of the global knowledge economy. It has also been ensured that citizens have the requisite means and the necessary knowledge for using the sophisticated technologies to their advantage, this would result in making the position and finances of public libraries more secure. If only public libraries could position themselves as inevitable in the learning scenario, economic and knowledge society, there will always be a strong and vibrant future for their services and systems. It would also be interesting to ascertain the probabilities of strategic partnerships in order to enable them for providing the services which are deemed essential to the community being catered by them.

The survey results from the Navigating the Economy of Knowledge, it was observed that the majority of the Australians who were included in the surveys, both users and non-users, would use the library in a reflexes, as a source of new information, if they desired to 'find something out' and that a major role of the library was imparting education and contributing to lifelong learning. It was thus concluded that neither of these were new roles for the library.

The self-improvement model devised by the Mechanics Institutes and Carnegie libraries has been an important motivation for public libraries. The role of public libraries in information infused literacy is documented significantly in the research literature. There have been conscious efforts by public libraries to undertake various programs either themselves or with other agencies to provide the essential modalities, resources and impetus in order to ensure that their local communities have access to the training based on information literacy.

## BENEFITS OF KNOWLEDGE SUSTAINABILITY

The beneficiaries of strong and innovative public library services will be both the libraries and the population as a whole. If a nation has access to information through a strong network of public libraries, then it has the basis for an informed citizenry, a sound democracy and the foundation of a strong, informed work force. Thus it becomes more competitive in the world economy. The theory that the public library is all things to all people has been largely restructured and has become proactive towards what its readers expect. This conviction has been effectively espoused by managers of public libraries around the world. They endeavor continuously for keeping public library services convenient, relevant and competitive in the environments that demand efficiency and customer assisted services. There is a new role being ascertained for the public libraries and it is based on lifelong learning and continuing education, while a different perception maintains that this is not at all a new role for the public libraries across the world. The idea of public library has always occupied a distinctive place in field of education, since its establishment as a knowledge centre to harness reading habits in the urban population belonging to working classes during the nineteenth century.

## FUTURE OF PUBLIC LIBRARIES

Although numbered in North India, public libraries need nothing less than renaissance to be able to exist in the days to come, whether being updated with sophisticated technology or outreach projects by going among the target audience and create awareness about resources and learning experiences libraries have to offer. Increasing number of social gatherings within libraries are quite an evidence that libraries have been preparing themselves to be alive while being among us, more like becoming a person. Several TED events have been focused upon the public libraries across the world and North India has not been an exception.

Rise of privatization has changed the way people read but still there is no alternative to presence of a book physically, with advent of e-readers like *Kindle* and *iBooks*, things have become less complicated but that surely has made the libraries vulnerable. Digitization of manuscripts and resources has played a pivotal role in the up gradation of libraries but there remains a lot to be done in order to make these knowledge centers truly sustainable.

Thus it could be summed up that public libraries have a greater role to play in shaping the societies, as in the yesteryears great movements were started on basis of proactive journalism, the current of thoughts flowing through minds of individuals made them aware of what was going on and why things needed to change. At present when libraries in India as a whole suffer for readership, it is inevitable to increase the permeability of the premise of libraries in order to become more user friendly, subsequently contributing in better ways of nation building, because a nation is nothing but its own heritage. There is a great need of enacting upon knowledge sustainability through libraries so as to achieve the goals in line with sustainable development goals.

## REFERENCES


1. Asogwa, Brendan E. Knowledge Management In Academic Libraries: Librarians In The 21st Century. Journal of Knowledge Management Practice, Vol. 13, No. 2, June 2012. *http://www.* tlainc. com/articl301. htm.
2. Batt, Chris (1998), Information technology in public libraries, 6th ed., London, Library Association, p. 53.
3. Borrowed time? The future of public libraries in the UK (1993), London, Comedia, p. 20.
4. Bhattacharjee, R. (2002). Public Library Services in India; Systems, Modernization, Networking and Deficiencies. National Round Table on the Modernization & Networking of Libraries in India edited by H. K. Kaul. New Delhi: DELNET.
5. Cameron, K. S. & Quinn, R. E. (2011). Diagnosing and changing organizational culture:Based on the competing values framework (3rd ed.). San Francisco, CA: Jossey-Bass.
6. Ciganek, Andrew P. Organizational Culture for Knowledge Management Systems: A Study of Corporate Users. *http://www.* irma-international. org/viewtitle/41855.
7. Drucker, Peter. (1993). Post-capitalism Society. Oxford, Great Britain: Butterworth Heinemann.
8. Gandhi, S. (2004), Knowledge management and reference services. The Journal of Academic Librarianship, 30(5), 368-381.
9. Heim, Kathleen M. and Wallace, Danny P., eds. (1990), Adult services: an enduring focus for public libraries, Chicago, ALA.
10. Kalpana Dasgupta, 2000. "Libraries and librarians in India on the threshold of the third millennium: Challenges and risks," IFLA Conference Proceedings (Jerusalem, Israel, August), athttp://www.ifla.org/IV/ifla66/papers/039-120e.htm, accessed 17 September 2017.
11. Khursid, Anis (1972). Growth of Libraries in India. Quoted by Jashu Patel and Krishan Kumar.In. Libraries and Librarianship in India. Westport: Greenwood, 2004, p.6.

12. Kidwell, J. J. Linde, K. M. V. & Johnson, S. L. (2000), Applying corporate knowledge management practices in higher education, Educause Quarterly, (4), 28-33.

13. Kumaresan Chidambaranathan, Knowledge Management and Organizational Culture in Higher Educational libraries in Qatar:An Empirical Study. Volume 37, Issue 4, October 2015, Pages 363–369, Library & Information Science Research. *https://www.* researchgate. net/publication/ 281740934.

14. Kumbar, B. D. (2005). Growth and Development of Public Library System in India with Special Reference to Karnataka. Retrieved Nov 19, 2005 from http://www.nigd.org/libraries/ mumbai/reports/article-4.pdf.

15. Lee, Hwa-Wei, Knowledge Management and the Role of Libraries hlee@lc. govhttp://www. white-clouds. com/iclc/ cliej/cl19lee.

16. Madge, Dr. Octavia-Luciana, Knowledge Management in Libraries *http://www.* lisr. ro/en14-madge. pdf

17. Maponya, Pearl M. Knowledge management practices in academic libraries: a case study of the University of Natal, Pietermaritzburg Libraries *http://citeseerx.* ist. psu. edu/. viewdoc/download?doi=10.1.1.137.8283&rep=rep1 &type=pdf.

18. Marshall, C. Prusak, L. & Shpilberg, D. (1996). Financial risk and the need for superior knowledge management. California Management Review, 38, 77–101.

19. Martin, Lowell A. (1983), Public library: middle age crisis or old age, Library Journal 108, January 1, 1983, p. 17–22.

20. Nagar, Murari Lal (1983). Foundation of Library Movement in India. Ludhiana, Indian Library Institute and Bibliographical Centre.

21. Navigating the economy of knowledge: a national survey of users and non-users of state and public libraries (1995), Brisbane, Griffith University.

22. Nazim, Mohammad. Mukherjee, Bhaskar, Journal of Knowledge Management Practice, Vol. 12, No. 3, September 2011, Implementing Knowledge Management In Indian Academic Libraries Banaras Hindu University, India. *http:/ /www.* tlainc. com/articl269. htm.

23. Nonaka, Ikujiro. (1991). "The Knowledge-Creating Company,

"Harvard Business Review (Nov.-Dec. 1991):96-99.

24. Omotayo, Funmilola Olubunmi. Knowledge Management as an important tool in Organisational Management: A Review of Literature, Library Philosophy and Practice (e-journal) Libraries at University of Nebraska-Lincoln Spring 4-10-2015. *http://digitalcommons*. unl. edu/cgi/viewcontent. cgi?article=3330&context=libphilprac.

25. Panda, B D. (1993). Handbook of Public Library System. New Delhi: Anmol. http://www.nmlindia.nic.in/ (accessed on 21.09.2017)

26. Ranganathan, S. R. (2011). Five laws of librarianship. In Wikipedia the Free Encyclopedia. *http://en.* wikipedia. org/ wiki/Five_laws_of_library_science.

27. Sahib, S. (2003). Library and Literacy Movement for National Development. New Delhi: Concept.

28. Sanchez, R. (2001), Knowledge management and organizational competence. Oxford University Press, New York.

29. Sharma, J. S. (1965). The Substance of Library Science. Bombay: Asia Publishing.

30. Sharma, Pandey S K (1987). Libraries and Society. New Delhi: Ess Ess.

31. Sharma, S. K. Pandey. 1996. Public Libraries in India: Trends and Status. In Public Libraries in Developing Countries: Status and Trends. Ed. P.K. Mahapatra, 121-127. New Delhi.

32. Smith, Vincent A. (1981). Oxford history of India. 4th. Ed. Delhi: OUP.

33. The role of libraries in a learning society (1998), London, Library and Information Commission.

34. Thomas, V.K. (1997). Public Libraries in India: Development & Finance. New Delhi.

35. Townley, C. T. (2001). Knowledge Management and Academic Libraries. College and Research Libraries, 62(1), 44–55.

36. Vikas. Verma, I.N., & Agarawal, U.K. (Eds.) (1994). Public Library Services in India. Udaipur.

# 8

# Knowledge Management Technologies : A Great Survey

**Dr. Pankaj Kumar Singh**
*Asst. Pro. Library Science, DSN PG College, Unnao (UP)*
**Nibedita Choudhury**
*Librarian, Nowgong Polytechnic*
*Nagaon - 782003, Assam*

## ABSTRACT

Knowledge Management is related to the field of Library Science. It is an in conclusive process of creating, sharing, using and managing organisationl knowledge and information. It utilizes knowledge with a multi-disciplinary approach. Launched in Lasi, it covers a wide sphere which includes business administration, information system, management , library and information science etc. It significantly contributes knowledge, management research and therefore, it has been gaining currency day by day. The paper undertake to make a general survey of knowledge management technologies with a new to pointing out now KM can be utilized to the maximum benefit of mankind.

## INTRODUCTION

As a library personnel, I have so far felt that knowledge management is a key to the best functioning of a library and other organizational institutions where knowledge is required. To me, it KM is the foundation of a library where knowledge and information is created, shared, used and managed. No media, business centers and information system can survive without KM. both colleges and universities have felt the need to promote KM , therefore , the technologies of KM become important for every library personnel like me. In the present paper, an attempt has been made to a make a general survey of knowledge management technologies with a riew to making it beneficial for mankind.

Knowledge Management (KM) as is known to all and sundry related to the field of library science is an endless process of creating, sharing, using and managing the knowledge and information of an organization or institute. In a way it is a multidisciplinary approach to realizing the goals of an organization by way of utilizing knowledge in the best possible way. It is an established discipline since 1991 and it incorporates subjects and courses taught in the spheres of business administration, information systems, management, library and information sciences. These are some other fields like information and media, computer management research. The field of knowledge management has been gaining so much importance that there are many universities which offer dedicated master's degrees in knowledge management.

Today there are many companies, public institutions and non profit organizations which have resources dedicated to internal knowledge management efforts, often as a part of their business plan, it ur human resource management departments. The efforts of KM focus on better and integrated performance, faster a healthy competition and encourage innovative steps. Moreover , KM points but the basic need to share earned knowledge. In this way.KM enables and improves organization learning and work culture.

Having outlined the meaning and importance of KM, the study non shifts to the knowledge management technologies which may be grouped as under.

**(A) Groupware :** It includes technologies that facilitate collaboration and sharing of organizational information. Lotus notes is one of the earliest successful products in this category that provided tools for threaded discussions, sharing of documents, organization wide uniform email etc.

**(B) Workflow :** These tools allow the representation of processes associated with the creation, use and maintenance of organizational knowledge, e.g., the process to create and utilize forms and documents.

**(C) Content/Cocument Management :** It consists of systems that automate the process of creating web content and /or documents. Robs such as editors, designers, writers and producers can be explicitly modelled alongwith the tasks in the process and validation criteria.

**(D) Enterprise Portals :** These are web sites that aggregate information across the entire organization or for groups such as project teams.

**(E) e Learning :** It enables organization to crate customized training and education software. This can include lesson plans, monitoring progress and online classes.

**(F) Sheduling & Planning :** It serves to automate schedule creation and maintenance , e.g. Microsoft outlook. The planning asput can integrate with projects management tools such as Microsoft project.

**(G) Telepresence :** It enables individuals to have

virtuel 'free to face' meeting without gathering at one location. Videoconferencing to the best example.

## CONCLUSION

From the foregoing discussion it becomes apparent that with the adoption of internet standards KM technology products such as lotus notes defined proprietary formals for email , documents and form etc. have proliferated. The internet drove most vendors to adopt internet formats. Open source and freeware tools for the creation of blogs and wikis non enable capabilities that used to require expressive commercial tools. Overall, KM promotes the use of such technologies in order to enhance the capabilities and performance of the organization.

## REFERENCE

1. Givand, John P:, girand, JoAnnL.(2015) online Journal of Applied Knowlegement , 3 (1): 14
2. Maier, R (2007) Knowlegement Management Systems: Information And Communication Technologies for knowledge Management (3rd edition). Borlin: Spriger.
3. Rosner, D:, Grote,B; Hartman, K: HoblingB: Guerieke, O (1998). "from natural language documents to sharable product knowledge: a knowledge engineering approach" In Borghoff, Vwe M:, Pareschi Remo. Information Technology for Knowledge management. Springer Verlog PP 35-51.

# 9

# Knowledge Management

**_L D Nagda_**
*B.L.I.Sc., M.L.I.Sc., CPDL*
*Janardan Rai Nagar Rajasthan Vidyapeeth*
*Udaipur, Rajasthan*

## 1. INTRODUCTION

In the era of information technology and knowledge, knowledge has become the key. The traditional function of the Academic Library is to collect, process, disseminate, store and use information to serve the affluent community. However, the environment in which the academic library operates today is changing. Academic libraries are squeezed by both parties: budget reductions, and learner demand increases. The success of academic libraries depends on their ability to use information and knowledge to better meet academic needs. Knowledge management is a viable tool for academic libraries to improve their knowledge-based economy.

This can be achieved by creating an organizational culture that shares knowledge and expertise in the library. However, the organization faces numerous challenges in developing and managing knowledge. The challenge arises because part of the knowledge can only be internalized by the organization; the other is internalized by the individual. The library is the gateway to knowledge. A gateway is a digital means of accessing the required information source. The gateway provides services that enable users and researchers to navigate to access resources. The gateway is a place for individuals and groups to learn, and is the center of interactive learning using digital resources and networks. Gateway goal is convenient, efficient, timely, unified program. Making the library a gateway to innovation into digital knowledge.

## 2. OBJECTIVES OF KNOWLEDGE MANAGEMENT IN ACADEMIC LIBRARIES

The main goal of knowledge management is to ensure that the right information is available in a timely manner in order to take the most appropriate decision. The objectives are as follows:

- Promote the collection, processing, storage and distribution of knowledge
- Promote scientific research
- Promote the relationship between the library and the learner
- Protect intellectual property in the information age
- Create a knowledge base and manage knowledge as an asset
- Organize the value of knowledge and strengthen effective research

## 3. ROLE OF LIBRARY PROFESSIONALS IN KNOWLEDGE MANAGEMENT

1. The traditional role of libraries and information professionals is to collect, process, disseminate, store and use information to provide multidisciplinary services to the individual and professional needs of library learners. But now their

role is not limited to information management. They play a major role in the knowledge management program,

2. Acquire, develop, resolve, store and share information. Libraries and information professionals must manage relationships with external information and knowledge providers and should negotiate with them. Knowledge management has created new opportunities for libraries and information sciences. Library professionals should have the following knowledge: Academic Library Knowledge Management
3. Journal of International Journal of Parallel and Distributed Systems
4. Understand the information sources of library assets, products and services.
5. Know where these sources are stored and its use.
6. Knowledge of the user, including the teaching staff, the researchers, and the use of these sources and how to increase their use.
7. What are the current uses of these sources and how are they used
8. Innovative and capable, learning and adapting new technologies, providing better service to customers, and the ability to create, share, use and use information
9. Understand the impact of knowledge creation and information production
10. Information literacy skills to create, discover, share and use
11. Understand the principles of "organizational knowledge"

**4. SKILLS NEEDED BY THE LIBRARY & INFORMATION PROFESSIONAL**

Teng and Hawamdeh summed up the skills needed by the Library & Information professional in a knowledge based environment:

- IT knowledge, know how to use appropriate technology to capture, catalog and disseminate information and knowledge to target audiences, and learn how to import accessible information into a central database so that employees of the organization
- keen analytical thinking;
- Innovative consulting;
- Make knowledge, communication and communication within the organization and between employees and the public possible.

It is important that academic libraries encourage librarians to constantly update their skills and learning environment.

## 5. NEED FOR KNOWLEDGE MANAGEMENT IN LIBRARIES

Increasing the exponential of various forms of human knowledge leads the library to develop resources to access and share strategies from printing to electronic and digital resources. To provide effective funding for the library, to easily acquire technology, personnel and space, to carefully analyze the needs of learners, and to seek a cooperative acquisition plan to better achieve results.

In fact, the majority of the library budget is allocated to the acquisition and cataloging of its staff and library materials. Effective use of staff (HR), improve the efficiency and effectiveness of technical service operations is the basis of academic library knowledge management.

The goal is to make full use of the knowledge that exists in the organization and improve operational efficiency and productivity.

## 6. PRINCIPLES OF KNOWLEDGE MANAGEMENT

Thomas H Davenport has formulated ten principles of knowledge management as listed below:

- Knowledge Management is expensive
- Effective management of knowledge requires hybrid solutions of people and technology
- Knowledge Management is highly political
- Knowledge Management requires knowledge managers
- Knowledge Management benefits more from maps than model, more from markets than from hierarchies
- Sharing and using knowledge are often unnatural acts
- Knowledge Management means improving knowledge process
- Knowledge access in only the beginning
- Knowledge Management never ends
- Knowledge Management requires a knowledge contract

## 7. COMPONENTS OF KM

The knowledge management environment centered round three components-

1. People – Technology experts
   Knowledge professionals
   Knowledge managers
2. Process - Creation, capturing, storing, sharing, application, and
3. Technology- Hardware and software packages
   (Robertson and Brun, 2005)

**1. People :** All members of the organization are the focus of knowledge management; they are the creators and users of knowledge assets (explicit and implicit). They are the target groups, they are involved in the creation, sharing and use of knowledge generated within the organization, and external knowledge is related to human cognition. The main requirement of knowledge management is information sharing culture. There are three types of people related to knowledge management, namely:

A. *Technology experts* : are those concerned with design and development of tools and services for knowledge discovery. They build applications, databases, networks that allow the organization to do its work with accuracy, reliability and speed. (Kim, Seonghee 2000)

B. *Knowledge Professionals* : What are the people in the organization who have the skills, training and expertise to organize information / knowledge into systems and structures that contribute to the efficient use of information resources.

   For a long time, LIS professionals have been serving as information managers And knowledge managers are concerned about the different knowledge managers Public domain knowledge, and knowledge managers for institutional implicit / tacit knowledge.

C. *Knowledge managers* : are the groups of people, who focus on the achievement of organizational goals. Identify present needs and problems, initiate practical and manageable activities to achieve set goals. Most important feature of knowledge management is motivation of staff to contribute and share their knowledge (not an easy task). Large portion of the knowledge in any organization is tacit, embedded with in individual experience, judgments and intuition (Ahmed, Lim, & Loh, 2002). Some staff may have difficulty in expression and communication. Some staff may not want to share their knowledge for the fear that once their knowledge is shared, they might no longer be valued/ indispensable. Some staff may not share their knowledge for free, as there are free riders who take others knowledge for granted but never share their own. (Susarla, Liu & Whinston 2003).

**2. Process :** Knowledge management process consists of several stages:

A. *Environmental Creation* : People who work in an organization must change their way of thinking, share their acquiescence, develop and understand more information about the system, system users identify and integrate people, and processes and technologies.

B. *Knowledge creation* : knowledge in the public domain is clear and open. In the personal field is the default. Information is human capital.

   Identify new knowledge, create new knowledge, add value and vision for new information and its application, and be the essence of KM

C. *Knowledge organization* : traditional and current knowledge-oriented organizations have a common direction, namely, the establishment of semantic relations, the provision of grammar, hyperlinks (data collection, classification knowledge database to create content mapping, etc.) (library professionals with professional knowledge).

D. *Knowledge sharing* : knowledge sharing involves creating one value of intangible assets (HR / tacit knowledge)

E. *Knowledge synthesis* : the intrinsic value of knowledge creation is applicable to the appropriate situation. Applications can be made from top to bottom, even in the middle. Each strategy has its own advantages and risks.

**3. Technologies :** Do you need to interconnect personal (ie intranet) gadgets (hardware and software)? Internet internal and external processing, storage and retrieval of the required technology and suppliers to provide a variety of KM solution package.

We use existing technology to store and retrieve knowledge and promote knowledge management of library business. Open source technology and software are ideal. But these require a high level of programming skills to use. In contrast, most libraries / librarians have installed Microsoft Office Suite on their workstations.

MS Word helps create operating procedures and other documentation related to library business. MS Excel helps keep statistics and create charts at the department / department level. MS Access can be retrieved by storing data from a custom query, or it can be converted to web pages (static / dynamic), easy to retrieve, and most employees are familiar with MS Word and Excel. In addition, the portal, online help desk, virtual reference desk and so on. All information is accessible via Wi-Fi network.

## 8. KNOWLEDGE MANAGEMENT PROCESS

Knowledge management is a process involving knowledge creation, acquisition, packaging and application or knowledge reuse. It consists essentially of the following four steps:

- Knowledge Collection
- Organization
- Data protection and presentation
- Dissemination of Knowledge Information

Knowledge management is the way to maintain knowledge growth through sharing, and this sharing is best done in a material or human way. With the help of the following flowcharts, you can understand the relationship between knowledge and social development:

- Knowledge creation knowledge
- Knowledge processing pricing knowledge
- Knowledge - enhancing knowledge distribution

**Definitions**

According to Srinivasan, *"Knowledge Management refers to a collection of process, technologies and principles that serves to promote a learning environment supportive of the search community goal."*

Knowledge Management is the process of capturing value, knowledge and understanding of corporate information, using IT systems, in order to maintain, re-use and re-deploy that knowledge. [Source: OIC document management.]

## 9. THE CONCEPT OF KNOWLEDGE MANAGEMENT

The concept of "knowledge management" began to flourish in the business world in the last decade of the twentieth century. The business world first recognizes the importance of knowledge in the "global economy" of the "knowledge age".

In the new knowledge economy, with relevant strategic knowledge and constantly updated, so that enterprises gain a competitive advantage. The application of knowledge management has now been disseminated to other organizations, including government agencies, research and development departments, universities and library information occupations.

As early as 1965, Peter Drucker already pointed out that "knowledge" would replace land, labor, capital, machines, etc. to become the chief source of production. His foresight did not get much attention back then. It was not until 1991 when Ikujiro Nonaka raised the concept of "tacit" knowledge and "explicit" knowledge as well as the theory of "spiral of knowledge" in the Harvard Business Review that the time of "knowledge-based competition" finally came. IN his latest book, Building Organizational Intelligence: a Knowledge Management Primer, Jay Liebowitz stated as:

"In today's movement towards knowledge management, organizations are trying to best leverage their knowledge internally in the organization and externally to their customers and stakeholders. They are trying to capitalize on their organizational intelligence to maintain their competitive edge." "The thrust of knowledge management is to create a process of valuing the organization's intangible assets in order to best leverage knowledge internally and externally. Knowledge management, therefore, deals with creating, securing, capturing, coordinating Information.

## 10. TOOLS FOR KNOWLEDGE MANAGEMENT

The following are the key types of knowledge-related tools that effectively manage and process information and knowledge to maintain a knowledge base organization:

- Intranet / extranet
- Electronic document management
- Data Analysis Data Warehouse
- Helpdesk technology
- Drawing tools
- Machine learning
- Workflow management system

### Groupware

- Information retrieval tool
- Data Warehouse: Metadata
- Portal

- Agent technology
- Ontology (based on computer)

## 11. THE STAGES OF DEVELOPMENT OF KNOWLEDGE MANAGEMENT (IN SHORT)

Looking at KM historically through the stages of its development tells us not only about the history of KM, but it also reveals a great deal about what constitutes KM.

### First Stage of KM : Information Technology

The initial stage of KM was driven primarily by IT, information technology. That first stage has been described using an equestrian metaphor as “by the internet out of intellectual capital”. The concept of intellectual capital provided the justification equestrian metaphor as “by the internet out of intellectual capital”. The concept of intellectual capital provided the justification and the framework, the seed, and the availability of the internet provided the tool. As described above, the consulting community jumped at the new capabilities provided by the Internet, using it first for them, realizing that if they shared knowledge across their organization more effectively, then they could avoid reinventing the wheel, underbid their competitors, and makes more profit. The first use of the term Knowledge Management in the new context appears to have been at McKinsey.

They realized quickly that they had a compelling new product. Ernst and Young organized the first conference on KM in 1992 in Boston (Prusak, 1999). The salient point is that the first stage of KM was about how to deploy that new technology to accomplish more effective use of information and knowledge.

The first stage might be described as the “If only Texas Instruments knew what Texas Instruments knew” stage, to revisit a much quoted aphorism. The hallmark phrase of Stage 1 was first "best practices," to be replaced by the more politic "lessons learned."

**Second Stage of Knowledge Management: HR and Corporate Culture**

The second Stage of intellectual property has shown that simply deploying new technologies is not enough to effectively achieve information and knowledge sharing. Need to address the human and cultural dimensions. The second stage may be described as "if you build it, they will come" is a fallacy "stage - admit that" if you build their future "is a recipe that can easily lead to quick and embarrassing failure if the human factor is not Fully considered.

It is clear that the implementation of knowledge management will involve changes in corporate culture, in many cases is a significant change. Consider the situation of the new pediatric drugs mentioned above, and find the effect of adding orange juice to the recipe. Pharmaceutical sales representatives are not primarily based on salaries, but on sales-based bonuses. The sales representative in the sharing of her new discovery, the most likely result is next year her prize will be greatly reduced? The change in corporate culture that promotes and encourages information and knowledge sharing can be significant and profound. As a result, KM is far beyond the structured information and knowledge and makes it easier to access.

As this recognition unfolded, two major themes from the business literature were brought into the KM fold. The first was Senge's work on the learning organization (Senge, Peter M., 1990 The Fifth Discipline: The Art and Practice of the Learning Organization.) The second was Nonaka's work on "tacit" knowledge and how to discover and cultivate it (Nonaka, Ikujiro & Takeuchi, Hirotaka,

1995 The Knowledge Creating Company: How Japanese Companies Create the Dynamics of Innovation.) Both were not only about the human factors of KM implementation and use~ they were also about knowledge creation as well as knowledge sharing and communication. The hallmark phrase of Stage 2 was "communities of practice." A good marker of the shift from the first to the second stage of KM is that for the 1998 Conference Board conference on KM, there was for the first time a noticeable contingent of attendees from HR, human resources, departments, and by the next year, 1999, HR was the largest single group, displacing IT attendees from first place.

**Third Stage of KM: Taxonomy and Content Management**

The third stage developed from the awareness of the importance of content, and in particular the awareness of the importance of the retrievability of content, and therefore of the importance of the arrangement, description, and structure of that content.

Since a good alternative description for the second stage of KM is the "it's no good if they don't use it" stage, then in that vein, perhaps the best description for the new third stage is the "it's no good if they try to use it but can't find it" stage. Another bellwether is that TFPL's report of their October 2001 CKO (Chief Knowledge Officer) Summit reported that for the first time taxonomies emerged as a topic, and it emerged full blown as a major topic (TFPL, 2001 Knowledge Strategies – Corporate Strategies.) The hallmark phrases emerging for the third stage are content management (or enterprise content management) and taxonomies.. At KMWorld 2000 a track on Content Management appeared for the first time, and by the 2001 KMWorld Conference, Content Management had become the dominant track. In 2006, World added a two-day workshop entitled Taxonomy Boot Camp, which still exists today. The hallmark terms for the third stage of KM are taxonomy and content.

#### Other KM Issues

One query is the need to retain the knowledge of retirees. Of course, this baby boomers have been rumbling, and now has to retirement age, this problem is particularly prominent. KM technology is very relevant to this problem. One technique is the application of lessons learned - just retiring as a long term project and creating a large-scale data dump follow-up report. This idea seems obvious, but only in exceptional circumstances it may be very useful.

More likely to help keep the retiree involved, keep him or her in the CoP, and find it through the Expertise System. In the information left by retirees, the real situation may not be direct, but the new knowledge created by the interaction of retirees and current employees. Retirees said: "This happens to me ..." and leads to a similar "yes, but here ..." response, a discussion unfolds, retirees provide some of the required expertise And produce a solution. The solution is not directly from the retiree's knowledge, but from the interaction.

Another major development is the knowledge management beyond the 20th century knowledge management vision, as the organization's knowledge, as defined by the Gartner Group's knowledge management definition. Increasing knowledge management is considered to ideally encompass the overall bandwidth of information and knowledge that may be useful to the organization, including knowledge generated outside the organization - knowledge generated by suppliers, suppliers, customers, etc., as well as from the scientific and academic communities the knowledge of the traditional world of the library world. From this point of view, KM extends to environmental scanning and competitive intelligence.

**Is KM here to stay?**

The answer is definitely yes. The most compelling analysis is bibliometrics, which simply calculates the number of articles in the business literature and compares it with other business zeal. Most business enthusiasm grew rapidly, reaching a peak in about five years, and then the rate of decline was almost as fast as the growth rate.

## 12. BARRIERS TO KNOWLEDGE MANAGEMENT IN ACADEMIC LIBRARIES

Every library professional working in academic, public, or any special library wants to use knowledge management techniques to achieve organizational goals and provide better service to their users, but because they cannot use the following obstacles:

- There is no co-operation between senior and junior staff.
- Generally, the junior staff cannot share their knowledge and ideas when they feel there is no benefit of this in terms of salary increases.
- Every library cannot participate in terms of modern technology and its management
- Lack of communication skills.
- Lack of staff training.
- Lack of sufficient budget / funds
- Lack of tool and technologies
- Lack of Centralized policy for Library cess

## 13. BENEFITS OF IT IN KNOWLEDGE MANAGEMENT

A computer, databases and telecommunications, particularly in relation to the Internet, provides administrators with an incredible selection to improve the way the organization. As long as,

IT provides management systems and professional

approach to IT services. Adopting its guidance offers users a wide range of benefits, including:

- Reduce service costs
- Time users and staff
- Improve the quality and quantity of
- Better customer service
- Provide a more professional approach to service through better customer / user satisfaction
- Increased productivity
- Information technology helps maximize profits
- Provide management and trust to cover risks in order to achieve organizational objectives
- Retrieve data faster and more easily and disseminate information
- Reduce the risk of errors and

## 14. RESOURCES REQUIRED BY KM

KM is a useful resource. Qualified and dedicated personnel are required for a successful KM effort, as a supporting technology. One of the resources required for a successful KM effort is personnel. KM requires not only knowledgeable employees, but also specialized knowledge workers. A KM worker requires varying depths of knowledge in particular areas (Sky me, 1998):

**Technical skills :** information (resources) management, information technology skills.

**Business knowledge :** industry, markets, 190 ICAL 2009 – VISION AND ROLES OF THE FUTURE ACADEMIC LIBRARIES customers, competitors, and general business context.

**Interpersonal skills :** networking, listening comprehension, challenge, teamwork, communication.

**Management skills :** incentives, counseling, promotion, impact.

**Corporate / organizational knowledge :** procedural and cultural knowledge.

**Personal characteristics :** integrity, confidence, openness, trust, support, honesty, willingness to learn.

## 15. SIGNIFICANCE OF KNOWLEDGE MANAGEMENT IN ACADEMIC LIBRARIES:

KM is defined by Gartner Group (2000) as a discipline that promotes as integrated approach to identifying, capturing, evaluating, retrieving and sharing all the information assets of organization. Balcombe (1999) defines:

"Knowledge management is systematically capturing, sharing, using and creating knowledge to add value to the organization." It also refers to effectively identifying, acquiring, developing, resolving, using, storing and sharing knowledge, to create an approach for transforming tacit knowledge into explicit knowledge (Shanhong, 2000).

For the purposes of this document, according to the above definition, KM can be defined as the process of identifying, capturing, storing and utilizing knowledge (default and explicit). In order to determine the value of the Intranet as a KM tool for the University of Karnataka, a small survey was conducted to understand their understanding of knowledge management.

Their understanding of knowledge management is "the process of identifying, acquiring, organizing, and sharing packets in a user group."

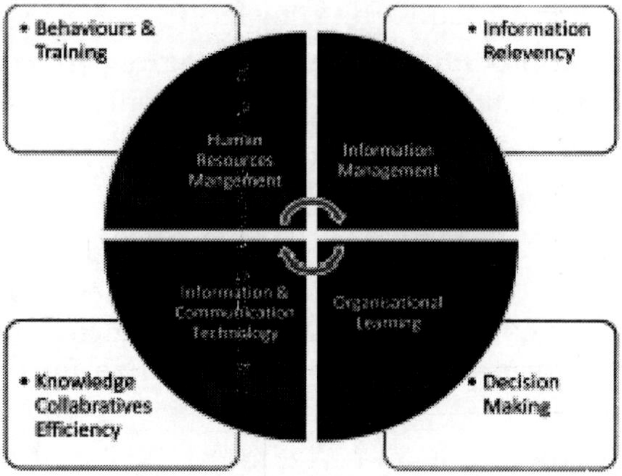


**16. RECENT ADVANCEMENT OF KM FOR INSTANT COMMUNICATING WORLDWIDE**

1. Cloud computing
2. Social network
3. Information sharing App and Web
4. Free electronic resource tools
5. Library free reference

**17. LOOK FOR ADVANCEMENT IN KM**

Information technology and knowledge need to work together to focus on getting the right information in the right time transfer to the right person. Librarians and information scientists must have the community as a whole knowledge management strategy or framework, as a means of disseminating the required information.

With the following items, in order to better implement the knowledge management library, especially in academic libraries:

- Provide adequate budget
- Provision of a special fund for new technologies

- Library processing with new technologies with network facility
- Change of professional staff between organizations / libraries
- Staff participation to develop their professional skills
- Organize a training program for me and change staff at the present time at the national level (at least once every two years for two months)
- The Center could establish a monitoring center specifically for libraries to monitor library standards and provide assistance

## 18. INTERCONNECTING KNOWLEDGE MANAGEMENT DATABASE NECESSITY FOR FUTURE OFFSPRING

We provide an approach to knowledge-building through structured exploration of large temporal temporal datasets. First, we provide the context of our problem and define both (GV) and discovery of knowledge in databases (CKD), and source areas for methods being merged. After that, we review and compare the recent GV and CID developments and consider the possibility of integration, emphasizing that the iterative process with user interaction is the main focus of attention and revealing meaningful patterns through each. We then present an approach to the design of an integrated HV-K-environment oriented to exploration and discovery in the context of temporal spatial environmental data. The approach emphasizes a matching of GV is and KDD meta-operations. Following description of the GV is and KDD methods that are linked in our prototype system, we present a demonstration of the prototype applied to a typical spatiotemporal dataset. We conclude by outlining, briefly, research goals directed toward more complete integration of GVis and KDD methods and their connection to temporal GIS.

## CONCLUSION

Academic libraries play a vital role in crossing borders, the key to opening all doors to knowledge. Librarians should train themselves and their staff to develop appropriate knowledge management systems and use information technology for equipped libraries to provide better, faster and more accurate services to their customers.

Knowledge management helps library and information professionals improve the services provided to their users. Information professionals have to transform their roles as knowledge professionals.

The role of librarians should not be limited to information keepers, but they must acquire the skills to be updated in order to intelligently and objectively face the efficient and effective knowledge management in academic libraries.

## REFERENCES


1. International Journal of Parallel and Distributed Systems Volume 1, Issue 1, 2011, pp-05-08 Available online at: *http://www.bioinfo.in/contents.php?id=107*
2. Davenport, T. H. (1997a), Knowledge Management at Ernst and Young, 1997, http://knowman.bus.utexas.edu/E&Y.htm, 1997a.
3. Davenport, T. H. (1997b), Some Principles of Knowledge Management
4. Sharon Teng, Suliman Hawamdeh, (2002) "Knowledge management in public libraries", Aslib Proceedings, Vol. 54 Issue: 3, pp.188-197, *https://doi.org/10.1108/00012530210441737*
5. Jennifer Rowley, (1999) "What is knowledge management?", Library Management, Vol. 20 Issue: 8, pp.416-420, *https://doi.org/10.1108/01435129910291175*
6. Robertson, Shaunagh and Brun, Caroline De (2005): Developing the Knowledge Management
7. Environment. NLH Knowledge Management. Specialist Library (Jul-2005) *http://www.library.nhs.uk/*

*knowledgemanagemet/ view Resource.aspx?*

8. doi: 10.5465/AMR.1981.4287793 ACAD MANAGE REV April 1, 1981 vol. 6 no. 2 225-230 Senge, Peter. "The fifth discipline." (1990).
9. Reid, I.C (2000): The Web and the Universities. http// :ausweb.scu.edu/aw2k/papers/reid/ accessed on 6/4 / 2008.
10. Naidoo, V. (2002): Organizational culture and subculture influences on the implementation and outcomes of aspects on internal quality assurance initiates. http//:www.edu.on/ conmferences/herdsa/ main/papers
11. DiMattia, S and Oder, N (1997): Knowledge Management: Hope, Hype or Harbinger? Library Journal,. 122(15), 33-35. Table: Services through Intranet KM - services Intranet services Intranet services No Intranet, UL in J&K(4) UL in Karnataka UL in J&K Ser.
12. Branin, J.J (2003): Knowledge Management on Academic Libraries: Building the knowledge bank at the Ohio State University. Journal of LibraryAdministration, 39(4), 1-56.
13. Robertson, Shaunagh and Brun, Caroline De (2005): Developing the Knowledge Management Environment. NLH Knowledge Management. Specialist Library (Jul-2005) *http:/ /www.library.nhs.uk/knowledgemanagemet/ view Resource.aspx?*
14. Kim, Seonghee, (2000): The roles of knowledge professionals for knowledge. Management. INSPEL 34,1 (2000),1-8 *http:/ /www.ifla.org/ VII/ d2inspel/ index.html*
15. Ahmed, P. K., Lim, K. K., & Loh, A.Y.E. (2002): Learning through knowledge management. Oxford: Butterworth-Heineman.
16. Susarla, A., Liu, D, & Whinston, A. B. (2003): Peer-toPeer Enterprise knowledge Management. In Handbook on Knowledgement. Pt.2: Knowledge Directories, Berlin: Springer, pp.129-139.
17. Garterner Group (2000): Knowledge Management. available at: *www.stevedenning.com/ what_is_knowledge_ - management.html*
18. Balcanbe. J. (1999): "Getting out of Box: the role of the information professional in Knowledge management". The Law Librarian, 31(2), 91-94.

19. Shanhong, T. (2000), "Knowledge management in libraries in the 21st. century", 66th IFLA Council and General Conference, Jerusalem, Israel, available at: *http://ifla.inist.fr/IV/ifla66/*

20. Blackmore (1997): "The development of an Intranet within college of further and higher education". ASLIB Proceedings, 49 (3), 67-72.

21. Curry, A and Stancich , L (2000): " The Intranet: an intrinsic component of strategic information management". International Journal of Information Management, 20, 249-68.

22. Yen, D.C and Chou , D.C (2001): "Intranets for organizational Innovation". Information Management and Computer Security. 9 (2), 80-87.

23. Skyrme, D. (1998), "Knowledge management – a fad or a ticket to ride?" available at: *www.skyrme.com/pubs/iis0298.htm*

24. Robinson, H. (1999), "The development of an intranet as a knowledge management tool", The Law Librarian, Vol. 30, No. 2, pp. 95-7.

25. Jussilainen, M. (1999), "Intranet as a tool for knowledge management: the case of the Council of State in Finland", International Online Information Meeting, 23, 111-16.

# 10

# Internet Literacy Among P.G. Students: A Case Study

***Reena Anand***
*Assistant Librarian*
*The IIS University, Jaipur*

## ABSTRACT

Information communication technology, through the computer internet has brought about a revolutionary change in the ways we used to seek information traditionally. The effects have primarily been on the stupendous range of database that can be made available in a very short span of time, with authenticity. Internet literacy thus becoming an integral part of education and research in institutions of learning all over the world.

The object of this present study is to find out the usage pattern of internet searching, satisfaction levels of the available information services along with their authenticity, evaluation and implementation among P.G students.

The study was undertaken with a view to know the extent to which internet literacy is being put to use by students of P.G course, and to what extent the students felt it helped them in furthering their cause. Accordingly, a self-designed questionnaire was prepared by the investigator and distributed among the aspirants for the course.

## 1. INTRODUCTION

The Internet, if one were to say in one word, is a formidable application tool! Formidable, I say in the sense of a boon. Just imagine! Can we conceive of a life without the Internet! Internet is the one single-most factor that has taken the world's imagination by storm. Suppose the Wi-Fi connectivity is not there for a day, that day the world will have almost come to a standstill.

This global resource is available to all, at one – anyone, anytime, anywhere. Its applicability is universal. Great advances, specifically when we see it in the field of research, industries, business, banking, ticketing, buying of goods and services, it facilitates all and sundry - electronic exchange of ideas with a host of latest information and has been an invaluable source of collaboration among the scholarly communities' connectivity of the world. Study, research and development has acquired a speed and proficiency that opens up vistas of user-friendly accesses; this being the sole objective to modernize and make Libraries equipped as an all-encompassing centre for Research and information. Statistical analysis of the use of Internet and e-resources has thus become an irreplaceable necessity in the sphere of Library studies. Internet has brought people on a common platform beyond the isolated telephone, fax and computer to a organized networking of exchanges of news, views, events, and browsing through library catalogues, a networked information frontier.

Internet can be likened to a transport vehicle integral to an information store in files and documents to be transported from one computer to the other. It carries together various information and services, such as electronic mail, online chat, file transfer and the interlinked Web pages and other documents of the World Wide Web. Without these key operations possible which, unfortunately, is still a reality in many of the South (undeveloped) countries of the world of Library information access facility. Just as human hunger is satiated with food grains, so is the intellectual hunger appeased by Internet.

The present study is an urge to bridge the gap of library facilities available in the advanced countries vis-à-vis the developing countries. If we do not focus our attention and display an indifferent or lackadaisical attitude in improving on this front, we are sure to lag behind and the chasm would go on to becoming a gulf which, as developing countries we cannot afford or allow.

## 2. OBJECTIVE

1. To know frequency of using Internet
2. To find out the different purposes for which the Internet is used by users
3. To identify most visit website use by the users
4. To know the favorite search engines used by the users
5. To find out the satisfaction levels of the available information services through Internet
6. To identify the type of problems faced by the users

## 3. METHODOLOGY

In the present study, questionnaire method was adopted to collect information from the respondents. Keeping the well defined aims and objectives of the present investigation, a well – structured questionnaire was prepared and distributed to the users. For the purpose of the present study, information pertaining to the "Internet Literacy" was collected from 100 P.G students of The IIS University, Jaipur.

## 4. DATA ANALYSIS

The present study was conducted to ascertain the Internet Literacy among P.G Students. The collected data are tabulated and analysed to reach meaningful conclusions.

*Table 4.1. Frequency of using Internet*

| S.No. | Response | No. of Respondents N-100 | % |
|---|---|---|---|
| 1. | Daily | 75 | 75% |
| 2. | Once a week | 19 | 19% |
| 3. | Once a fortnight | 5 | 5% |
| 4 | Once a month | 1 | 1% |

Table 4.1 show that 75% respondents used Internet daily, followed by 19% respondents who used the internet once in a week, while 5% respondents used internet once a fortnight and 1% used internet once a month.

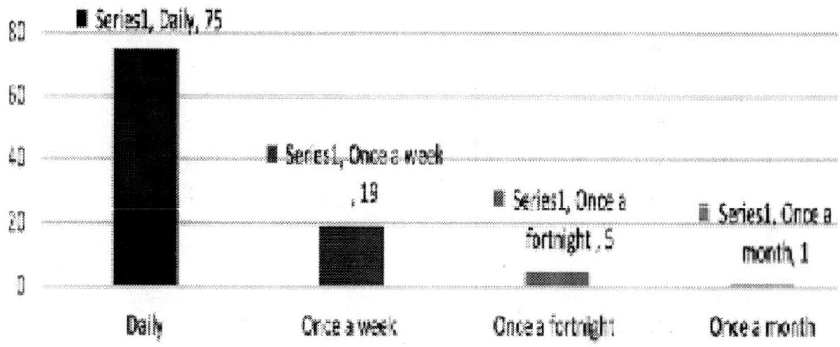


**Fig. 4.1. Frequency of using Internet**

*Table 4.2. Location of Internet use*

| S.No. | Response | No. of Respondents N-100 | % |
|---|---|---|---|
| 1. | At Library | 20 | 20% |
| 2 | At home | 40 | 40% |
| 3 | At cyber café | 5 | 5% |
| 4 | At on seat | 35 | 35% |

**Table 4.2** show that 40 % respondents used internet at home , 35 % users used internet at on seat, 20% respondents used internet in the library, 5 % respondents used internet at cyber café.

**Fig. 4.2. Location of Internet use**

*Table 4.3. Purpose of Internet use*

| *S.No.* | *Response* | *No. of Respondents N-100* | *%* |
|---|---|---|---|
| 1. | For seeking required information | 11 | 11% |
| 2 | E-mail | 20 | 20% |
| 3 | Communication with friends | 18 | 18% |
| 4 | Entertainment | 13 | 13% |
| 5 | Bibliographical information | 08 | 08% |
| 6 | Searching journal | 20 | 20% |
| 7 | Day to day information need | 10 | 10% |

Table- 4.3 show that purpose of Internet use 20 % respondents use internet for E-mail services and searching e-journals, communication with friends mentioned by 18%, 13% respondents access Internet for entertainment, 10% respondents use internet for Day to day information need and 08% use internet for Bibliographical information.

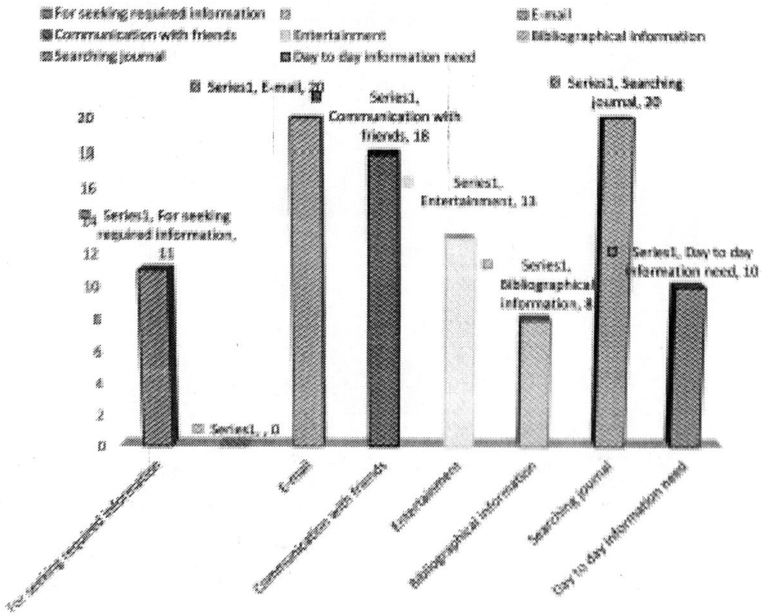


**Fig. 4.3. Purpose of Internet use**

*Table 4.4. Most visit website*

| *S.No.* | *Response* | *No. of Respondents N-100* | *%* |
|---|---|---|---|
| 1. | Commercial website | 15 | 15% |
| 2. | Educational | 40 | 40% |
| 3. | Entertainment | 35 | 35% |
| 4. | News websites | 10 | 10% |

Table-4.4 show that a majority of respondents 40% consider information websites like Wikipedia as useful for accessing the lasted information on a particular subject and 35% mentioned entertainment / community – based websites such as facebook.com, 15 % respondents access commercial website and 10% respondents news website.

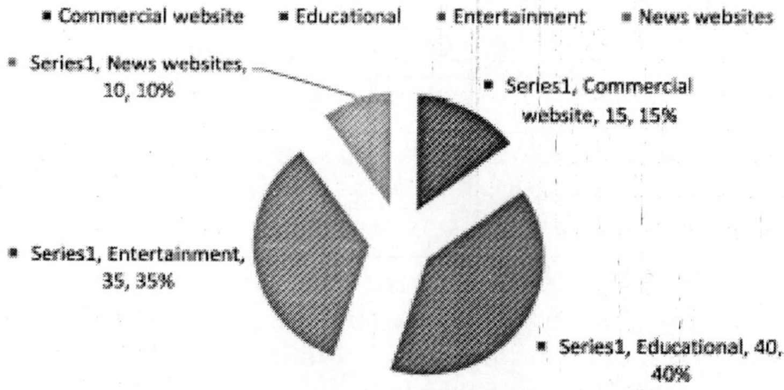


**Fig. 4.4. Most visit website**

*Table 4.5. Favourite Search Engines*

| ***S.No.*** | ***Response*** | ***No. of Respondents N-100*** | ***%*** |
|---|---|---|---|
| 1. | Google | 75 | 75% |
| 2. | Yahoo | 18 | 18% |
| 3. | Bing | 3 | 3% |
| 4. | Rediff | 4 | 4% |

Table 4.5 shows that Google.com is the most preferred search engine with 75% positive responses, followed by Yahoo with 18%, Rediff with 4% and Bing with 3% .It is clear from the analysis of data that Google.com most used search engine among the respondents.

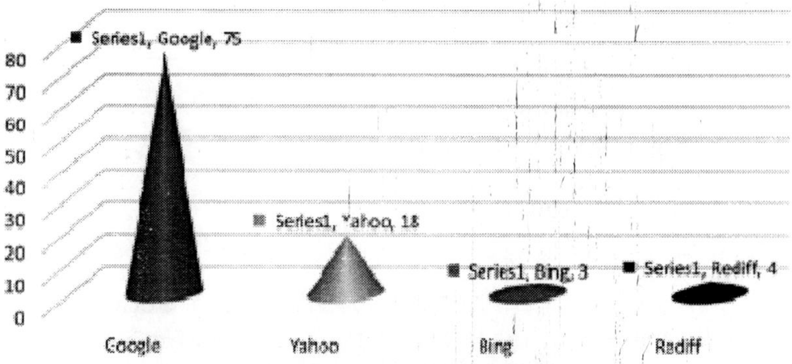


**Fig. 4.5. Favourite Search Engines**

*Table 4.6. Satisfaction with Internet facilities*

| S.No. | Response | No. of Respondents N-100 | % |
|---|---|---|---|
| 1. | Fully satisfied | 55 | 55% |
| 2. | Partially satisfied | 35 | 35% |
| 3. | Not satisfied | 10 | 10% |

Table 4.6 indicates that a majority of the respondents 55% fully satisfied with internet facilities, 35 % respondents partially satisfied and 10 % users are not satisfied with internet facilities.

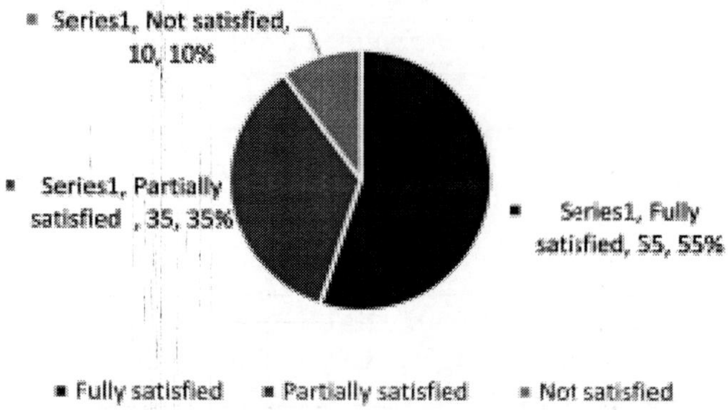


**Fig. 4.6. Satisfaction with Internet facilities**

*Table 4.7. Problem faced while searching the information on Internet*

| S.No. | Response | No. of Respondents N-100 | % |
|---|---|---|---|
| 1. | Lack of Time | 10 | 10% |
| 2. | Lack of Expertise | 18 | 18% |
| 3. | Slow speed of the Internet | 19 | 19% |
| 4. | Lack of Knowledge about important sites in the subject area | 45 | 45% |
| 5. | No problem | 8 | 8% |

Table 4.7 - The above table also depicts some problems, 45% users faced the most common problem like Lack of Knowledge about important sites in the subject area, 19% complained about the slow speed of the Internet, 18% suffering this problem, 19%.

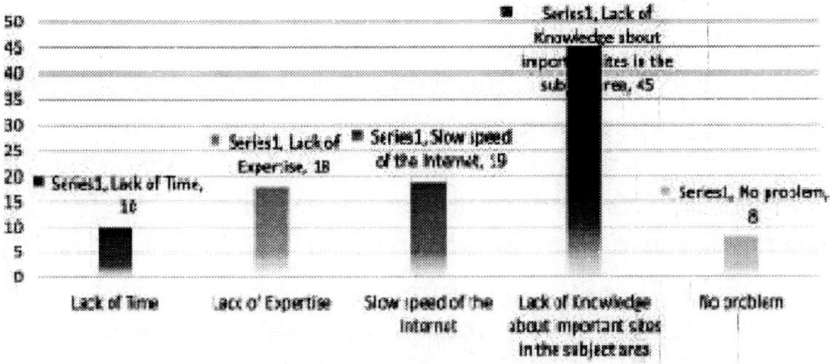


**Fig. 4.7. Problem faced while searching the information on Internet**

The Internet has changed much in two decades since it came into existence. It was conceived in the era of time sharing, but has survived into the era of personal computers, client server and peer- to – peer computing and the network computer. It was designed before LANs existed, but has accommodated that new networking technology, as well as the more recent ATM and frame stitched services switched services.

This study gives a snapshot of the Internet Literacy among P.G students. This study shows that most of users use the Internet services daily for accessing information quickly. It was found that a maximum number of users were satisfied with the use of Internet and the information available on the net. Mostly user preferred Google.com search engine. We can conclude that the users have a positive attitude towards the Internet 45% users faced the most common problem like Lack of Knowledge about important sites in the subject area.

The parameters on which the study was evaluated showed that the application of Internet use is growing at a rate that what was done in a decade is now replaced by a year. Redundancy rate shows the growth of use very clearly. The students, too, felt that their reports are now more accurate and pin-pointed over any range of study. In other words so to say, the satisfaction levels of the users was very high and appreciable.

Moreover, the ICT technology which is being upgraded and modernized every day benefits the aspirants in a way that they would like themselves to keep pace with the advantageous growth by, often, their own efforts and willingness rather that on to depend on some outside help for their orientation purposes.

Lastly, it places a greater need as well as responsibility on the libraries to keep itself updated with well-stacked information so as to facilitate any work of different disciplines to come to seek help for their information collection needs.

## REFERENCE

1. Anand, Reena and Agarwal, Umesh. 2017. Information - Seeking Behaviour of Research Scholars in ICT Environment. Research Reinforcement, 4(2),60-63.
2. Kaur, A. (2000), Internet Facility at GNDU: A Survey. *National Seminar on Academic Libraries in the Modern Era,* Organised by IASLIC, December 4-6, 2000, Bhopal. 119-124.
3. Mahajan, P. 2005. Internet Use by Researchers: A study of Punjab University, Chandigarh. Library Philosophy and Practice. 8(2).
4. Rajeev, K. and Kaur, A (2005): Use of Internet by Teachers and Students in Shaheed Bhagat Singh College of Engineering & Technology: A Case study. *Journal of Library and Information Science,* 29(1/2),81-94.

# 11

# Bibliotherapy : An Introduction

***Dr. Kunwar Surendra Bahadur***
*Regional Director UPRTOU Allahabada*
*147, A Civil lines, near Circuit house,*
*OPP- Allahabad Bank, Bareilly- 243001*

## INTRODUCTION

The Ancient Greeks were the first to recognize that people could use books as potential therapeutic tools. The inscription over the library at Thebes bore the inscription: "The Healing Place of the Soul" [1] . In the 20th century, this concept of using books for healing, currently termed "bibliotherapy", has undergone significant development. This paper examines bibliotherapy in the library science field with a particular focus on the use of differences between bibliotherapy and reader's advisory, the effectiveness of bibliotherapy, the different types of bibliotherapy, and the responsibility of the public library to provide bibliotherapy. The final section provides the librarian with some guidelines for practicing bibliotherapy with children.

A basic definition of the term bibliotherapy can be

derived from its etymology. Bibliotherapy is a combination of two Greek works, biblion meaning book and therapeia meaning healing. In semantic terms, bibliotherapy means, “healing through books”[3]. Although the concept of using word “bibliotherapy” first appeared in 1916. Essayist Samuel Crothers created the term bibliotherapy to describe “a technique of prescribing books to patients who need help understanding their problems”. Since its inception, the definition of bibliotherapy has become more complex. Several professions have adopted the use of bibliotherapy including psychiatry, sociology, psychology, education and library science. Each field interprets and practices bibliotherapy differently. Furthermore, within each profession, there are disagreements about the interpretation and application of bibliotherapy [4]. In the library science field, for example, confusion has developed over the distinction between reader’s advisory service and bibliotherapy.

Many librarians state that bibliotherapy is simply a more specialized form of reader’s advisory [5]. Both reader’s advisory and bibliotherapy transaction involve librarians recommending books for patrons to read. In a recent article, Brian Sturm elucidates an important difference between reader’s advisory and bibliotherapy. Sturm explains that “the reader’s advisor suggests what the patrons say they want; the bibliotherapist suggests what he thinks the patrons may need [6]. An illustration of a basic reader’s advisory transaction would be a librarian recommending books to a child about their favorite hobby. A bibliotherapy scenario would be a librarian recommending books to a child about divorce because the child is having problems accepting the divorce of his/her parents. In 1966, the American Library Association officially accepted the following definition of bibliotherapy: “Guidance in the solution of personal problems through directed reading” [7]. The presence of a “personal problem” is another element that distinguishes bibliotherapy from reader's advisory. In bibliotherapy, a librarian recommends books that they believe a child may need to help them overcome a personal problem. Some of the books that librarians recommend to children have actually been nicknamed "problem novels" [8].

An examination of the problem novel reveals how bibliotherapy work and some of its limitation. The development of problem novels can be traced back to the 1950's. [9]. In 1951, J.D. Salinger published his seminal novel, The Catcher in the Rye. Through the eyes of his protagonist Holden Caufield, Salinger was able to explore in a candid manner how adolescents feel alienated from society. Lauren Myracle argues that The Catcher in the Rye "heralded a new frankness in young adult literature ..... Soon afterwards, young adult novels were tackling such topics as teenage pregnancy, abortion, alcoholism, divorce, suicide, homosexuality, and more recently AIDS". Barbara Chatton points out that the development of problem novels was a reflection of a societal treand that involved being more open with children about "once-forbidden topics" [10]. The problem novel "genre" became relatively extensive in term of the variety of topics that the novels discussed [11]. Chatton argues that the expansion of the genre stimulated the use of bibliotherapy the children because librarians could match a book to almost any problem that a child was experiencing [12]. Michael Warner provides a straightforward explanation of how bibliotherapy works in theory.

The underlying idea of bibliotherapy is that is person dealing with a specific problem - e.g. peer pressure - might be helped by reading a piece of fiction in which a character is dealing with a similar problem.... Proponents of the use of bibliogherapy explain the process in this way:

1. A form a bond with the character facing a problem similar to the reader's own.
2. The character deals with the problem, most times successfully, sometimes not.
3. In a vicarious sense, the reader does the same and experiences the accompanying rise of self-esteem gained from successfully coping with the problem If the character fails to handle the problem successfully, the reader can come away from the story having tried one approach and seeing the outcome without suffering the negative consequences. The reader is then able to reflect on personal circumstances and practice the behaviours that now seem to stand the best chance of success [13].

Warner's explanation actually reveals one of the limitations of bibliotherapy. A librarian can attempt to match a book to a child's situation but there is no guarantee that the child will identify with the novel's characters, reading is a subjective experience and a librarian cannot predict hot a child will react to a novel. The recommended book itself is another critical factor in determining the effectiveness of bibliotherapy. Many problem novels offer "bandaid" solutions that are too simplistic for real world problems [14]. Beth and Carol Doll point out that "when these simplified solutions are ultimately unsuccessful, young readers can become discouraged and give up prematurely in their attempts to deal with important personal problem".

Considering these limitations, is bibliotherapy an effective form of treatment for children? Richard Riordan and Linda Wilson conducted a literature review on bibliotherapy in 1989. They concluded that studies on bibliotherapy are inconclusive because the published studies do not examine bibliotherapy as an isolated treatment [16]. Beth and Carol Doll discuss the effectiveness of bibliotherapy in a more recent book, Bibliotherapy with young People: Librarians and Mental Health Professionals Working Together. They state that librarians and mental health professionals disagree about this issue. The library field generally believes that bibliotherapy is an effective tool for children. However, some mental health professional argue that the evidence supporting the benefit bibliotherapy is "primarily anecdotal and so is scientifically unconvincing" [17]. Doll and Doll also state some studies have concluded that bibliotherapy can be effective when used in combination with other forms of treatment such as counseling. Using bibliotherapy in conjunction with counseling is a logical solution to overcome some of its previously discussed limitation. For example, discussing the novel with the child may help them to identify with the characters is the novel.

Librarians have legitimate professional concerns about providing counseling services to children. Most librarians are not trained mental health professionals and have to consider issue of liability if they attempt to offer formal counseling services18. Many to Lynch, director of ALA (American Library Association) Library and Research Center state that "[American] librarians... have never called themselves 'bibliotherapists'. We don't use that title. It isn't addressed this particular issue by formally adopting some specialized categories into their bibliotherapy paradigm. The basic category is bibliotherapy which means "guidance in the solution of personal problems through directed reading" [19]. This paper has been focusing on this type of bibliotherapy and will refer to it as "basic bibliotherapy" from this point on. However, within the library field exist two specialized forms of bibliotherapy, clinical and developmental bibliotherapy.

Clinical bibliotherapy is used by doctors and hospital librarians with persons with emotional or behavioral problem to encourage self-understanding or behavioral change. Developmental bibliotherapy is used with a wide variety of individuals in schools or in public libraries to promote self-knowledge, personal growth, and the successful completion of 'developmental' tasks associated with various life stages [20].

Public librarians provide development bibliotherapy to patrons because it does not require advanced clinical skills. Librarians usually engage in developmental bibliotherapy with groups of children and adolecents. The group factor is another important distinction between developmental bibliotherapy and reader's advisory [21] .This paper also previously stated that a key difference between bibliotherapy and reader's advisory is that librarians use bibliotherapy to help a child with a problem. The "problem element" is generally present in development bibliotherapy as well. The difference is that the problem is a potential one that children may face such as drug abuse or suicide. Michael Warner provides as explanation of how development bibliotherapy works.

A group of students read and discuss a novel or other piece of fiction in which a character of their age deals with a problem common to their age level. Since the problem faced in this book is likely not one they are facing at the moment, there is likely to be more willingness by readers to explore the steps taken in dealing with the problem. Follow-up activities to reading must include some aspect that will allow readers to express or work through their reaction to what they have read, completing the process of decision-making and putting a value of themselves on it [22].

Developmental bibliotherapy is not widley practiced mainly because librarians must receive specialized training to conduct it. For example, librarians have to receive training in programming in order to develop suitable interactive follow-up activities for the children. Furthermore, from a public library perspective, providing developmental bibliotherapy on a regular basis would involve the expenditure of considerable library resources. Considering these factors does developmental bibliotherapy belong in the public library? The answer is yes for various reasons.

An unfortunate trend in modern Canadian society has been the closure of school libraries and the subsequent loss of full-time teacher-librarians, Without these resources, the only opportunity for students to receive developmental bibliotherapy from a trained librarian is through their public library. Another issue that public libraries face on an ongoing basis is budget cutbacks. Public librarians may discover that they will be able to effectively advocate the value of their public library to their community through providing developmental and basic bibliotherapy. Catherine Morris, a public library manager in the United Kingdom, supports this argument.

Any librarian in a lending library is aware of the uplifting and cathartic power of fiction of mental health and well being ... Back in the 17th Century Samuel Johnson wrote : "The only end of writing is to enable the reader better to enjoy life, or better to endure it." I find it amazing that it has taken us librarians, the prime practitioners in the dispensing of fiction for the last 150 years, so long to start seriously researching the validity of this statement and shouting about it! it's akin to manufacturers of moisturising cream omitting to tell their female customers that the product reduces wrinkles—unthinkable! Let's hope it doesn't take another 150 years before every library service in the country sees the value of bibliotherapy [23].

Another argument for the place of bibliotherapy in public libraries relates to the altruistic mission of public libraries. Generally, most public libraries are committed to the idea of providing people with equal access to information. For example, Vancouver Public Library has this motto "Access for All" on its website .One can view public libraries as "social equalizers" as they provide individuals from low economic backgrounds with access to informational resources that they could not afford on their own. In terms of bibliotherapy, individuals from low economic backgrounds may turn to the public library for assistance with personal problems because they cannot afford to go to a therapist to obtain assistance for their child. Librarians have to be cautious because bibliotherapy is not a substitute for a professional therapist. The literature advises public librarians not to provide clinical bibliotherapy. Clinical bibliotherapy should be provided by trained medical librarians and therapists because clinical bibliotherapy is intended for "aiding persons severely troubled with emotional or behavioral problem". However, librarians should remember that for low economic individuals, the public library may be one of their only options to seeks some form of assistance with a personal problem. An analogous situation would be a patron who comes to the public library for legal information because they cannot afford a lawyer. Many public librarians deal with this type of situation frequently. In these cases, the librarian does not provide the patron with legal advice. They do however assist these patrons by informing them about the legal resources available to them at the public library.

Arguably, a public library has a "social responsibility" to provide bibliotherapy to patrons. Based on their educational background, public librarians may only feel qualified to provide basic bibliotherapy. This would mainly involve recommending books to patrons to assist them with a personal problem. The following guidelines may help a librarian provide effective bibliotherapy service for children.

**1. Always Recommend More than One Novel**

The development of the problem novel has lead to

the misperception that there is always a perfect book for each problem. Barbara Chatton uses the topic of divorce as an illustration of this point. She states that there are an extensive number of problem books about divorce.

There are books written for various ages of readers with protagonists of both sexes, and several different cultural and ethnic backgrounds. They cover a number of possible permutations of the problem. More and more novels on the topic of divorce continue to appear....But this approach to the topic of divorce implies that there can be one perfect book for each child that will parallel the situation of any child living through a divorce [24].

The librarian should recommend more than one book even if a librarian finds a book that closely parallels the child's situation.

### 2. Recommend Different Types of Books

Each child has their own coping strategy for a personal problem. Referring to the divorce example, some children will want to read a book that closely parallels their own family situation. They want to read about characters that they can identify with in order to overcome feelings of isolation. Other children wanted a temporary escape from their personal problems. This may involve reading about a happy family where the parents are still married or they may want a science fiction novel. Other children may desire a book that will provides a humorous perspective on divorce. Librarians should recommend different types of books for children. For example, librarians should recommend different types of books for children. For example, a librarian could recommend both a novel about divorce and non-related fantasy novel that feature a strong protagonist that may inspire the child.

### 3. Know Your Collection

Librarians should familiarize themselves with the.

collection ideally through reading the books. Chatton states that ideally "we should never suggest books that we have not read ourselves, especially not "problem novels". Chatton argues that "We need to read widely so that we can offer a range of books not necessarily on topics but on themes which may be healing for children suffering all kinds of problems with growing up".

**4. Develop A Diverse Collection for Children**

Librarians should attempt to develop a diverse collection for children. This involved dedicating time to reading collection development resources and networking with other librarians.

**5. Encourage the Parent/Child to Provide Feedback**

Through encouraging feedback about the recommended resources, librarians can learn which resources are particular effective for specific problems. Furtheremore, there always the possibility that child may be unstatisfied parent or child to provide feedback provides the librarian with another opportunity to help them.

## CONCLUSION

Public Libraries should strive, as their resources permit, to provide bibliotherapy to individuals and developmental bibliotherapy to groups. Through providing bibliotherapy, public libraries will be providing as invaluable service to their patrons. In order for public libraries to thrive in the 21st century, public libraries must ensure that they find ways to remain a vital part of their community.

## REFERENCES

1. Encyclopedia of Library Science, Vol- III(5,14,24,26,28).
2. Proceeding of ALA Bibliotherapy work shop, - W.K. Beatty, St Louis , June 1964(6,18,20,21,25,32)
3. Bibliotherapy : An Application of Psychoanalytic Theory,

Caroline Shrodes, American Image, 17, 311, 319 (1960).

4. Bibliotherapy : Microsoft 2007(9,22,30,35,)
5. Bibliotherapy : Does it work ?(1,2,3,4, Riordem, Richard and Linda S.Wilson 1989, 506, 19.-Riordan and Wilson 1989, 507.)
6. Will the real bibliotherapist please stand up, Journal of youth services in Libraries, 2(3), 241-49, EJ 395-489. (11, 12, 13, 15, 17, 23, 33, 34, 36, 37. (Chatton 1988, 334,335,337)
7. Bibliotherapy how it work -Rubin 1978,1. www.google.com
8. Bibliotherapy how it work - Warner 1989, 34 www.google.com
9. Bibliotherapy how it work -Warner 1989,35 www.google.com
10. Bibliotherapy how it work -Hynes 1987, 170 www.google.com
11. Vancouver Public Library, 2004
12. burgess, gelett. "How to not read," the critic,36:33-38, jan.1900.
13. lbid., p.295
14. Robinson, G.S. "INSTITUTE LIBRARIES OF LOWA," Mordern hospital, 6:131-132,feb.1916.
15. Hospital libraries.Cambridge conference.The Lancet,2:777-778,oct.4,1930.
16. Du Bois,Isabel. "Book as a Solace for the Sick," Hygiea,10:55-58,jan.1932.
17. Foreman, Emma T. "Carefully Chosen Books Have Therapeutic Value' Modern Hospital,41:69-70,nov.1933.
18. Jones, E Kathleen. Hospital Libraries Chicago,American Libraries Association,1939
19. ibid, p. 210
20. Kinney, Margarett M. "bibliography and the librarian," Special Libraries,37:175-180,july August.1948.
21. Bry, Ils. "Medical Aspect of literature," Bulletin of the Medical Library Association, 30:252-266, April 1942.
22. Allen, Edwrd B. "Books Help Neuropsychiatric Patients," Library Journal, 71:1671-1675+,Dec..1, 1946.
23. Condon, Minette. "Library Therapy,'Hospital Progress, 27:14-16, jan.1946.
24. Hannah, Ruby. "Navy bibliotherapy; Library programs," Library journal, 80:1171- 1173,May 15,1995.

# 12

# E-learning & Virtual Learning to Smart Class

**Nisha**
*Reserch Scholar (LIS), Baba Mastnath Unversity*
*Astal Bohar Rohtak (Haryana)*

**ABSTRACT**

The Virtual Learning is defined as intstuctional learning and experiences or enabled by electronic technology terms that are commonly used included "Internet learning" "Networked learning" "Wed based learning" "Virtual learning". Computer and internet has changed the procedure and patterns of education today.Today educational insititution are embracing it with rapid speed across the globe. The focus of the paper is to highlight the advantages and disadvantages of e-class and to prove its status in today's education.

**Key Word :** E-Learning, Virtual Learning.

Today the grim education picture is being replaced by e-goverances, class room, e-tutorials. It is a matter of right for the countery in agencies in particular for the popularization of the mission mode programmes on e-governance.Arrival of computer nd Internet in the field of education has changed the pattern of education. Now, education knocks at the door of the students and reserchers.

New technological terms are replaced old terms, such as banking into e-banking, commerce into e-commerce, money into e-money, education into e-education. E-Education is a new sensation in the field of education. E-learning is internet enabled. e- education refers to the use of internet technologies to deliver abroad array of solution that enhance Knowledge & performance.

## 1. NEED AND IMPORTANCE OF E-LEARNING RESOURCES

Today educational insititution are embracing it with rapid speed across the globe. In corporation of e-resources in the learning experience, cotinues to evolve.It has certainly improved the outcomes of the individuals by personalizing the learning experiences. A very common and vital drawback of traditional class room teaching is students having low mental ability and inability to keep pace with the teacher.Proper learning experiences as well as output and outcome are essential for the learner to be successful in life .

### A. Main Characteristics of E-learning Resources

- Flexible
- Learner autonomy
- Error free and speedly technology
- MoreLarge and qualitive content
- Practically teaching learning
- Large mask coverd
- Access and sucess for all
- Transparent and authentic system of education

### B. Advantages of E-learning

- Learners may have the option to select
- Reduces travel cost and time to and from school
- Flexibility to join discussions in the bulletin board
- Different learning styles are addressed and faciliy of learning occurs throught varied activities

- Class work can be scheduled around personal and professional work
- Self paced learning modules allow learners to work at their own pace

## 2. VIRTUAL LEARNING OF THE CONCEPT

Virtual Learning is defined as instructional content or learning and experiences deliverd by electronic technology terms that are commonly used included "Online learning" "Networked learning" "Virtual learning" "Web based and distance learning" All of these terms imply that the learner is at a distance from the tutor or instructor. It is righty said that Virtual Learning is Internet-enabled learning.However, broadly speaking Virtual Learning is all abilities.

- Virtual classroom learning
- Virtual Learning scanning of graphics and pictures
- Downloding the files from the net
- Knowing and working the computer
- Knowing and surfing the Internet
- Downloding of print material and uploading the same on web

### A. Essentials Of Virtual Learning

- Moderating and facilities
- Feedback
- Student Evaluation

### B. Advantage of Virtual Learning

- It is cost effective and time saving
- Instruction- quality is consistent
- The information can be shared be more than one user at a time
- It has an edge over print media

### C. Disadvantages of Virtual Learning

- Knowledge of computer harware is required
- Virus and data corruption hinders the programme
- Information on websites is not assured informaion as the sites are not uploded in time
- Technology is changing at a faster rate and its incorporation in the system is not that easy

### D. Modes of Virtual Learning

- Internet and Extranet
- Satellite broad cost
- Audio -Video tape
- Ineractive TV
- Interactive CD-ROM

### E. Virtual Learning Tools

- Web blog
- Social book marketing
- RSS
- Wiki
- Text Chat
- Instant Messaging

### F. Delivery Methods for Virtual Learning

It delivers material irrespective of physical location, time digital reception devices are Listed below:-

**Audio :** This includes various audio tapes.

**Video :** This includes video tapes, satellite and cable - tranmission.

**Print Media :** This include textbook and e-text.

**Asynchronous Method :** This includes e-mail, Web-based and web form.

**Synchronous Methods :** This includes chat, video-confrence and tele-confrence.

### G. Limitations of Virtual Learning

- Students may feel isolated and miss social interaction
- Show speed
- Student respectively unmotivated students
- Students should be well varsed in knowledge of computer and technology

## 3. INDIAN SCENERIES OF VIRTUAL LEARNING

The future of Virtual Learning seems to be very brought in India as no. of internet users is growing in the country at quite a high pace but there are same barriers such as cost of computer durability, standards, Internet speed, connectivity etc. in fact, if we are able to overcome these barriers, then Virtual Learning can do wonders in India. The following are the major aspirations for promotion of reading habits:

**Role of Mass Media :** Newspapers and magazines, radio can help advertise reading project, workshop, village libraries and interviews of reading authorities/ teachers and organizations involved in the reading activities to promote reading.

**Role of Universities :** University may take part in community information services throught their libraries and library department. library teaching staff and student volunteer groups occasionally visit rural libraries, providing technical advice and requesting donations of library materials.

**Chatting Society But Not Reading :** Traditionally scholars of the ancient time would give animated narration of written words from book to illiterates throught reading aloud, animated reading. Now the process and habit of chatting on electronic media has squeezed the interest of reading in most of the sections of society.

- Role of Public Libraries
- Role of Family
- Factors Affecting the Reading Habits

## 4. THE RESOURCE CRUNCH

- For public use or student's use
- Libraries located in urban areas rather than rural area
- Insufficient or shortage of collection of books and reading materials
- Limited budget leading to back of collection resources
- Insufficient libraries,public libraries, school libraries or special

## 5. SMART CLASS" PROGRAMMES A DIGITAL INITIATION TO E- LEARNING

Smart class is actually a hight and educational technology in which the traditional class room becomes all the more interactive with loads of streaming, animations, videos and others digital contents. A digital initiative which is repeatedly transforming, the way teachers teach and students learn in school with innovative and meaningful use of technology.The content can be streamed into the class and shown by teachers in the class room to make abstract concepts real. this makes learning an enjoyable experience for students while improving their overall academic performance in school.

Teachers get the relevant digital resources such as animation and reduce interactive virtual labs etc. and used them as part of their lesson plans in every class. The classrooms are equipped with custem design, white board, interactive, electronic,PCs and UPS.Teachers used the digital resources while teaching inside the class rooms and better understanding of the concepts taught.Towards the end of the class, the teachers displayed a set of questions on a large screen and the students grt ready to answers the questions while the teachers is too able to get a score sheet for every students. At the end of the class, the teacher repeat those part of the lesson which were not understood well by the students. This result in faster and accurate understanding the concepts and helps improve the overall academic performance of the students.

The traditioal class rooms can become interactive and more insteresting. No doubt, the smart class programme is a comperehensive solution,designed to assist teachers in meeting with class room challenges .

## REFERENCES


- Chaurasia, Neeraj and Kumar, Ganesh; E-education and online prospective, 2nd international caliber-2004, New Delhi, 11 to 13 Feb.
- Singh, Akash and Kumar, Vinod; Next Generation Libraries: Issue and Challenges, National Conference proceeding-2015, Kumaun University, Nainital,22 March.


## WEBSITE VISITED


1. *WWW.brandan-hall.com*
2. *www.e-learningmag.com*
3. *www.masic.com*

# Part III

# 13
# Brief Historical Background of Library Automation

***Dr. Mehtab Alam Ansari***
*Associate Professor in Deptt. of Library Information Science at Aligarh Muslim University, Aligarh*

## 1. INTRODUCTION

Library automation has brought remarkable changes both in terms of technology and the involvement of people. This chapter will review the history of library automation and how it progressed in the developed world. Application of technology to library started in 1930s when a few libraries began to incorporate IBM unit-record equipment into their circulation section. This development had taken place even before the invention of computers. International Business Machines (IBM) and Remington Rand introduced equipments such as keypunch machines and electromechanical card sorters and collators. Though these devices can not be called computers, however possess certain traits resembling computers [1]. In the 1940s, two innovative methods viz. photo charging and audio charging were introduced for the circulation purpose. Photo charging is credited to Ralph R. Shaw at the Gary, Indiana, Public Library while audio charging was introduced by Stewart W. Smith in Country Public Library at St. Louis, Missouri [2]. Significantly, the application of computers to libraries first appeared, in 1950s in the United States of America [3]. Notably, pioneering work in the application of computers to libraries was done in the USA followed by UK and other countries of Europe due to the availability of best infrastructure in telecommunications and other technologies [4].However, the interest in the application of computer to libraries which was noticed in 1950s reached at a broader level in the next decade and began to culminate in the actual implementation of systems in libraries. Significantly, this decade had witnessed widespread applications of computers that were never seen before 1960s. However, apart from the growth in technological capabilities, other factors such as increased student enrollments combined with relative prosperity in education and social services resulted in more number of library users and more library funds that were never available earlier [5].

A remarkable development during this decade that continued to influence library automation in the following years was the initiation of the Library of Congress, America in the form of the Machine-Readable Cataloguing (MARC) format in 1961. The MARC format made it possible to record complete bibliographic information based on cataloguing code such as the AARC-II. The Library of Congress conducted a pilot project since 1966 and started the MARC-II distribution service in 1968. The Library of Congress also had a collaboration with the British National Bibliography (BNB) toward another pilot project namely UK MARC that led to the international exchange of records between America and

England [6]. Significantly, in the latter half of this decade, the establishment of Ohio College Library Centre (OCLC) took place which was later re-christened as Online Computer Library Centre and had a noticeable impact on resource sharing as well as library automation. Significantly, computer application in libraries during the 1960s involved primarily offline batch processing. Computers, notably, were used to increase efficiency in acquisitions, cataloguing, circulation and serial control. The main impact of computers, however, was limited to carry out the same operations but with faster speed and lesser human interventions [7]. A survey conducted by creative Research Services for the America Library Associations and the Special Libraries Associations found that by the mid-1960s, more than 80 libraries in the United States of America were using computerized circulation systems [8]. Another survey conducted a few years later for the Special Library Association showed that more than 150 were using computers for circulation control [9]. It is apparent from the findings of both the surveys that the use of computers first started in the circulation section.

The first commercial Selective Dissemination of Information (SDI) system and the Automatic Subject Citation Alert (ASCA) service was introduced by the Institute of Scientific Information (ISI) in 1965. In the same year the System Development Corporation (SDC) introduced the COLEX online experimental system that was later became the basis of the commercially available SDS, ORBIT system. A similar system was ordered by the National Aeronautics and Space Administration (NASA) from Lockheed Missile. In 1965, an experimental work had begun on the Remote console or RECON system that became operational in 1969 for NASA. It was later developed into the Lockheed DIALOG service [10]. In the subsequent years, DIALOG became very popular Online Retrieval System.

Undoubtedly, the use of computers in circulation section and the creation of a standardized MARC format were significant achievements in 1960s however; the most important breakthrough was seen in 1966 with the introduction of an integrated library system in the University of Chicago. This system consisted of acquisition, cataloguing, and serial control and became fully operational in 1968 [11].

Though during 1960-1970 many important developments have taken place in the field of library automation, nevertheless, much greater improvements would have to be seen in the years to come. The cornerstone of these developments was a radical change in computer technology characterized by faster processing, increased storage capability and decreasing hardware prices. Systems such as the IBM 1401, popular in library use during 1960s were much better than those used earlier. In the same way, the successors of IBM 1401 were for better in many ways than (IBM 1401) these computers. In a 1977 issue of *Library Technology Reports*, William Schultz put the comparison in perspective:

In 1960, the IBM1620 computer needed a room that was approximately 20 by 30 feet. In 1974, a similar machine in terms of capability took up a space that was approximately 3 feet by 3 feet [and] would perform identical tasks to those performed by the IBM 1620 in about to buy the 1974 machine was about what is cost to *rent* the IBM 1620 for one month [12].

The chief implication of these technological advancements was the tremendous increase in the number of libraries adopting computers for different applications. In USA, UK and other parts of Europe, there was rapid growth in the number of libraries automating their operations during the latter half of the 1970s and first half of the 1980s. This development also took place due to availability of large number of automated library systems. Before that, library wished to automate their collection had to depend on local expertise of computer professionals.

This radical shift in the use of computers by libraries has been narrated beautifully by Maurice in an issue of *Library Journal*: appeared way back in 1984.

Most libraries could not even fantasize about automation in the 1960s. It became possible for them, in a limited way, in the 1970s. In the 1980s, it will be tough to keep libraries away from automation. The 1960s were dominated by the mainframe computers and their use by the nation's largest research libraries: The New York Public Library, Stanford, Chicago, Yale Columbia and some others [13].

Computers available in the later period were basically the results of morphosis. These are much faster and more accurate in comparison to their predecessors. From the early experiments in the field of library automation, it was learnt that the needs of automation are revealed in many areas. Some of these are technical processing, circulation control and information storage and retrieval.

Taking into consideration, many computers programmes have been written to solve these complex library problems. One of them has to do with the use of computers for supporting the clerical functions found in technical processing and circulation operations. Many libraries used the programs that enabled them to perform certain routine work such as inter filing entries in a catalog, ordering books from publisher, written request letters to the Library of Congress for cards, preparing serial records lists, monitoring circulation operations printing book catalog, and analyzing increased the efficiency and productivity of the organization [14].On the hardware side, the period 1970-1990 was dominated by minicomputers as mainframe were being only used by the large corporations.

Meanwhile, evolution of commercially available library automation systems could be viewed as important development in the field of software. These commercially available library automation systems had many similarities because of an emergence of common understanding regarding functionalities within these systems. While the early systems were based on proprietary hardware, software and database structures, the marked moved toward systems that adopted library and computing standards. A shift was observed from in-house development to go for commercially available software and from closed system based on local practice to open systems compatible with technical standards, particularly the MARC format [15].

Significantly, online catalogues also started appearing in libraries in the mid-to-late 1970s. However, their use was made available on local area networks in the early 1980s and by the late 1980s these catalogues were accessible via internet [16].

Online catalogues became very popular due to many qualitative improvements these have brought about in access to library resources. Online catalogues provided new searching facilities such as keyword search, use of Boolean operators and refining search by publication year, language and form of material [17, 18].

By 1980s, the online system allowed access by author, title, a combination of author and title, call number, subject etc. An important public service feature of online catalogue based on circulation system was that they provided the user not only bibliographic and holdings information, but also information whether an item was presently available for circulation [19].

## 2. PACE OF TECHNOLOGICAL DEVELOPMENT

With the advent of micro computers during 1980s, the computer industry made rapid advances. Libraries have embraced micro-computers in a big way as these became cheap particularly during 1990s. In the beginning, a variety of makes of micro-computers were available and major manufacturers such as Apple Computers, Digital Equipment Corporation and IBM designed their own systems. However, there was little or no interoperability between these systems. This anomaly had been overcome in the later years with the standardized micro-computer. Popularly these are now known as PC. Significantly, the PC outsmarts the Apple Macintosh, the other make available in the market. The operation system for the Macintosh pioneered the Graphical User Inter face (GUI) long before Microsoft Windows made its presence in the late 1980s [20]. It is important to note here that libraries have shown no hesitation in adopting latest available technology.

## 3. GROWTH OF NETWORKS

Library networks in different forms have spread rapidly from the mid 1960s. In 1967, an online catalogue for member use was introduced by the Medical Research Library, Downstate Medical Centre of the State University of New York. The work associated with the catalogue formed the basis of the SUNY Biomedical Communication Network in the following years [21]. The New York State Library FACTS network was set up in 1967 to examine methods of graphic transmission as a means of improving document delivery. The pilot project financed by New York State covered 15 libraries peaking at 30 request deliveries per day. However, this facility was withdrawn due to poor equipment performance [22]. In the same year Washington State Library set up a system to support shared bibliographic services for other libraries. Moreover, the Northwestern online Total Integrated System (NOTIS) was also started in 1967 that offered an integrated Cataloguing, Acquisitions, Serials Control and Circulation control system. UNESCO and the International Conference of Scientific Unions set up

UNISIST in 1967 to assist the bibliographical control of periodicals that led to the foundation of ISDS (International Serials Data System) in 1972. The centre promoted standards and communicates data between libraries [23].

In the U.K., the office of Scientific Technical Information (OSTI) stimulated Computer based information provision by awarding a grant to the institution of Electrical Engineers and the Physical Society. A preliminary study into the feasibility of producing the Science Abstracts series using computer was carried out in 1965. The earlier work by MIT on the Technical Information Project was used in the Information transfer Experiments (INTREX).Sponsored by the National Science Foundation, the Council on Library Resources and the Carnegie Foundation, the system attempted to place information retrieval at the user's desk [24, 25]. With these developments, remote terminals could be used to search a catalogue of twenty thousands journal articles in the fields of material science and engineering, using natural language techniques. The full of retrieved item became also available online [26].

In 1968, the Bell Laboratories Library introduced a real time system, giving three remote libraries access from two terminals each with a catalogue and issue system [27]. An online acquisition system was introduced in the Washington State Library in 1968 using a purchase order number as the key. In 1969, a co-operative bibliographic movement began in the United Kingdom. OSTI supported financially the Birmingham Libraries co-operative Mechanisation Project (BLCMP) and the South West Area Library Cataloguing Project (SWALCAP) till the time they became self-supporting.

**MINITEX :** One of the least-tiered networks came into being during 1960-70 was the Minnesota Interlibrary Teletype Exchange (MINITEX). Instead of different levels of communication hierarchy and a multiplicity of referral centres at the highest level, libraries in Minnesota communicated directly with a single centre, the MINITEX offices headquarter located at the University of Minnesota. MINITEX drew upon the collections of the university and surrounding libraries in the Minneapolis-St. vicinity to fill requests. Delivery to eight locations in the state was done through MINITEX-funded couriers and delivery to other locations was by United Parcel service. In 1973, fill rate in the MINITEX was around 85 percent and in majority of these cases, the materials lent or copied had been delivered to the requesting library and awaiting patron pickup within three working days after the request had been received at MINITEX [28].

Telecommunication networks both public and private had been expanded rapidly in the United States. The Advanced Research Project Agency (ARPA) sponsored by Ministry of Defence, used interface message processors to link computers *via* leased times, at various universities and research institutes associated with the Defence Ministry. Tymnet was introduced in 1971 using leased lines, followed by Telenet in 1975 [29]. Tymnet and Telenet were important packet-switched data networks which used the lines of the Public Switched Telephone Networks (PSTN) to provide data communication pathways between computers. All the major cities in the USA had local telephone numbers through which a customer's computer could dial-in to the network and access remote computers as well as databases. The telephone company had charged the customer for the local call while the network i.e. Tymnet or Telnet charged customers depending upon the volume of data that was transmitted. Furthermore, the databases provider e.g. DIALOG charged the customer for having access to one more of its databases and also for the outputs produced. During the 1970s, organizations that need to connect their headquarters with the branch offices located in different cities usually leased telephone lines or satellite channels from telephone companies at substantial expense. Leased Lines provided speed and assured availability. However, this alternative was not a viable one for libraries and they were by and large, dependent on the PSTN and network such as Tymnet or Telenet to connect with remote users, with utilities such as OCLC, or with other libraries. Significantly, this all has changed with the appearance of Internet [30].

Another technological development during the 1970-80 has been witnessed in the form of Local Area Networks (LAN). These networks can be established in a single building or in a group of closely located buildings for the purpose of connection computers, file servers, printers, disc drives and CD towers. LANs became favorites in libraries along with business and educational organizations. A large number of libraries started using LANs for sharing of data and files between the different library subsystems. LANs established in the libraries enhanced communication and interaction between users and the staff of library. Access to library catalogue was made possible through Online Public Access Catalogue (OPAC) terminals. Furthermore, user located far away from the library could connect to the library LAN via communications links to the organizational network. Online searching to the catalogue of library and other databases became popular among the users because of these technological developments.

## 4. THE BIRTH OF THE INTERNET AND THE WORLD WIDE WEB

The development in networking, however, remains incomplete without the mention of Internet. The person who probably had the greatest long-term influence related to computer networks was Paul Baran, an American electronics engineer who had a shaky start in computing and television in the late 1940s joined the RAND Corporation, Paul Baran, at RAND was encouraged to develop his ideas about networks, finally conceptualizing the idea of subdividing information into small packets, able to be transmitted *via* telecommunication networks between computers. The idea came due to Baran's sound background in information. This was also made known that information was an entity that could be described, analysed and processed. However, this idea and related developments could not find favour from the telecommunications companies but the military were very much interested. The Advanced Research Projects Agency (ARPA) had the nuclear defence of the USA at the top of its agenda. Its computer scientists came across Baran's work and commissioned him look at its defence potential [31].

In October 1969, working the University of California at Los Angles (UCLA), ARPANET successfully established a network initially linking four academic computing sites, an event now regarded as the moment when the internet began [32]. Developments in the UK and France followed within a year and international networking came shortly after-wards [33]. Networking outside the defence community, nevertheless, had been confined to academic organizations until the late 1970s, when the potential of PCs was beginning to be recognized. The National Science Foundation in the USA, the sponsor of much of the science that had created ARPANET, agreed in 1979 to allow commercial exploitation of the network, a challenge taken up first by the establishment of CompuServe, and then that of the rival America Online (AOL) [34].

Throughout the 1980s, the internet grew steadily, although largely within the scientific and academic communities. Users still needed considerable skill in the use of computers. Telecommunications links were not always reliable and were often slow. Due to these shortcomings, a simple, universally understood interface was needed that would allow users with no or less skills in computers to access the internet. The solution was of course, the World Wide Web (WWW) [35].

Physicists and Computer Scientists, notably, Tim-Bernern- Lee launched the WWW project in 1989 at the CERN, the European particle physics research centre in Geneva [36]. The system that Tim Berners-Lee developed was based on the use of hyper-text, a mechanism to link related information located on different networks anywhere in the World (provided the information is available on a machine connected to the internet) into a seamless web of information. The team of Berners-Lee proposed the use of a markup language called HTML that would point to another HTML page on some other computer connected to the Internet. The link also known as hyperlink clicked by a user would open the page to which link pointed. This all is possible due to the concepts of HTTP (Hyper Text Transfer Protocol) and a URL (Uniform Resource Locator). The URL is a unique identifier of a document or page on a particular computer connected to the Internet.

It was Nelson who coined the phrase 'hypertext' in 1965. Hypertext worked, and was beginning to be use in some networked applications by 1980's [37]. For Bernern-Lee, hypertext provided the ideal medium for his new information system. Because it was driven by the way people work rather than the way computers work; to device a system that was at once logical and fuzzy. Interestingly, the ability of hypertext to switch between documents could, in a networked environment, easily be transformed into the ability to switch between different computers. The familiar framework and language of the web emerged rapidly along with servers, sites, and search engines and so on. The Web took-off dramatically since 1992, the year it was launched. The Mosaic Browser became available in 1993 that helped in navigation of the internet via the links. This first such software or Internet browser proved to be the ideal interface and provided the final-stage booster for Bernern-Lee's electronic rocket [38].

In 1994, Mosaic was taken over and marketed by a commercial company called Netscape Communications Corporation. Netscape browser was provided free of cost to the users. Significantly, Microsoft also launched its product *viz.* Internet Explorer and made available it free of cost. In subsequent years, Internet Explorer got wide popularity because of Microsoft backing.

The Internet and the web added new dimensions in the use of library resources. Significantly, information generated in any corner of the globe could be accessed from any where also as long as it was hosted on a web server. In this way, networked environment made access to resources of the libraries and information centres much easier. Simultaneously, the relationships between information providers, including librarians and information users became more complex. The use of the web became important in many forms of scholarly communication. Preprints and technical reports became widely distributed on the web, democratizing access to this vital information and speeding up the rate communication. Monographs and reference works became available in datasets became vital resources in the Physical and Life Sciences, the Social Sciences and even in some areas of the humanities [39].

Due to Internet and the World Wide Web, the information access, delivery and knowledge provider no longer remained the sole domain of libraries and information centres. The way these technological developments brought changes has been described by Abbas in the following words:

Perhaps no other recent innovation has impacted the library profession to such a great extent as the Internet and other networked resources. Not only is our world becoming an interconnected global community, but this early use of the internet has changed the fundamental roles, paradigms and organizational culture of libraries and librarians as well [40].

## 5. LIBRARY AUTOMATION SOFTWARE

The first integrated library system from a commercial supplier, the CL systems LIBS100 systems became available in 1973 [41]. The University of Toronto Library Automation System (UTLAS) was inaugurated in 1973. The system provides online cataloguing support from a data base of over 6 million records. In 1975 a stand alone circulation system was developed to run on a minicomputer. Within a decade, services were made available to over 600 libraries. The British Library was formed in 1973 from the British Museum library, the National Lending Library and other national collections. In 1974, the British Library launched its automated Information Service (BLAISE) starting with the Local Cataloguing Service and has been offering the Medline service since 1977 in addition to an electronic version of the national bibliographic database files [42]. The Research Libraries Group (RLG) was incorporated in 1975 to provide a catalogue processing facility for the universities of Columbia, Harvard, Yale and the New York Public Library. The system which used software developed for the BALLOTS system, later became the Research Libraries Information Network (RLIN).PRESTEL, the UK public access view data system was introduced in 1979 [43]. Between July 1981 and July 1982 the National Library of Canada produced a number of video disc programme linked to a minicomputer [44].
However, the landmark breakthrough came during 1970s when the International Labour organization (ILO), an organ of the United Nations had taken the initiative to design and develop the Integrated Set of Information system (ISIS) software for the libraries in developing countries. The software provided support to variable

length records, repeating fields and proved very helpful in creation bibliographical data bases. More importantly, the ISIS software and training was provided free of cost in order to promote the library automation process in developing nations.

When mini-computers became more widely and cheaply available; the International Development Research Centre (IDRC) established by an act of Parliament provided support to enhance the capability of developing nations in the field of information management and thus developed MINISIS. MINISIS had the same features as ISIS but suits the environment of minicomputers and played a vital role in bringing IT into the libraries and information centers of several developing countries.

By mid-1980s, micro-computers became quite cheap and libraries of developing countries could afford to purchase these computers. UNESCO, another UN body has developed a PC-based version of the mainframe ISIS in 1985. This was also known as Computerized Documented System/Integrated Set of Information System (CDS/ISIS). Like ISIS it was also made available free of cost. More importantly, UNESCO, along with other agencies, conducted training programmes to develop skills in using CDS/ISIS these initiatives computer and database technology into many libraries [45]. In India, CDS/ISIS was distributed through erstwhile NISSAT (National Institute of Information System for Science and Technology).Notably; a large number of libraries in India also created their databases using ISIS software prior to the installation of proprietary library automation software package. Significantly, the data base created in ISIS had been imported in other software.

The first use of computers in India was reported in 1965 in Indian National Scientific Documentation Centre (INSDOC), now known as National Institute of Science Communication and Information Resources (NISCAIR),

New Delhi. INSDOC initially computerized the Author and Subject Indexes of 'Indian Science Abstract' and in 1967 brought out, "Roster of Indian Scientific and Technical Translators' using computers [46]. Later on, several Indian libraries particularly those attached to Scientific and Industrial Research organizations used mainframe computers of their parent bodies in 70's.

It is worth pointing out here that not only the technology advances that have made automation feasible for libraries but also the situation in which they have found themselves has encouraged them to consider automation seriously. Funds particularly in academic libraries have been reduced but the numbers of users are increasing with each passing year. The knee-jerk reaction to such dilemma is to reduce services but on the whole librarians try to give as good a service as they can and their professionalism encourage them to do so. Automation to large extent has come for their rescue as a way of reducing manual routines improving the accuracy of routines which replace them and re-deployment resources to enable services to be retained and even to provide new services [47].

Technological developments have changed the complexion of services being provided by banks and insurance companies etc. and some ways these are analogous to changes in libraries. Automation, for instance, has allowed these service providers to open up cash points whilst libraries have provided users OPAC terminals. Moreover, more attractive and helpful publicity materials are provided in the organizations termed as service providers. This is made possible with the help of automation and aimed to influence certain group of users. In the same way, libraries also impress their clients with the increased use of their services possible through automation. Furthermore, automated systems generally provide much improved management information. Regarding the advantage of being able to make use of centralized data, Rowley focused in the following paragraph:

One element in many computerization programmes is the availability of external data which can be exploited to a greater effect on a computer-based system. Centralized data and its availability is a significant factor in the move to computerized cataloguing systems. The ability to share records andsome of the burdens of planning and designing a system has had a significant effect in most house-keeping operations [48].

## REFERENCES


1. Dennis, Reynolds, *Library Automation: issues and applications,* (New York: R. Bowker, 1985), p.4.
2. Ibid, p.12
3. Roy J., Adams, *Information Technology & Libraries: a future for academic Libraries,* (London: Groom Helm, 1986), p.1.
4. L.J., Haravu, *Library Automation: Design, Principles and Practice,* (New Delhi; Allied, 2004), p.2.
5. Reynolds, no.1, p.22.
6. Avram, H.D. MARC: *its history and implications,* (Washington DC: Library of Congress, 1975).
7. Reynolds, no.1, p.22.
8. Cited in C.D. Gull, "Automated Circulation System", in *Library Automation: A State of the Art Review,* Stephen R. Salmon, ed. (Chicago, American Library Association, 1969), p.139.
9. Barbara Evans Markuson, "Application of Automation in American Libraries: an analysis of the LARC Survey Returns", in *Survey of Automated Activities in the Libraries of the US and Canada,* (Arizona: LARC Publication Office, 1971), p.2.
10. R.K., Summit, 'DIALOG: An operational on-line reference retrieval system' in *Proceedings of the 22nd National Conference of the Association for Computing Machinery,* Washington DC: Thompson, 1967, p.51-56.
11. Adams, no.3, p.4-5.
12. William H. Scholz, "Computer-Based Circulation Systems- A current Review and Evaluation", *Library Technology Reports* 13, (May, 1977), p.243.

13. Maurice J. Freedman, "Automation and the future of Technical Services", *Library Journal,* (June 15, 1984), p.9.
14. Joseph Becker, Current Trends in library automation available a *http://www.ideass.uivc.edu/bitstream/2147/1759/2/Becker16.pdf*
15. J.Hallmark and C.R., "Garcia System migration experiences from the field", *Information Technology and Libraries,* December, 1992, pp.345-358.
16. Haravu, no.4, p.10.
17. J.R. Matthews; S. Lawrence and D.K.Farguson, *Using online Catalogue: nationwide survey,* New York: Neal-Schuman, 1983.
18. A. O'Brien, "Online Catalogue: enhancements and developments", *Annual Review of Information Science and Technology,* Vol.29, (William, M.E. ed.), New Jersey: Medford, pp.219-242.
19. Dennis, no.1, 97-98.
20. Haravu, no.4, p.15-16.
21. Roy J. Adams, no.3, p.5.
22. Nelson Associated Incorporated, "The New York State Library's pilot programme in the facsimile transmission of library materials, a summary report" Nelson Association, New York, 1968.
23. Roy J. Adams, no.3, p.5.
24. J.F. Reintjes, 'System characteristics of Intrese' AFIPS Spring Joint Conference, Vol.34, *Proceedings,* pp.457-459.
25. C.F.J. Overhage, 'Project Inters: a brief review', MIT, Massachusetts.
26. Roy J. Adams, no.3, p.6.
27. R.A. Kennedy, 'Bell Laboratories library real time loan system (BELLREL)', *Journal of Library Automation,* 1, 2, June 1968, pp.128-141.
28. Roy J. Adams, no.3, p.6.
29. A description of the early workings of MINITEX is provided by Alice E. Wilcox, "Networks Descriptions of Operational System-MINITEX", in *Networks and the University Library,* Le Mayne W. Anderson, ed. (Chicago: Association of College and Research Libraries, 1974), p.23-29.

30. Haravu, no.4, p.18-19.

31. Jerry Everard, *Virtual States: the intenet and the boundaries of the nation state,* (Routledge, 2000), p.12-13.

32. Brian Winston, *Media, technology and society: A history from the telegraph to the Internet* (Routledge, 1998), pp.328-9, see John Navghton, *A brief history of the future: the origins of the internet,* (Weidenfeld & Nicolson, 1999), p.117.

33. Jerry Everard, no.31, p.14-15.

34. Brian Winston, no.32, p.333.

35. James Dearnley and John Feather, *The Wired World: an introduction to the theory and practice of the information society,* (London: Library Association Publishing, 2001), p.30-31.

36. The story of the Web is now well known and has been recounted by, among others, its inventor, the English Physicst, Tim Berners-Lee; see Tim Berners-Lee, *Weaving the Web: the past, present and future of the World Wide Web,* (Orion Business Books, 1999).

37. Jon Naughton, no.32, pp.218-221.

38. Berners-Lee, no.36, p.75-80; Jon Naughton, no.32, pp.243-46.

39. C. Lynch from automation to transformation: fourty years of libraries and information technology in higher education, EDU CAUSE (Jan/Feb, 9, 2000), p.60-68.

40. *http://alexia.lis.uiuc.edu/review/5/abbas.html.*

41. Roy J. Adams, no.3, p. 10.

42. Ibid, p.10-11.

43. J. Marten, "PRESTEL and public libraries: an LA/ASLIB experiment", *Aslib Proceedings,* 31, 5 (1979), pp.216-236.

44. S.S. Sonnemann, 'Videodisc, a new resource for library information storage and retrieval' videodisk/videotext, 4, 1, Jan-Feb, 1984, p.63-73.

45. Haravu, no.4, p.17-18.

46. Pandey S.K. Sharma, *Library Computerization: theory and practice* (New Delhi: Ess Ess, 1993), p.91.

47. Noragh Jones and Peter Jordon, *Case Study in Library Management,* (London: Clive Bingley, 1988), p.51-52.

48. J. Rowley, *Computers for libraries,* London: Bingley, 2nd .ed. 1985.

# 14

# Library Automation and Networking : An Indian Scenario

***Naurin Ashraf***
*Librarian, Urdu Academy*
*Malerkotla, Sangrur (Punjab)*

Libraries and information centers are custodians of information and knowledge for the posterities. Libraries are repositories of cultural heritage. The prime purpose of a library is to generate, manage, process and distribute information and knowledge at the local, regional, national and international heights. This very aim can only be attained with the sustain and appliance of information and communication technology (ICT) in libraries. ICT enables access to digital information to anybody, anywhere and anytime. Open dissemination of information and knowledge at the doorstep of the group of people is the major purpose of the library.

The latest growth in the area of information, communication and technology has also altered the prospect of the patrons in many ways. Therefore, there is a larger accountability on the library staff to find out and take on the best and effective practices to convene the demands of end-users. The use of Information Communication and Technology with inventive/ pioneering ideas leads to developing best practices in library environment which can be replaced in library and information centers.

Due to the information explosion, a huge number of documents in variety of subjects are being published now-a-days. This exponential growth of knowledge has lead to a great problem of information management and handling. Library users are increasing with strain for knowledge in multi-disciplinary subjects or the subject explosion.

## 1. CONCEPT OF LIBRARY AUTOMATION

Library automation means the utilization of peripheral devices to automate the traditional housekeeping operations of libraries such as acquisition, cataloging and issue/return (circulation) etc.

Library automation is a procedure in which the artificial intelligence is used for the ease in functioning and saving the manpower and time of the staff as well as the user. The prime objective of adopting automation in the library is to spare the librarians and other library personnel so that they contribute more enthusiastically to disseminate the knowledge and information.

The word 'library automation' has been used in literature for the last four decades. Many of the authors of library and information science did not tried in the direction of describing the term clearly. They use the term 'Library automation' in the sense of the applying computers as to assist for library operations. However, many authors and library scientists have defined the term as follows.

## 2. DEFINITIONS OF LIBRARY AUTOMATION

(1) Library automation is the technology that is

apprehensive with the planning and progress of the procedure and system that lessens the requisition of human involvement in their operations. (Dictionary of Library Science)

(2) "Library automation is the use of automatic and semi-automatic library activities as acquisition, cataloguing, and circulation. Although these activities are not necessarily performed in 90 traditionally associated with libraries; library automation may thus be distinguished from related fields such as information retrieval, automatic indexing and abstracting, and automatic textual analysis." (Salmon (1975))

(3) "Linguistic purists have argued rightly that the term 'automation' applies more correctly and narrowly to automatic process control... and 'library automation' is now far the most commonly used term for mechanization of library activities using data processing equipment." (Salmon (1975))

(4) "Library automation in the broadest sense can be taken to mean the employment of machines for library processes. In general, however, library automation has come to mean the application of computers and related data processing equipment to libraries." (Markers (1967))

It can be observed from the first part of the above definition that the term 'Library Automation' means just to perform routine operations of the library with the help of Information Technology. It means the routine tasks of the library which earlier were done manually, now are done by adopting computer applications in the library.. In other words this definition is limited just to the routine tasks of the library, of course justifying that these are cost effective and accelerate library performance. However if we goes to the depth of the library science literature the concept of library automation is very vast which is beyond these routine tasks.

Following definition, in fact, defines the area of library automation at some extent;

i. The application of data processing equipment to do/to support the clerical/repetitive functions found in technical processing circulation control and serials control.

ii. The application of data processing equipment to the fields of information storage and retrieval, automatic indexing and abstracting and in reference work; and

iii. The application of computers/data processing equipment for operation research and system analysis.

(Reference: Hayes and Becker (1970))

It is experiential that most of the efforts have been done in the first two areas of the above mentioned definition and in the third part the literature of studies is very limited.

It provides many chances for improving services to the users. Besides of other advantages, finding information is made uncomplicated for users along with library staff who can provide better services to the users. Staff tasks such as acquisition, cataloguing, circulation and reference services can be performed better with library automation rather than manual system.

Staff training is a must to implicit the automated library system with its full potential. Strategic version is the next to the staff training. It means priority wise selection of the library functions to be automated.

Deciding the operations that are to automate and their preferences in relation to each other is significant for all kinds of reasons. If wants and preferences are apparent, operations can be automated in phases, allowing for more successful utilization of often in short supply funding. Furthermore, it is a method to expand trustworthiness with financial support agencies and be able to get benefit of "unexpected" funding opportunities. At last, evaluations of systems and options will be easier and more dynamic if we are in a place according to fit our ideal practical priorities against the consequent modules on hand within the market.

### 3. PROMINENT ASPECTS OF LIBRARY AUTOMATION

- This process is electronically based which is done by human beings
- It helps in providing library services better than manual
- There should be consistency in library operations
- Rightness is a must in efforts
- Knowledge should be communicated speedily
- Duplication must be avoided in the library work
- There should be trained staff in the library
- Availability of information is a must
- It may be called time-saving system
- It is also a user-friendly system
- Networking is also one of its features

On the basis of the above information we can briefly define the Library Automation as;

- It Provides Easy & Efficient Management
- Proper and updated information is provided to the library users
- It keeps a check on the obsolete and less useful resource
- It motivates library users
- It increases usage of the available resource
- It refer to the right resource
- It provides exact information at the exact place and at the exact time

- It presents a picture of the changing roles of librarian

## 4. BRIEF HISTORICAL BACKGROUND OF LIBRARY AUTOMATION

The background of library automation has become very old now. While investigating the historical background of Library Automation, one must be to look back in the past centuries when idealists invented devices before the computer age for assisting their book lending system.

A great explosion in Library Automation and Networking was noticed in 1970s when integrated computer chip and storage devices were developed.

The online library networks, i.e. Research Libraries Information Network (RLIN) and Washington Library Network (WLN) were established. During this decade, many of the information centres adopted information technology by using the computers of their institutions. Libraries were seeking technological aids for the facilitation and enhancement of their processes and support since very long.

During the 1980s, with the rapid development of lower-cost microcomputers, the automation became a possibility for every kind and of library, whether big or small. There were so many library automation softwares appeared in the market. The advent of Compact Disc Read Only Memory (CD-ROM) in late 1980 reformed the system that information centres used to apply, databases stored in CD-ROMs, software, and facts which earlier were obtainable only by printed media, got obtainable in the market. These non-print media made the information more accessible to the users. The advent of typical typewriter in1800s and inventions starting from an earlier printing press to microcomputers simulated a huge gamut of library operations (Reynolds, 1985). Studies show that library automation has introduced in the beginning of 1930s, having the use of purchased cards equipment (invented by 'Herman Hoolerith' of US Census Bureau) in routine tasks of library. Soon after this major discovery, other IT based applications were adopted in the library procedures. Though, the growth was very lethargic and the most of the practical data processing applications were restricted to library circulation (Riggs, 1992).

The 1990s the rise of computer networking caught the attraction of libraries. In a library network, two or more computers were linked together via the internet in which the access could be provided from distance as well as locally, and the many resources available on the networked computers could be shared. Libraries and information centres also initiated internet and the World Wide Web on large-scale, supplying faster services to their clienteles. Hardware-specific automation packages and packages with web-interface, appeared into the marketplace. A large accessibility of general purpose computers in the 1960s replaced all and facilitated the second millenium of library automation systems. Punched cards were not completely deserted, but their part slowly and gradually slumped (Salmon, 1975). USA, UK and later on Continental Europe took the major initiatives towards library automation just because of the accessibility of best infrastructure in telecommunication and information technology. It is said that the beginning of library automation is noticed in three different phases: the first, during 1954-70; the second, during 1970-90; and the present from 1990 onwards. The hardware and software available in the past have swayed each of these phases (Haravu, 2004).

In the new technologically advanced era, whether it is small, medium or large, every information centre is now using peripheral devices for its various routine operations and services. Online Public Access Catalogues (OPACs) are largely substituting manual library catalogues. Latest technologies are opening new challenges and opportunities for libraries and information centres to provide well-organized and comprehensive information services using worldwide computer networks. Technological advances adopted in library to implement automation system are barcode technology, digital library system and security system using RFID.

## 5. NETWORKING

When two or more libraries are connected via a computer network to exchange their data, information and knowledge, it is called Networking. Networking allows member libraries to share their resources and to exchange data. A union catalogue is maintained for that purpose. Networking avoids unnecessary duplication of resources, saves finance and gives effective library services. Library users can approach to a wider range of information resources, saves time of users and library staff, and establish a new common platform where they can interchange their expertise, skill and talent.

The areas of Library Networking in India have been witnessing remarkable changes and made considerable progress with the establishment of a number of library and information networks in India during the late 1980s and early 1990s. The library and information networks are playing an important role in collection development and resource sharing, organization of information, retrievals and the dissemination of information across the country for the benefit of academic community of India. Due to financial crisis and resource crunch in Government as well as in private sectors, emphasis was given on the idea of resource sharing among the libraries and information centers through the library networks. The prime motive of all these networks is to get reading materials altogether, evade copying, resource sharing system for expensive foreign journals and databases, to enhance the utilization of reading materials, available in libraries and information centres of a particular locality or region.

### Some Renowned Library Networks in India

On the basis of sponsoring agencies the library & information networks may be categorized / classified (Sinha and Satpathy, 2004 A, B ; Sinha and Sahay, 2006, Sinha, 2008) under following types :

### General Networks of India

**SIRNET :** Scientific and Industrial Research Network. Sponsored by CSIR (Commissioned Agency-NCST, Bombay)

**ERNET :** Education and Research Network. Sponsored by Department of Electronics, Government of India

**INDONET :** Data network sponsored by CMC, 1996 COALNET : Coal India Ltd., 1993

**NICNET :** National Informatics Centre Network. Sponsored by Planning Commission, Government of India.

### Library and Information Networks Sponsored by NISSAT

- *DELNET* : Developing Library Network
- *MYLIBNET* : Mysore Library Network
- *BONET* : Bombay Library Network
- *ADINET* : Ahmadabad Library Network.
- *PUNENET* : Poona Library Network
- *CALIBNET* : Calcutta Library Network
- *MALINET* : Madras Library Network
- *BALNET* : Bangalore Library Network

### Library Network Sponsored by UGC

- *INFLIBNET* : Information Library Network, Ahmadabad (Now in Gandinagar, Gujarat)

## 6. NEED AND PURPOSE OF LIBRARY AUTOMATION AND NETWORKING

Ranganathan, the father of library and information science in India, has initiated five laws of library science. Among which the fifth law of library science states that the library is a growing organism. The growth of library is continuous in every dimension such as size, documents, users, building, equipment and staff. It results in increased number of routine operations and transactions also. Every library must increase the staff to handle the increased number of routine activities and transactions in the specified ratio. Shortage of financial resources, documentary and human resources is creating several problems for the libraries. Library managers are finding it difficult to manage and provide efficient and effective staff and services to the satisfaction of their users. Even the same libraries are turning into warehouse and consequently their image is at stake. To achieve the stated objective and improve the services, libraries felt the need of computers. The use of these machines helps to improve the existing services and also supported additional features, which would have been unthinkable as these libraries depended totally upon manual system.

Several authors have given various reasons for the automation of libraries.

As per Clayton (1987) the reasons for consideration of automated library system are as under:

"There is a problem with the existing manual systems which knowledge and experience does the librarian might be solved by automation. However, it is increasingly the case that systems are short in order to expand the automated services already offered to replace existing systems which have reached the end of their useful life."

According to Borgman, libraries are adopting automatic library systems due to the reasons as follows:

1. Evolving International workflow and catalogue sharing.
2. Interaction of information system, i.e. efforts towards real-time interaction between peripheral devices disseminated worldwide and LANs (Local Area Networks), by means of different standards, such as Z39.50 and the World Wide Web protocols, etc.
3. Providing access to other collections and to other online services for operating bibliographic and other information services, document delivery, online data exchange and integrating online resources.
4. Making accessible the local library resources, for instance, online public access catalogue.

Needs and purpose of library Automation may briefly be described as;

- Multi format availability of information, i.e. documentary sources and non-documentary sources etc.
- Varied approaches and needs of user
- Scarcity of library timings, space and human resources
- Repitition in routine operation
- For good management and information retrieval
- For the searching national and international database of information
- Influence of ICT
- Increment in the numbers of users
- For the improvement of the quality, speed and effectiveness of services
- Due to information explosion
- For the improvement of the approach to the information sources on different types of networks and systems, as well as the Web

- For improvement of the management of physical and financial resources of libraries.
- Maximum dissemination of information sources, products and services
- Promoting resource sharing, library consortia etc. via library networks
- Accelerating speed in library operations
- Establishing a good storage and retrieval system
- Providing quality services for saving time and human power
- The development of library cooperation and coordination
- For maintaining ease and simplicity in library management
- Complete and proper utilization of manpower in the library
- Growth of the latest library services to users
- Composing the reports and correlation
- Convenience for resource sharing and networking
- Growth of human resources

## 7. FACTORS RESPONSIBLE FOR LIBRARY AUTOMATION AND NETWORKING

1. Awareness and action of the managing authority
2. Approach and awareness of Users
3. Availability of suitable resources
4. Availableness of suitable software
5. Efficiency of library personnels
6. Building location of the library

### 1. Awareness and Initiative of the Management

Awareness and action by the managing authority have performed a prominent role in adopting automation system in the libraries in India. The Library management and the librarian himself as a secretary of the managing committee make the library management. The decisions took by the executive bodies of the parents organization of the library are carried out by management committee. The Librarian can convince the authorities about this emergent need only if he wants to take the initiative. The initiative may also come from the top and the Librarian is forced (or bypassed) to do it. But the best compound is that when the initiative of both the Librarian and top authorities are accorded. But the progress remains zero if there is no initiative taken from both the ends.

**2. Approach and awareness of Users**

A library and information centre may be as advanced as its users. If the users are technologically advanced and cognizant they may compel the library authorities to think towards library automation. If the users are well aware about the latest technology, they can automatically help in enhancement of the use of computers in the library to a great extent. Decision making process may not be ineffective by faculty of its parent institute, for example, libraries of IITs and other engineering institutions.

**3. Availability of suitable resources**

Resources available in the libraries are the third important factor. Both financial and human resources are included in the same. The funds are given for the purchase of books and journals only almost in every library. Many libraries do not need more books to be purchased some time, but these are not allowed to spend the funds anywhere except books and journals, even not for any library software. However the guidelines of University Grants Commission (UGC) allow a certain percentage of funds for such resources (It was 15% in VIII Plan and 10% in IX plan). It was not a logical distribution under this project.

Another problem that can be more serious than the financial one is the lack of trained staff. Most of the library science curriculums are based on the automation requirement of the libraries in this technologically advanced era. Many of the library science schools are teaching outdated library science syllabus. Not even a single library science school produces an aspirant who can directly go for the library automation in a University Library and can independently work without any further training. The diversification of the library science schools from actual libraries are may be the one of the main significant reasons for that. It can be said that it is the only profession where the teaching is lagging behind than the practice. In the world people are talking about digital libraries, RFID and web-OPACs and our library science schools are teaching fundamental of computers.

**4. Availableness of suitable software**

Suitable software for library automation plays a very important role. However there are many library automation softwares available in the market but most of them are non-standard softwares. The actual reason is that the most of these softwares are developed without the consultation of a qualified librarian.

That is why there is a gamut of non-standard softwares available in the market. Some of the big corporations like CMC, have also developed such library softwares but have not been proved very successful yet. The software developed by institutions like DESIDOC, INSDOC etc. could not be proved very successful due to lack in marketing and service after sales. The librarians are always confused as they are not in a position of selecting suitable software.

**5. Efficiency of library personnels**

An efficient library staff also plays an important role in library automation. There are no standard in India for the level of subordinate staff to be recruited in libraries. The educational and professional qualification of library personnels vary among different states of the country. In many cases the library restorers are recruited with $12^{th}$ pass and a six months certificate in library science while in some other institutions like IITs and Central Universities etc. the eligibility is bachelor's degree in library science. The institutions having better and more qualified staff go ahead while others lag behind. This point emphasizes that there should be uniformity in eligibility of library staff.

**6. Building Location of the library**

Physical location of library also played a very important role. The library in a metropolitan city is enriched with the availability of more resources than the library located in a rural or remote area. Libraries in developed and big cities have better approach to hardware and software market and also the better manpower. They have better training facilities too.

## 8. LIBRARY AUTOMATION AND NETWORKING: COMPONENTS

An automated library system is an employer aid planning system for a library. Automation means the use of computer and other machines for various library operations. However Library Automation and Networking refers to the implementation of computer software that allows formerly manual obligations to be completed by computer system. The fundamental components of an integrated or automated Library system are as given below:

1. Computer system and other peripheral devices
2. Networking tools and devices
3. Library Software
4. Library Record Database
5. Server

**1. Computer system and other peripheral devices :** A computer system is an electronic device that has the potential to simply accept records, save records, and mechanically execute a training, to perform mathematical, logical or manipulative operation to produce output. A computer system includes some of character components appearing a selected characteristic. Other peripheral devices includes mouse, keyboard, scanner, printer, etc. that help in different computer operations

The basic elements or peripheral devices of a computer system are input, output, storage and processing devices. Some of them are given below:

(a) **Input device :** An input device is a device that converts human thoughts, ideas and language in machine readable language or in artificial language. A number of common input devices are:

- *Keyboard* : It seems like a key board of a kind creator that allows us to enter information into a computer. Keyboard is the most popular and generally used input tool.
- *Mouse* : In computer system, a mouse is a pointing device. It looks as if a small plastic field with buttons and a scroll wheel and connected via cable with PC. Now the wireless mouse is likewise available in the market.
- *Optical Character Reader (OCR)* : It is a technique of analyzing character that have been printed or typed in a special type front. By means of a picture electric scanner device, this converts the mild styles into virtual signals for computer.
- *Optical Mark Reader (OMR)* : It is a special scanning device that may read cautiously marked pencil marks on specifically designed files, like form, answer sheets, and so on.

- *Bar-code Reader* : A bar-code reader is a digital device for reading printed barcodes on paper by the help of computer. This is very beneficial device for a librarian to find out the fundamental information of an e-book.
- *Scanner* : Scanner allows a pc to attach a drawing or photograph into digital format. This device is useful to build-up an automatic library collection.
- *Voice data entry* : Voice or speech statistics access system that accepts the spoken word as enter facts or commands through a microphone.

**(b) Output device :** An output tool is any peripheral tool that converts system readable facts into human beings readable language. Some typically used output gadgets are:

- *Monitor* : A monitor is a generally used show tool. It output signals as image format or display. It is very useful device for automated library system.
- *Printer* : A printer is an output tool that produces a tough replica of data on paper sheet. We can prepared / print catalogue card or bibliography with the aid of the usage of printer.
- *Central Processing Unit (CPU)* : The CPU is a main part of a computer in which operations are managed and executed. It consists of maximum important hardware of a computer. It additionally referred to as the brain of a computer.
- *Storage device / Memory* : A computer system consists of a ramification of storage devices to store data and information for its operation.

This is mainly of the following kinds:

i. Primary Memory, e.g. RAM, ROM etc.

ii. Secondary memory, e.g. Compact disc, Magnetic disk, Hard-desk, Floppy disk etc.

Those devices are very critical for computerized library machine, due to the fact you could shop books, journals and files in virtual format on storage device.

**2. Networking tools and devices :** Networking tool and devices include the following devices:

**Modem :** An electronic communication system that allows two or more inter connected computers and terminals to share information and resources.

**LAN :** A network for data communication, that connects the computers of a particular building or institution is called LAN or Local Area Network. It normally covers the area up-to 10 square km.

**MAN :** A network that connects the computer networks of a small city or a large campus, i.e. university is called MAN or Metropolitan Area Network. It usually interconnects many Local Area Networks.

**WAN :** A data communication network that connects computers located across a wide geographical area is called WAN or Wide Area Network, for instance 'Internet'.

**Cable :** The cables which are used to connect one networking device to another or which connects two or more computers to share printer, scanner etc. But with the advent of Wi-Fi cables are not required any more.

**3. Library Software :** Library software is a set of PC applications and associated statistics that provides the training for telling a computer what to do and a way to do it. To build-up an automatic library collection, use of computer software may be very crucial. Without using library software we cannot build-up an automated library collection. Basically it is an Application Software which is basically designed to manage different library operations.

Some of the popular library softwares are:

- Libsys
- CDS/ISIS
- E-Granthalaya
- D-space
- Koha,
- OpenBiblio,
- Evergreen,
- Green Stone Library Software, etc.

**4. Database :** A database is an incorporated collection of logically related information or items. Database is very essential for an automated library system, because all of the basic facts and data of books are saved on database. It can be as writer database, Bibliographic Database, and so on.

**5. Server :** A computer system or library software that manages or controls the access to centralized aid or service in a community. By way of the usage of server one could percentage his/her library e-sources with different libraries which are connected with the server.

## 9. STAGES OF LIBRARY AUTOMATION AND NETWORKING

Library Automation mission may be grouped underneath the subsequent three stages:

- Planning Phase
- Designing Phase
- Implementation Phase

### 1. Planning Phase

The first and leading step in library automation is the idea to instigate an undertaking. Valid reasons need to help such initiations, in particular so in libraries due to the fact they are non–profitable agencies. To emphasize this truth Salmon (1975) has rightly opined that projects should not be started for the reasons that the library should be "modernized" so that it can keep up with the Joneses of the Library world or just to promote the reputation of the library."

Further step in the plotting phase is to do a workability study about the intended undertaking. The outcome of such a study should help the management in determining whether or not proposed project is feasible. The undertaking is to be thought workable only if the intended projects can be beneficial to the parent institution.

In this way, the motive of a workability study is "to gather, analyze and document the data needed to make an informal, intelligent decision regarding a system's practicability" (Silverand Silver,1976).

There are following types of workability studies that can be done before proceeding ahead:

1. Technical workability
2. Functional workability
3. Economic workability

The activities in the drafting phase are initiated, if the inclusive outcome of workability study shows that the proposed project is feasible.

## 2. Designing Phase

The study of the existing system is a must before designing a new automated system. The study in which the evaluation of current working methods and their problems involved there in are identified. The result may be assumed to decide the traits that must be comprised in a suggested system.

The study of existing system must be structured by finding that what is being done, the purpose of the activity, procedure, steps to perform, its frequency of occurrence, time taken by it, status of the volume of transaction, factors to be changed, etc.

The result of such a study helps to identify features of the new system including both the information and the system. It generates the functional aspects, i.e. processing controls, response time and input and output ways.

There are many ways to design an automated library system. However, the future of the library depends on this one–time project. So, with enough care and caution, the best solution has to be arrived after considering the advantages and disadvantages of all other possible alternatives.

Experience of other libraries and information centers that have already done library automation and networking must be shared before adopting the same technology in a particular library. Emphasizing this aspect Salmon (1975) gives a caution that in early enthusiasm and eagerness to get started, it should not be forgotten to search the literature, to learn (through various means, including contacts with professional association) of similar projects which have been attempted or implemented, and then to take experience of these projects into account.

The next pace in designing an automated system is normally cited to as 'logical design' in comparison with the procedure of growing real source code, i.e. program or software, which design is referred to as 'physical design'. System specifications are made in this state of designing. It is relatively unfamiliar to librarians due to the technicalities involved in this phase. Details of output, input, files, database interaction, controls and procedures are included in these specifications.

The terms also contain hardware feature of the structure. In fact, many design tools are used to portray the design accurately, i.e. as charts, tables, data diagrams, data dictionaries, etc.

Logical design is followed by the physical design which refers to the development of 'software' for automated systems. The backbone of any automated (computerized) system is its software which decides the success or failure of a system.

Literature of the field identifies six principles which may be deemed as the characteristics of good software design (Senn, 1989). These are top–town partitioning, loose coupling, functional grouping for cohesion, limited span control, manageable module size, and shared modules. There is likelihood of achieving acceptable levels of reliability and maintainability of the software if one follows these principles.

Software development has two approaches. There are so many readymade softwares available in the market. Beside of this one can develop new customized software too. Both approaches depend on cost of the software, choice and time etc. Whatever the case may be, the software should be aimed at fulfilling the customer objectives and principles.

Further, to ensure easy use of the system and help in the future development, the software should be well documented.

### 3. Implementation Phase

If two stages which are discussed above are passed through satisfactorily, a good result in the operational stage may be expected. The substantial mechanisms of the organization are sited in their outfitted surroundings first time in this stage. This stage in fact consists of two steps, i.e. implementation, and evaluation.

**Implementation :** Putting the new equipment to use, train the users, install the new application, and construct the data files required is called implementation.

System exchange is very important operational implementation. The shifting from the old system to the new one is called conversion/exchange. The adoption of any one of the following methods depends upon the resources and availability of personnel.

**Evaluation :** At this stage the evaluation of the conducted system is normally termed as "post–installation evaluation". It involves the inspection of the performance of the structure. They have to be monitored and evaluated once the computerized structure is adopted in libraries or library and information centers. Evaluation of the system is that the results can also be adopted for proper improvements in the system to modify by and large effectiveness of the system and thus to derive maximum benefit from the system. Not only is it assessed in such evaluations that how well the computerized library system is planned and implemented. Instead it provides valuable information for the outlook projects in the similar library and for the related projects in other organizations too.

## 10. ADVANTAGES AND DISADVANTAGES OF LIBRARY AUTOMATION AND NETWORKING

Some of the main advantages of library automation and networking are as follows:

- It provides ease in searching of information
- It is Time-saving. Thus fulfill the fourth law of library science.
- It speeds up the communication
- It is helpful in stock verification
- The working is very easy in automated system
- It promotes resource sharing
- It motivates to library staff
- It helps in the technological growth and development of human resources

However the library automation and networking is very useful but there are some of its disadvantages are as follows:

- It is time consuming and very lengthy process
- It is monetary expensive
- Nonstop human resource training is required for it
- There may be security problems at some extent
- It is completely electricity dependent
- Its conservation is very costly
- Most of the users are untrained

## 11. TRENDS IN LIBRARY AUTOMATION AND NETWORKING

The following are the brand new automation traits that can be viewed for the library automation software:

### Integrated Library Management System

An automation system in which a number of applications share one Bibliography database is called an integrated library management system. As well as the additional modules each device has a set of core modules, which, if critical or affordable, can be added on.

### Core Module

Core Modules or primary standard modules include circulation, cataloguing and on line public access catalogue. Some additional modules are developed on demand of the purchasers, which often cost extra charges. Thus these are need oriented and are less responsive. Some of the main examples of additional modules are acquisition, information courses reserves, community, imaging, materials reserving, inter-library loan and serials control modules. Acquisitions and serial control modules are the most of the required additional modules as part of the core package, e-learning and content management, etc.

### The Architecture of Client-server

Turnkey systems are becoming outdated now a day. Database manipulation and retrieval system is handled by a client/server system which is very effective that leaves the individual interface to the laptop client software. It offers the user a higher journey through a quicker interface and shares the computational load between the client and server computers.

### Z39.50 Protocol

Z39.50 is a protocol or common platform for several online databases around the world that helps in the information retrieval from one computer to another computer located at far of places. It allows the library users/library staff to access another library's catalogue by using this common interface. Client and server both computers should be Z39.50 compliant to visit each other's catalogue. Client computer with Z39.50 compliance can access other same compliant server computer's catalogue and vice versa. In this way access goes both sides.

### Graphical User Interface (GUI) for all models

Most of the Indian computers use windows as operating system but in the early days, computers were only used to work in console mode, that is, one could not see things and he/she did not see any work on the computer to do this, he/she used to command it to work, then obviously there were so many limitations. Everyone could not easily learn to run a computer as it was completely command driven. But now we can edit photos or videos using the mouse so that we can see them and it is possible to change them and we know this system by the name of GUI (Graphical User Interface).

Only after the introduction of the GUI (Graphical User Interface), the computer becomes very useful for everyone, whereas now we only work on seeing the screen, to create a file first. We had to give a long command earlier. Now using the mouse, we can create a file in a few seconds and work on it.

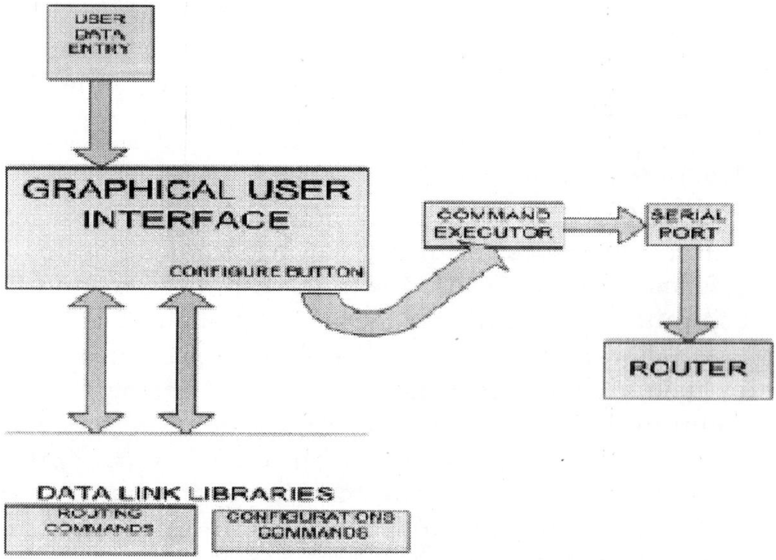


**Cataloguing formats (MARC 21 and non-MARC compliance)**

Library systems are the pioneer to develop to use MARC records. Now cataloguing formats are must allowed by systems, for instance, no MARC formats yet exist alongside MARC records for internet resources.

**Online Public Access Catalogue (OPAC)**

Online Public Access Catalogue is a catalogue which provides remote access to the users. Users can access any particular library's catalogue at their home or at any place through internet.

Password-protected systems are better incorporated to allow the access to library users to parts of their own archives distantly.

**UNICODE protocol**

UNICODE protocol helps in typing in none roman

language using the same computer keyboard. It can encode 65000 exceptional characters unlike the extended ASCII character set of 256 characters. Not only every vendor has completely applied this yet, though most are working on it.

### Radio Frequency Identification Technology (RFID)

RFID is very modern technology used in libraries not only for security purpose, but beyond the same. Electromechanical (EM) and Radio-Frequency (RF) systems are used in libraries for security purpose for decades, but RFID-based systems go beyond security for the monitoring systems that includes security with additional efficient monitoring of library materials. It includes very easy and faster charging and discharging system, recording, and handling etc. Following are the benefits of RFID system i.e. rapid charging/discharging, easy library user self-charging /discharging, elevated consistency, speedily inventorying, long-term life, automatic library-materials handling, etc. Basically, libraries must plan to use a library automation management system as a gateway for attaining right of entry to sources.

## 12. THE INDIAN SCENARIO

In comparison with the technologically advanced era, the adoption of information and communication technology in Indian libraries took place too late. INSDOC (Indian National Scientific and Documentation Center) did the first effort in this direction in 1965, when author and subject indexes of 'Indian Science Abstract' soon after two years INSDOC (Now National Institute of Science Communication and Information Resources (NISCAIR)) computerised (Sharma, 1993). However, computerization progress was too slow to pace with the modern world. Due to the financial obstacles, the important movement towards automation in Indian libraries accelerated the impetus with the declining prices of hardware, great accessibility of various software packages and ever-increasing interest towards automation among library professionals. Instead of the slow past, many libraries in India connected with Research and Development organizations developed lots of library software packages. LibSys, OASIS, e-Granthalaya, Sanjay, SOUL, Suchika, DELMS, DELDOS, TLMS, LIBMAN, Delsis, Libman, Librarian, Libris, Library Manager, Maitreyi, Library Management, Loan Soft, Salim, Slim 1.1, Trishna, Tulib, Ulysis, Wilisys, etc. are examples of some renowned Indian library softwares (Saxena & Srivastava, 1998). Though, SOUL and LibSys versions are generally adopted in Indian libraries because these are upgraded hysterically. Besides, many international standards are also fulfilled by these softwares. It must be noted here that most of the academic and special libraries in India are presently applying some international softwares such as 'Alice' for Windows, 'Virtua', 'Techlib-Plus', etc. to upgrade the status of their library tasks and services. Considerably the prompt towards using foreign softwares especially 'Virtua' software of VTLS (Virginia Technology Library Solutions) Company is developing very rapidly among Indian libraries.

The information retrieval system is the most crucial module of the whole project in every library automation endeavor. It has a direct connection with the library users. In actuality, the success of the entire automated library system of a particular library depends upon an efficient and effective information retrieval system.

## 13. BARRIERS IN THE WAY OF LIBRARY AUTOMATION AND NETWORKING IN INDIA

In the developing countries like India finance and lack of awareness and lack of library staff is a major barrier in the way of library automation and networking. All the barriers creating problem in implementation of library automation and networking in Indian libraries are as follows:

**1. Phobia regarding unfavorable effect on employment :** If it is assessed that library automation replaces human resources with information technology, then it is just a phobia. Human resources are required during each and every library operations i.e. acquisition, technical processing and circulation, etc. Cataloguing is the only area where manpower can be saved in automated library system. Data entered while retro-conversion data entry can be used for cataloguing too. Many classified entries that are time consuming can also be generated with a single click. But this is post-data entry stage, thou data entry requires manpower. Thus there is no need to worry regarding the adverse effect of library automation on employment. Machines cannot perform alone, until the human resources execute them.

**2. Misconception regarding the cost of technology :** Normally a misconception regarding the cost of hardware as well as software is a great issue of concern. However it depends on the level of automation. To overcome this apprehension INFLIBNET developed integrated library management software 'SOUL' at very reasonable charges. Besides there are so many open source library management softwares, i.e. 'KOHA', 'D-Space', 'CDS/ISIS', etc., available free of cost. So cost should not actually be a constraint in the way of library automation.

**3. Extensive training required for library personnel :** Library automation is considered a very tough job while working in a manual library system. Library management and sometimes library staff assume that they must undergo extensive training before working in an automated library system. This is not completely true, because as the technology is getting advanced day by day, the use of information technology and library softwares are becoming very easy. A little bit training and in some cases there is no training required to jump to an automated library system. In most of the cases training for operating and handling the library software is often provided by the vendor who supplies the software. The level of automation also decides training of library staff.

**4. Financial constraint due to the lack of support from the top management :** Lack of financial support from the library management is a big constraint in the way of library automation. Here the role of librarian becomes very crucial, as he has to use his convincing power to bring the management on a common platform of adopting library automation. He/she must convince the management that library automation system is not only for the ease of library staff, but it also helps in providing better and fast library services to its users. The users of the library are the major beneficiaries of the same.

**5. Retrospective conversion of old library data :** Due to the auto-generated the analytical cataloguing and other library operations, the saved human resources could be utilized for retrospective conversion too. Though, many libraries and information centres are taking time bound project for the same.

## 14. E-GRANTHALAYA: A DIGITAL AGENDA FOR LIBRARY AUTOMATION AND NETWORKING IN INDIA

National Informatics Centre, (NIC), Ministry of Electronics and Information Technology, Government of India developed an Integrated Library Management Software called 'e-Granthalaya'. E-Granthalaya was developed jointly by IT professionals as well as library professionals for the automation of various housekeeping operations of the libraries. It also provides various online member services to the libraries. Libraries can publish their catalogue with the help of built-in web OPAC interface over world wide web. It is UNICODE Compliant therefore supports data entry in local languages also.

The advanced version of e-Granthalaya i.e. Ver.4.0 is actually a 'Cloud Ready Application' which provides a Web-based data entry compliance in business form with a centralized database for cluster of libraries. It uses PostgreSQL (an Open Source database management system) as epilogue database solution. NIC (National Informatics Centre) National Cloud made it available for the private libraries as well as government libraries as per NIC distribution policy.

This is a remarkable step of the government of India towards the library automation and networking especially for all the government libraries of India. It is totally free of cost to the government libraries. The government of India has tried to overcome all the barriers in the way of library automation and networking, some of which are discussed above.

**Salient Features of e-Granthalaya 4.0**

- It has the multi-Tenancy having single-sign up interface
- It clings to cataloging standards (AACR2/MARC) support data, domain specific Meta-Data, exchange standards, i.e. MARC21, MARCXML, ISO: 2709, EXCEL, CSV, etc.
- It support in downloading catalog records from internet.
- It has in-built Z39.50 protocol.
- It provides barcode, e-mail SMS, Smart Card Integration facility.
- It has digital library options.
- It provides e-books manager with e-books viewer
- User- defined data entry format helps in standard workflow.
- It provides adaptive business rules for circulation module.

- It accommodates multi-volume, multi-copies, auto-accessioning with retro-conversion of data.

Here we discussed almost every important point regarding Library Automation and Networking. On the whole can say that we live in a digital era and now-a-days library automation and networking is a topic of great concern. The libraries of India must implement the same to pace with the technologically advanced world. We live in the country like India where at one side the bullock cart and while on another side a car run on the same road. It means to say that there is a big gap in financial conditions, status of people and technology. Our government doing so many efforts to fill this gap, but some responsibility lies on the library staff and the common people too.

## REFERENCES


- Rupinder Singh. 2012, 'Status and Challenges of Public Libraries' Automation in Punjab', International Journal of Information Dissemination and Technology, Vol. 2, Issue 2, pp.146-152.
- Dr.K.H.Sunitha. 2009, 'Effective practices to enhance skills at the Learning Resource Centers', International Conference on Academic Libraries (ICAL).
- Dr. Hilal Ahmad. 2014, 'Library Automation in India: A survey of information retrieval system of central libraries of IIT Delhi, IIT Kanpur and Kashmir University', International Journal of Digital Library Services, Vol. 4, Issue 4, pp. 78-171.
- Dr. Yogendra Singh. 2003, 'Library Automation in Academic Libraries in India: Problems and Prospects', http://ir.inflibnet.ac.in:8080/ir/bitstream/1944/188/2/03cali_19.pdf
- Agarwal, Rajesh & Tiwari, Bharat Bhusan. 2001, IT Encyclopaedia. Com, 2nd ed. vol. 1, Pentagon Press, New Delhi.
- Balakrishna, Shyama & P.K. Paliwal (eds) 2001, Encyclopaedia of Library and Information Technology for 21st Century Series, Future Library Technology, Anmol Publication, New Delhi.

- Boralyan, R. & K.A. Ramadevi, 1995, 'Library Automation and Information Network System', Library Progress (International), vol. 15, no. 1-2, pp. 17-21.
- Cawkell, A. E. (1991a). Electronic document delivery systems. Journal of Documentation, 47(1), (p.41).
- Cawkell, A. E. (1991b). Electronic document delivery systems. Journal of Documentation, 47(1), (p.73).
- Dayal, Rameshwar. 2012, 'Recent Trends of using ICT in Modern College Libraries', International Journal of Engineering and Mathematical Sciences, vol. 1, Issue 1, pp. 55-59.
- Gopal, Krishan. 2006, Modern Library Automation, 1st ed., Authorspress, Delhi.
- Husian, S. & Ansari, M.A. 2007, 'Library Automation Software Packages in India: A Study of the cataloguing Modules of Alice for Windows, Libsys and Virtua', Annals of Library and Information Studies vol. 54, pp. 146-151.
- Joshi, P. & Nikose, Satyaprakash, 'Problems and Prospects in Automation and Networking in Libraries in India', http://eprint.relis.org/14339/1/ Problems and ... India pdf.
- Kochar, R.S. & K.N. Sudarshan. 2007, Library Automation (Issue and System), APH Publishing Corporation, New Delhi.
- Lazar, Peter.(1985). Information System design and Managment. Bangalore : Sarada Ranganathan Endowment for library Science. (p. 43).
- Line, Maurice. B. (1985). National Planning and the impact of electronic technology on document provision and supply. LIBRI, 35(3), (pp.190-191).
- Kent, Allen. (1989). Library Network: Bibliographic Database and Network, In S. S. Murthy et al. (Eds.), International conference on Bibliographic databases and Network organized by DESIDOC. New Delhi : Tata McGraw-Hill Publications. (p.27).
- Prabha, Neelam. (2004). Automation in Academic Libraries : A Suggested Model network, Agra : Y. K. Publishers. (p. 298). Satpathy, Kishor Chandra & R. Ramachandran. (eds). Networking of Library and Information Centre in Digital Era: Problems and Prospects, SK Jain and Son Publication and Distributor, Jaipur.

- Sen, P. 2005, 'Automation of a college library: Some issues', In Automation and Networking of the College Libraries, edited by Biswajit Banerjee. Maulan Azad College, Kolkata, pp. 125-26.

# 15

# The Role of ICTs in Changing Library Services in Universities

***Dr. S. M. Abbas***
*Documentation Officer (Sr.Scale)*
*MMAJ-Academy of International Studies,*
*Jamia Millia Islamia, New Delhi-110025*

## ABSTRACT

University libraries are providing information services to its users. ICTs have revolutionized the working style of most organizations nationally and internationally in digital era. University libraries have no longer legging behind in adopting ICTs advances for their management, services and information products. Because of this adoption the services of university libraries have changed drastically from traditional to electronic. In changing these services library professionals play role of catalyst.

**Key Words** : Role, ICTs, Library Services, University

## INTRODUCTION

There are two words coined together one is information another is technology. It means application of computers to store, retrieve and transfer of information in business offices or others is called information technology. It defines as "Information technology is the application of *computers* to store, study, retrieve, transmit, and manipulate *data*[1]" "Set of tools, processes, and methodologies (such as coding/programming, data communications, data conversion, storage and retrieval, systems analysis and design, systems control) and associated equipment employed to collect, process, and present information. In broad terms, IT also includes office automation, multimedia, and telecommunications[2]". It involves the development, maintenance, and use of computer systems, software, and networks for the processing and distribution of data.

## INFORMATION COMMUNICATION TECHNOLOGIES

"ICT refers to technologies that provide access to information through telecommunications. It is similar to Information Technology (IT), but focuses primarily on communication technologies. This includes the Internet, wireless networks, cell phones, and other communication mediums[3]".

"ICTs stand for information and communication technologies and are defined, for the purpose of this primer, as a "diverse set of technological tools and resources used to communicate, and to create, disseminate, store, and manage information[4]"

The American Library Association defines IT as "the application of computers and other technologies to the acquisition, organization, storage, retrieval and dissemination of information. The computers are used to process and store data, while telecommunications technology provides information communication tools, which make it possible for users to access databases and link them other computer networks at different locations. IT and ICT (Information and Communication Technologies) are used somewhat interchangeably.[5]" .

The term ICT is also used to refer to

the *convergence* of audio-visual and *telephone networks* with *computer networks* through a single cabling or link system. There are large economic incentives (huge cost savings due to elimination of the telephone network) to merge the telephone network with the computer network system using a single unified system of cabling, signal distribution and management.

## UNIVERSITY LIBRARY

University library is the library that is attached to a university which serves the Students, Researchers and Faculty to support the curriculum and research. It provides services to users which help in development of persons. Most universities libraries are at the center of the university. University library is called heart of a university. It is also called the sun around which teaching and research revolve. A *university library is a* collection of sources of information and the same resources, made accessible to students, teachers and researchers for reference or borrowing. It provides physical or digital access to the reading materials to the users. University library's collection can include books, e-books, journals, e-journals, reference books, e-reference books, reports, e-reports, dictionaries, e-dictionaries newspapers, e-news papers etc. University libraries are increasingly shifted their services and allowed users to get unrestricted access to information of many sources available in library or outside libraries. Their services have been extended beyond the physical walls of a building, by providing reading material accessible by electronic modes, and by providing the assistance of library professionals in navigating and analysing very large amounts of information. University library performs following main functions:

**Collection Development :** Collection development is a main function of a university library. The library supports in providing collections to meet the information needs of the students, researchers and faculty for learning, teaching and research. A wide range of different subjects is collected for the effective use. In today's time university libraries have become more active to develop its collection in print as well as in digital form. Collection should not be static but rather adaptable in response to past, current, and future information needs of the users.

**Organising Knowledge Material :** The second main function of the university library is to organize the knowledge material in such an efficient way that all the users students, researchers and faculty should access easily. This can be done through staff and technology. Knowledge material is maintained through consistency in selection and de-selection process.

**Providing variety of Library and Information Services :** University library provides a variety of library, documentation and information services. These services are both responsive and anticipatory. Basically university libraries are used to user-centric approach in providing library and information services. These services are designed in accordance to the information needs of users.

## ROLE OF ICT IN CHANGING LIBRARY SERVICES

In the last decade of 20$^{th}$ century and first decade of the 21$^{st}$ century a great change has been witnessed in the services of university libraries. This was only possible due to information communication technologies. The use of ICTs is widely replacing the traditional services and making use of digital information sources. Due to ICT, the concept of library is changing from physical to hybrid to electronic and digital. This brings the revolution in the services of university libraries. The focus is on how ICT has changed on delivery of Library services to students, Researchers and Faculty. In the specific context of library services, one of the implications of use of ICTs is that university libraries can reach out globally to provide their services 24-hours a day in a very cost effective manner. These services are worth to mention:

- Catalogue
- Circulation
- Inter Library Loan
- Reference Service
- Bibliographical Services
- Document Delivery and Electronic Document Delivery
- Current Awareness Services
- Translation Services
- Current Awareness Services
- Press Clipping

## CATALOGUE

The library collection is organized for easy access to reading material. The role of the library is to organize information resources and services in a way that supports user needs. Cataloguing and classification are basic processes in organizing information. Cataloguing is the process of describing material so it can be identified, while classification is the assignment of a call number that places material in order by subject. Manual Catalogue was used in the traditional library system; catalogue was manually prepared and provided access to the books through it. This was available alphabetically author, title wise. Through the use of ICTs user can access through:

**OPAC :** Is an online public access catalog or library catalog which serves the users in a library. It is an online database of reading materials collected and preserved by a library or group of libraries. Through this users can search the catalogue to locate the books and other material available.

**Web-OPAC :** It is the catalogue of a library available on web on 24/7. The users can search online on the different databases books, journals and manuscripts. It uses MARC-21 format to search databases.

**MobOPAC :** This is most important development which introduced by CR2, a revolutionary and innovative products in the field of library automation. The name is mobile based online public access catalog search engine. Facilitation of our products range, which allows management of your articles online. It allows easy to search and locate any article, catalog, book or any material held by your single or group of libraries.

## CIRCULATION SERVICES

The circulation of books, serials, and other materials has been one of the major works of library use for decades. Indeed, circulation and other outputs are viewed as more accurate indicators of a library's utility than the traditional input measures such as volumes added. This has become very effective and within time because of use of library software such as Koha ILS, MODRENLIB, LIBSYS, LIBRARIAN etc. This has made the decline in circulation to the library community.

**Bar-coding of Books :** Bar coding is used to identify an item. In university libraries it is used to identify and track the books. ISBN can be used to search the books by software.

**Reservation of Books :** Books not available on the shelves can be reserved for the user. Through ICTs, mail, messages deliver as soon as books available.

## INTER LIBRARY LOAN

The documents of library transfer from one library to another library physically, which require manpower and fund. The changes have taken place in this service by using ICTs advance. The same documents can be delivered in different modes such as e-mail, Whats App. and PDF forms in real time, saving time and money.

## REFERENCE SERVICE

The reference desk or information desk of a library is a public service counter where reference librarians provide library users with direction to library materials, advice on library collections and services, and expertise on multiple kinds of information from multiple sources. Reference services may vary from library to library, but most libraries have an information or Reference Desk where assistance from a professional is available. Almost all libraries provide reference services via the telephone and many libraries offer email, text, or chat services with a reference librarian. In digital era university libraries provide reference and research assistance to students, faculty and researchers in the following modes:

**E-reference service :** Reference services are now available electronically through use of ICT. Due to this the reference desk is also in transition from traditional realm to electronic. The reference service changes to e-reference service. The methods are used as

**E-mail Reference :** E-mail has become very common method to communicate. With the use of less threshold of technology, both library and user can use it and asked the question through this method. The replies of queries are also sending by mail.

**Chat Reference :** With the use of ICTs, reference librarian is now online connected with its user. Quarries are asked about their area of interest. The replies of the quarries are given in real time. It is a two way conversation between the users and reference librarian

## BIBLIOGRAPHICAL SERVICES

University Library also provides bibliographical services to its users on demand. A list of bibliographical references compiled by the library professionals on a given area of interest is catered. It was compiled manually. By adoption of ICTs in university library, this service is provided in real time Under this, a list of bibliographical references would be compiled on the given subject using the available electronic and online databases and sent to the concerned users through electronic mode.

## DOCUMENT DELIVERY AND ELECTRONIC DOCUMENT

In traditional libraries documents were delivered physically. Books, articles and reports etc were delivered through one person to another person or one library to another library. By the application of information & communication technologies delivery has become very easy from person to person, library to library state to state and country to country.

- From physical to virtually recorded information/ knowledge
- Access to information irrespective of location and format
- Progression from paper to paperless libraries
- Access to information without regard to location and format
- Electronic Document Delivery

## TRANSLATION SERVICES

Articles published in German, Russian and French etc, they translated into English and provided to the users of the library. It took much time to translate into English. Due to ICTs translation becomes very easy and with no time.

**Google Translate :** It provide translation services to more than hundred languages. This was developed by the Google in 2006.It caters free translation services from one language to another language. It serves more than 500 million people daily as of May 2017.

**Ginger Translation :** It is a free software which can translate forty languages.

**Current-awareness service** is an important service which keeps well informed to the students, faculty and researchers about newly acquired reading material or books in university libraries. Display boards and shelves are showcased to draw attention to recent additions.Throuh the use of ICT following services are used:

**Alert Services :** This is a kind of Current awareness service. It caters to the researchers, faculty and students in keeping up-to-date with current researches in their areas of interest.It may be send through SMS.

**Recent Addition :** A list of recent addition of books in the Library collection is prepared. The same list sends through electronic mode to users of the library.

**Table of Contents (TOC) :** The books are added in the library. Table of contents of these books of different subjects are prepared. These list of table of contents are sorted out subject wise, area of specialization wise and send to the users according to their area of interest.

## SERVICES FOR DIFFERENT ABLED PERSONS

If you personally know someone with mental or physical conditions, the best way you can help is to provide them unconditional love, support and patience. University library also provide services to the different abled persons through use of ICTs. Some of them are fallows:

- Google Translation
- Google Play
- Braille Library
- LibLouis is open source software and Braille translator, back translator and formator for a large number of languages and brail code
- *Digital Access Information System* : Digital Audio Books , Periodicals and E-books etc. It is a complete

substitute of printed material to the audio form. It is designed for the use of print disabilities like blind, impaired vision and dyslexia etc. DAISY multimedia includes news papers, periodicals, journals, books and encylopedias etc.

- *Sugamya Pustakalya-Online Library* : It is a online library for visually disabilities.

## PRESS CLIPPING

A press clipping service or clipping are the same. It provides clients with copies of media content, which is of specific interest to them. The university library provides news paper clipping to its users .This work involved paper cutting, paper pasting and arranging accordingly. With the help of Information Technology, the work of cutting, pasting and arranging is over. These clippings were taking place with the help of ICTs, news paper clippings are being sent to the users through electronically daily.

## CHANGING ROLE OF LIBRARY PROFESSIONALS IN PROVIDING LIBRARY SERVICES IN UNIVERSITY

Librarians were considered as a custodian of books. They were used to issue and return books and maintain daily records. These impressions about the librarians have changed with the pace of time. The applications of ICTs in the library in house operations and other services have shifted the role of library professionals. Due to this technology, the information access has become very easy and same is available in real time. The most of the library professional have changed according to the needs of the time and now they are expected to manage, maintain information, acquisition, and store and retrieval information. They are catalyst for the reorganization of the services of the university libraries. By doing so, they have to perform as:

**Librarian** : In addition to his work, they also perform in developing collection according to the need of the users, books, e-books, journals e-journals, dictionaries, e-dictionaries, reports, e-reports, consortium etc

**Information Manager :** Library professionals are not only librarian, they are information mediators, to collect information from producers and retrieve it to the users. They now how, which and when information is needed. The library professionals manage and deliver it according to the information needs of the users.

**Information Adviser :** Library professionals perform as adviser to the users for getting appropriate information at appropriate time. For that purpose they use their staff for getting required information in real time.

**System Designer :** The librarian has to perform as a system designer because knowledge of system and sub system is basically demand of time. They deploy staff according to the need of system and sub system. For the accurate and quick access of knowledge a system is perfectly required for which library professionals play a important role.

**Leadership :** Library professionals should lead their library and information centers on the fronts with keeping goals set for the organization. They should work positively for goals to achieve in the present and for future. Effective leadership is needed for creating and inspiring vision.

## CONCLUSION

The application of ICTs has increased the working capacity of the university libraries. Users' expectation has increased due to developments in technologies and university libraries have moved forward in this direction. The University Libraries must increase the numbers of computer available to enable the users to maximize the usage of ICT-based resources and services. Users can access digital resources using a number of different open source digital library software packages. In the end it can be said that university libraries have moved according to the time with the use of ICT and transformed their services globally. Internet has played a very significant role in providing universal access to information.

## REFERENCES


1. *Daintith, John, ed. (2009), "IT", A Dictionary of Physics, Oxford University Press.*
2. Busines Dictionary, *http://www.businessdictionary.com/definition/information- technology-IT.html* : Accessed on 1 June 2017.
3. Merriam Webster Dictionary , *www.merriamwebster.com/dictionary/information%20technology* : Accessed on 2 June 2017
4. *https://www.google.co.in/search?dcr=0&source=hp&q=icts+definition&oq=icts+definition&gs_l=psy-ab.12...0.0.1.122.0.0.0.0.0.0.0.0..0.0....0...1..64.psy-ab..0.0.0....0.MqJvs4OsQ58,* accessed on 6 June 2017.
5. American Library Association (1983), *The ALA glossary of library and information science.* Chicago. ALA.

# 16

# Changing and Challenging Skills (Role) of Academic Librarian in Digital Environment

***Dr. Jayaprakash G Hugar***
*Librarian, Dhyanprassarak Mandal's College & Research Centre, Assagao, Bardez, Goa*

## INTRODUCTION

Traditional librarianship is all about sitting down in the midst of books and expecting people to come and read. If they do not come, then, the librarian closes at the end of the day. This is the daily ritual. But a modern-day librarian in the Digital Age must be sound in the storage, retrieval and dissemination of information with the aid of information communication technology (ICT). This may be through computer, internet, E-mail, CD-ROM, slides, teaching aids, telephones, including the global system of mobile telecommunications (GSM), fax machines, etc.

The fast development of information and communication technologies has caused major changes in the movement of informational structures, the most noticeable and argued being those as regards the types of documents that form their collections and the services for users. Indeed, all activities in libraries have seen noteworthy changes in last twenty years, as well as the role of the institution and its library professionals. Change is necessary to a certain extent very often in this digital age, therefore organizations and people must constantly be willing and able to learn and get used to it.

Digital technology has revolutionized not only the way information is packaged, processed, stored, and disseminated, but also how users look for and access information. Academic libraries no longer confine themselves to print services such as collection development, cataloguing, classification, circulation, reference services, current awareness service, selective dissemination of information, and other bibliographical services, but have extended their efforts to interdisciplinary and multidisciplinary concepts, computer software, hardware, telecommunication engineering and technology. As observed by Campbell (2006:17), "numerous creative and useful services have evolved within academic libraries in the digital age: providing quality learning spaces, creating metadata, offering digital reference services, teaching information literacy, choosing resources and managing resource licenses, collecting and digitizing archival materials, and maintaining digital repositories".

In the Digital Age, librarians can no longer be simply information supplier or the keepers of knowledge. Technological progress and the use of electronically stored and retrieval information systems have altered the way students and researchers are capable to access, retrieve and use information. The direct access to information through the Internet has made limitless amounts of information and data accessible to anyone with a computer, a modem and a provider. The skills for the creation, management and use of digital information resources and services are certainly necessary, but given that technology, different applications and tools featured on the information market are continuously developed or replaced by others completely new, these skills must be constantly updated.

## DEFINITIONS

According to Wiederhold "A digital library is popularly viewed as an electronic version of a library where storage is in digital form, allowing direct communication to obtain material and copying it from a master version".

Ian Whitten said that the Digital Library is a "Collection of digital object (text, video, and audio) along with method for access and retrieval, [as far as users are concerned] and also for selection, organization, and maintenance (from the point of view of librarian)".

Yerkey and Jorgensin described as "Digital libraries are electronic libraries in which large numbers of geographically distributed users can access the contents of large and diverse repositories of electronic objects, networked text, images, maps, sounds, videos, catalogues of merchandise, scientific, business and government data sets as they also include hypertext, hypermedia and multimedia compositions".

The advent of digital libraries presents a surplus of challenges and opportunities to the digital librarian. Digital librarians add value and can make digital libraries really useful and user friendly. In future the digital librarian become the guardian of digital information and will be the intermediary to preserve democratic access to information. The digital librarian's role will be intensified towards recommending consultancy to the users in their attempts in providing digital reference services, electronic information services, navigating, searching and retrieval of digitized information through web documents that cover the Universal Digital Library or the Global Digital Library.

The digital librarian can be manager of a digital library, digital information centre or a librarian of the electronic library, which may be a division/section of a traditional library. A number of personal characteristics and the new skills and competencies are important for the digital librarians to build and administer digital library collections and services.

## TRADITIONAL LIBRARIAN

Traditionally librarian is identified as a person located in the library building carrying out the tasks like acquiring, organizing, preserving the printed documents in addition to it, helping the readers in locating the information needed by them. In the last century this picture has rapidly altered under the impact of advances in computer and telecommunication fields. Traditionally librarians have been information suppliers for centuries. They now have the chance to use modern apparatus to afford faster, more complete, and more difficult service to the users.

## DIGITAL LIBRARIAN

The apparatus used by the librarians in their day to day work have altered very much for the period of last twenty years. In addition to traditional card catalogs and microfiche readers, most libraries now present an Online Public Access Catalog (WEB-OPAC), public PCs equipped with CD-ROM and DVD drives, scanners, or terminal connected to the Internet. Currently, most of the libraries are providing services through their web pages on the World Wide Web from where users get in to a variety of services without physically entering into the library.

## NEED OF DIGITAL LIBRARIAN

With the introduction of Digital India, central government is forcing all business and education sector to reach out to public in an electronic mode. Now a day's students, research scholars, guides, teachers all are IT savvy people, they are in need of information in on online mode. So, ultimately all libraries have to provide digital library services to its users.

Digital libraries comprise distinctive characteristics that vary from traditional libraries and their approaches to information provision. Digital libraries are the future of academic and research institutions, and digital library professionals will require having more breadth and depth of knowledge and skills across the dimensions of traditional library knowledge, technology, and human relations. Now, additionally to their traditional library skills and knowledge, many of today's professional librarians are anticipated to possess the additional knowledge and skills necessary for work within the digital information world.

## DIGITAL LIBRARY REQUIREMENTS

Minimum requirement for the Digital Library is as follows:

- Audiovisual: TV CD/DVD, sound box etc
- Computers with multimedia kit
- Network-LAN/WAN/ Internet etc
- Printers, Laser, Digital graphic printer etc
- Scanners Flat bed, sheet feeder, Drum Scanners
- Digital Camera, Barcode Scanner
- Storage devices
- Freely available suitable software's

## COLLECTION DEVELOPMENT IN DIGITAL ENVIRONMENT

Internet and World Wide Web provides the

technology for the development and operation of digital library. So, Librarian of Digital Library should take care of the following points in developing and upgrading of his digital library:

- Storage capacity of the Hardware and its maintenance.
- Standards required in acquiring ICT tools.
- Funding or Budgets for hardware, software and electronic resources.
- He should be aware of latest development of technology so he can upgrade it immediately.
- Authentication of electronic resources and password management.
- Interface problems/navigation.
- Information Literacy.
- Copyright issues and others.

## TYPES OF DIGITAL RESOURCES

- Electronic Journals
- Electronic Books
- Electronic Newspapers
- Electronic Thesis and Dissertations
- Search Engines
- Library Networks / Portals
- Directories
- Digital Archives
- Discussion Forums
- Webinars
- Scanned images and images of photographic or printed text.
- Scientific data sets.
- Online databases with multimedia interactive video components.

- Databases available in CD/DVD's.
- Digital audio-video clips or full length movies.
- Websites of freely available electronic resources.
- Purchased, licensed or subscribed version of electronic resources such as NList, where one can find 31, 35,000 electronic books and 6000 journals.

## USE OF OPEN SOURCE SOFTWARE'S

Librarian has to think of automating of his library with freely available software's, because of increasing budget cuts for their libraries.

**1. Library Management Software's :** When we are moving towards creation of a digital library for the institution, librarian has to think of freely available open source management software's such as newgenlib, koha, openbibilio, PMB, Evergreen and others.

**2. Digital Library Software's :** Digital Library Software help librarians to control manage and disseminate digital content to the larger extent. Those Open Source Digital Library Software's are DSpace, GSDL, Eprints etc.

**3. Journals** such as DOAJ which was launched in the year 2003 provides 6833 journals searchable at article level. It has 300 open access journals on different subjects. 126 countries are contributing to the collection of DOAJ, by covering all areas of science, technology, medicine, social science and humanities. Like this, there are so many web portals (PUBMED, BIOMED and others) which will help readers as well as librarians to find their required articles in their field of study.

**4. Online Discussion Forums :** Online discussion forums significantly influence the knowledge sharing. Librarians can make use of these forums to cope up with new trend in librarianship. Such as LIS forum, MLOSC forum, LIS links, Info librarian, LISERT-India etc are active in India to solve the each other librarians' problem in a proper way. In this system, younger librarians get suggestions from knowledgeable and skilled library professionals and also, they will get authenticated freely available electronic resources etc. The information shared here reaches to the mass. These online discussion forums support librarians to obtain the knowledge of collection development, new resources and their links.

**5. Interactive Technology in Libraries :** Tools of web 2.0 such as blogs, wikis, podcasting, chats, RSS feeds, Mashups, Social Networking, email, listserve, Audio / Video Conferencing, NetMeeting, Newsgroups chat or Instant Messaging and other interactive technologies and applications will constitute substantive and significant changes in the library services. These all the tools encourage and increase the communication between the library staff and the library users. This will help in disseminating library collection to the larger extent; thereby you can increase and improve your library services.

## LIBRARY SERVICES IN THE DIGITAL ENVIRONMENT

1. CD-Rom Searching Service
2. Audio-Visual Service
3. Database Searching Service
4. Internet Browsing Service
5. Newspaper Clipping/Scanning Service
6. OPAC or WEBOPAC Service
7. Information Alert Service
8. Digital Reference Service
9. Real-time Digital Reference Service: Library Chat Rooms
10. Electronic Document Delivery Services
11. Service through Library Websites
12. Web-based User Education through Video

**BENEFITS OF DIGITAL LIBRARY SERVICES TO THE LIBRARY:**

- Access to existing information and services at less cost.
- Break the boundaries of space and time and enables optimal utilization and sharing of resources among the institutions. Digital library must provide the network to any additional resources of other digital library very easily thus a perfectly integrated resource sharing can be accomplished.
- Digital libraries can be retrieved at any time, 24 hours a day and 365 days of the year; provide faster access to the holding of libraries worldwide through automated catalogues.
- Digital technology proposes multiple, simultaneous user from a single original document which is not possible for materials collected in any other forms mainly printed books inside the traditional library.
- *Economy* : The cost of maintaining a digital library is much lower than a traditional library because it is saving large sums of money paying for staff, book maintenance, rent for space and other recurring additional expenses.
- Help to locate both physical and digitized versions of scholarly articles and books through single interface.
- Increased name and fame of the library as well as librarian.
- Increases the communication between the librarian, faculty and students.
- Information creation in digital format possible.
- It permit librarian for the insertion of materials only accessible on the Internet or in the digital format;
- It eliminates the drawback of a book being lost or off the shelf;

- It fulfills the $4^{th}$ law of library science, saves the time and manpower of the library and users also.
- It is less labor intensive; and
- It offer the user with the ability to download text and images;
- It saves preparation/ conservation cost, space and money of the library.
- Offering online learning environment and making short the chain from author to user.
- *Preservation and Conservation* : An accurate copy of the original can be made any number of times without any degradation in its quality. So librarian can protect the important documents, rare and distinctive collections of libraries.
- Produces an increased quantity of scientifically and technically trained persons
- Simultaneous information searches is possible over the Internet.
- *Space* : Where as traditional libraries are restricted by storage space, digital libraries have the capability to gather much more information, because digital information needs very little physical space to hold them. When the library had no additional room then digitization is the only solution to accommodate huge number of information in small space. It collect and/or decreases the physical space taken up by library resources;
- *Structured Approach* : Digital libraries offer contact to a large amount richer content in a more structured manner i.e.:- we can easily shift from the catalogue to the exact book then to a particular chapter and so on.
- The library resources are accessible at the user's desktop, despite of where the user is physically positioned;

- To get knowledge about latest technology related to the library.

## BENEFITS OF DIGITAL LIBRARY SERVICES TO THE USERS

- It enhances the teacher's ability to acquire and utilize knowledge; to get knowledge about latest developments, as well as to get knowledge about latest technology in their field of study.
- Encourages teachers to acquire higher education and work in teams.
- Increased users approach towards the library and demanding information on their interested topic.
- Improving the productivity of the faculty as well as the students.
- Enables the teacher to concentrate on other tastes such as research and consultancy.
- *No Physical Boundary* : The user of digital library not required to go to the library actually, persons from all over the globe can get access to the same information, as long as an internet link is accessible.
- *Information Retrieval* : The user is capable to apply any search term (word, phrase, title, name, and subject) to search complete collection. Digital library will provide very user friendly interfaces, giving click able entry to its library resources.
- *Freedom of Accessibility* : Digital library can be accessed at anytime and anywhere across the world with the internet facility. The same resources can be used at the same time by a number of users.

## ROLE OF THE LIBRARIAN IN THE DIGITAL ENVIRONMENT

Now the impression of the library doesn't remain as a structure or a physical repository that houses printed information resources. It has reached ahead of the four walls of structure. Librarians have a long history of accepting the technology to enhance their library services. Librarian transformed himself from using initial typewriters to the present internet. Though the digital environment is built as a system, which can be directly used by its end-users from their desktop/laptop, the role of librarians cannot be ignored. The accountability of the librarian or information professionals has boosted in terms of packaging and repackaging of information, electronic publishing, recommend users about the tactics to find out relevant electronic sources, etc. In such a contemporary environment it will be very challenging for the librarian to decide what should be organized? Which sources of information have to be acquired for the library? How to organize the collection? etc. Therefore librarian has to transform himself and obtain more skills and additional roles. The atmosphere in which librarians work is revolutionizing in terms of skillful access to a variety of information, improved speed in acquiring information, greater complexity in locating, analyzing and relating information, frequently changing technology and acclimatization.

In the prevailing electronic era, the library professionals have to carry out a different type of roles such as: - digital collection developer, resource sharing role, manager role, information professional role, network administrator role, information literacy trainer. The present day digital librarian is progressing to network specialty, information broker, system designer and knowledge manager. By and large competencies needed to create, store, analyze, organize, retrieve and disseminate digital information in digital libraries or any category of information centers. Libraries and librarians must manage with the demands of an information society. Librarian is a professionally trained person responsible for the care of a library and its contents, including the selection, processing and organizing of resources and the dissemination of information, and other services to meet the requirements of its users. In digital environment, the task of librarian is to manage and mediate access to information that may exist only in the electronic format.

The Librarian should have capability to deal with the changing and challenging environment of libraries and information systems and services in the prevailing electronic era with an importance on examining present-day problems, advances and solutions.

## SKILLS REQUIRED FOR INFORMATION PROFESSIONALS IN DIGITAL LIBRARY ENVIRONMENT

An ideal information professional should have the following skills.

**Librarian as a Facilitator :** Due to availability of electronic documents on internet and World Wide Web librarians have to take part in the job of facilitator in discovery, meeting and organizing information infrastructure such as network access, software access, licenses and passwords to use information sources. He should acquire necessary skills in effective use of software to identify and get back the broadly dispersed information in the digital environment.

**Librarian as a Content Manager :** Librarians act as content managers in the digital environment by designing the Library Web page to facilitate and supplement access to current information resources and services. Website of an institute gives an entry to outside resources, where web pages specific to their subject is existed. Librarian should locate, evaluate, and provide a link to information resources relevant to parent organization. The task of librarian while designing a web page is to disseminate information about the library resources and services. Overall, librarian will act as a guide in critical evaluation of relevant resources.

**Librarian as Information Navigator :** Librarian is an specialist in navigation, accessing and sorting, digital information services from the digital information sources.

The job of the librarians is carrying on the changes with the acceptance of Internet and World Wide Web into the profession of librarianship. They are the most suited professionals to guide scholars and citizens toward a better understanding of how to find valuable information online.

**Librarian as a search intermediary :** Intermediary is defined by Peter Ingwersen as "A person or mechanism placed physically between information retrieval systems and actual user with the purpose to transform interactively requests for information to query formulations that suit the retrieval components of one or several IR systems.

**Librarian as End User Trainer :** The number and different type of information sources available via internet and world wide web have led to train and retrain the end users in use of IT-based resources and services, such as email, ftp, telnet, internet browsers, search engines, Web-OPAC, scholarly discussion forums, mailing lists, assist users in using the databases etc. End user training would also include information searching skills, alerts to users on recent resources in their focused area of study. Therefore, the librarian is having a fundamental role in the digital environment as educator or end user trainer. Good Communication Skills are also essential to provide information to the users.

Along with this, librarian should have suitable subject knowledge of the parent organization and an understanding of the information sources and its users.

## LIBRARY WEBSITE AS A MEDIA OF INFORMATION DISSEMINATOR

Information contained in web pages is quite different. There is no reliability of what is to be included and how it has to be presented. However, library website must provie relevant information without extremely demanding the end user time by inserting huge amounts of textual material and unwarranted multimedia components.

## ESSENTIAL INPUTS TO DIGITAL LIBRARY WEBSITE

The following important information about a library should be provided in their respective library websites:

Information about Library vision and mission, Library Rules and Regulations, library committee, Collection: Print resources (Books, Journals, Magazines, Project Reports, Bounded Journals, Question Papers, Newspapers etc) as well as electronic resources (e-books, e-journals, e-newspapers, Audio-Video Lectures, CD/DVD's, Courseware, Open Access Resources, e-theses and dissertations, web portals etc) Contact Information / Library Staff Directory, various sections of the library, FAQ's, Library services especially e-services (Internet Access, Printing, Scanning, Reprography, Web OPAC, User education programme) Site / Floor Map, Home page, Subject gateways / Portals, Course materials, etc.

## VALUE ADDED SERVICES OF THE LIBRARY WEBSITE

The following information can be added to educational institute website, since these all are value added services of the library website. Faculty Publications or Institutional Repository, New Arrivals List, Photo Gallery, Library events and Updates, Inclusion of Web 2.0, 3.0 and 4.0 technologies, Job Opportunities and Useful websites for competitive examination, Website counter, Name of Web Administrator and date of update. Library website should have video of a library orientation as well as information literacy videos for their user's benefits.

## SCOPE OF THE INFORMATION PROFESSIONALS IN IT ERA

The distinctive role of Librarian is to procure, arrange and delivery information to its users. Further, use and safeguard publicly available information despite of the format in which it is packaged (print, CD-ROM, network form) in such a way that, whenever it is required, it can be traced and put to use. Ever increasing different type of information resources from which to choose the most appropriate vehicle, and librarians must widen their selection processes in order to decide on the right medium for right situation.

However, without professional support many searchers, particularly beginners (Internet-users), do not utilize the full potential of search engines and as a result, they do not get back all the related information accessible to them within short period of time. Librarians working for incorporating the new technologies to form the digital library are ascertaining a growing demand for their professional competence.

## CHALLENGES FACED BY THE LIBRARIAN IN DIGITAL ENVIRONMENT

Technology insists high level of technical skills required for library professionals in order to create utmost use of new hi-tech tools for providing useful and improved services to its users. Therefore, library professionals have to act in a proactive manner to support the changing society. The major challenges librarians faced in this digital environment includes :

**Digitization :** There is a lack of manpower and finance in almost all the libraries, and then it is a problem for the librarian to digitize their collection and put it on the websites.

**Growth in usage of Web Resources :** As number of users are growing day by day, then the librarian has to think of adopting new resolution technologies which again it is a burden on the parent organization to develop its infrastructure.

**Absolence of Technology :** A fast changes in information and communication technology (ICT) field requires frequent changes in the IT equipments. Very often new digital equipments are appearing in the market with better configuration and quality. So, librarian has to upgrade the technical gadgets' with changing circumstances.

**Collection Development of Electronic Resources:** As such there is no guidelines from the government or higher education institutions such as UGC, AICTE etc whether we have to procure materials in electronic form or not? In absence of selection policies in collection development, libraries are lagging behind in acquiring digital materials.

**Lack of IT skills :** Library staff has to undergo compulsory IT related workshops, seminars and other training programmes conducted by the universities, and other learned bodies. But, in some colleges there is only one librarian to look after the entire library and higher authorities are not promoting their library staff to do the courses from time to time. So, libraries are lacking in providing up to the mark / standard service to its users in a better and effective way.

**Frequent increase of Prices in Electronic Resources :** compared to printed resources, electronic resources price is high, so higher authorities are not willing to spend on the electronic resources.

## FUTURE OF THE LIBRARY PROFESSIONALS IN THE DIGITAL ENVIRONMENT

Dr. Ranganathan, father of Library Science has formulated the five fundamental laws, which are still holding well in the context of the Information and Knowledge Age. These five simple and distinctive principles of Ranganathan emphasise on linking people, libraries and information they use. In 1995, Crawford and Gorman have offered the new interpretation of the Five Laws of Library Science keeping in view of the changing role of the library in the knowledge society. These new five principles are:

1. Library serves humanity
2. Respect all forms by which knowledge is communicated.
3. Use technology intelligently to enhance service.
4. Protect free access to knowledge.
5. Honour the past and create the future.

Authors have visualized that, the future of the libraries clearly and expressed that the value of library is not defined by the collection but by the librarian. The central point of the new digital library is a well trained digital librarian who cares for the users. Therefore, in order to be an effective manager of information in the digital age, librarians have to act in a multiple role of knowledge mediator, information architect, hybrid librarian and knowledge preserver. Specifically, it is more desirable that digital librarians have to come out from the sphere of activity of gate keeping to the domain of gateways by equipping themselves with all information skills including technical skills and management skills.

## CONCLUSION

The world of information is experiencing fast changes. The day has arrived when it is most essential to be trained to get access to, analyze apply and check such information. As conventional custodians of information, librarians need to be aware of the implications of these changes and cultivate technological and managerial skills, which will facilitate them to make efficient use of information and to meet their institute changing information requirement.

Librarians are professionals qualified and trained in the procurement, arrangement, retrieval, and delivery of information. In essence, the practice of librarianship in the digital library environment should not be extremely different from that in the conventional print-based library. Digital age has brought a magnificent change in the way information contained and accessed. This has brought about a change in the impression of librarian, their collection and services. Many new terms viz. Digital Library, Libraries without walls, Virtual Libraries, are transpired to portray the libraries of digital age.

The character of librarians keeps on transforming with the adoption of Internet and World Wide Web into the profession of librarianship. While it is challenging to forecast with confidence, how active the job of librarians would be in this changing scenario. The conventional print-based libraries and their services will not disappear. But, as information professionals, we must allow modification and familiarize ourselves to the introduction of innovative methods and systems. Librarians are enthusiastic to offer new services to the users by using a number of facilities that are accessible by the worldwide website. Librarians / information professionals take care of selecting a relevant, qualitative and valuable resource to build up a library collection.

## WORKS CITED

1. (n.d.). Retrieved June 22, 2017, from www.elthamcollege.vic.edu.au
2. (n.d.). Retrieved June 22, 2017, from www.researchgate.net/publication/228408039
3. (n.d.). Retrieved June 20, 2017, from www.researchgate.net/profile/Mohsen_Sadeghi7/publication/236267812
4. Anunobi, C. V., & Okoye, I. B. (2008). The Role of Academic Libraries in Universal Access to Print and Electronic Resources in the Developing Countries. Library Philosophy and Practice , Paper 189.
5. Biradar, B. S., Vinaykumar, D., & Santhosh Kumar, K. T. (2013). Collection Development in Electronic Environment. In B. U. Kannappanavar (Ed.), Impact of Information Technology on Library Services (pp. 17-23). Shivamogga: Kuvempu University College Librarians' Association.
6. Campbell, J. D. (2006). Changing a cultural icon: The academic library as a virtual destination. Educause Review , 41 (1), 16-31.

7. Choi, Y., & Edie, R. (2006). What is Needed to Educate Future Digital Librarians: A Study of Current Practice and Staffing Patterns in Academic and Research Libraries. D-Lib Magazine, 12 (9).

8. Crawford, W., & Gorman, M. (1995). *Future libraries: dreams, madness & reality*. Chicago and London, American Library Association.

9. Jayaprakash, G. H., & Bachalapur, M. M. (2016). Academic Library Website: A Model. In G. Anandhalli (Ed.), Facets of Information Literacy (pp. 383-388). Siddalingeshwar.

10. Jayaprakash, G. H., & Kannappanavar, B.U., (2010). Role of Information Professionals in the IT Era. In 55th ILA National Conference held from 21st to 24th January 2010 on "Library and Information Science in the Digital Era" at Noida.

11. Karisiddappa, C. R. (2011). Future of Libraries in the Changing Digital Technology Environment. In B. H. Vishwanath, & H. A. Bhixavarthimath (Ed.), Digital Light (pp. 3-15). Harihar: S.J.V.P. College Autonomous.

12. Madge, O. L. (n.d.). Current Role of Librarians and Future Challenges for Academic Libraries in Romania. Creative Commons Attribution 4.0 .

13. Neil Yerkey A and Jorgensen, Corinne (1996) Course in Digital Libraries. DESIDOC Bulletin of Information Technology, 16(1), 31-39.

14. Obadare, S. O. (n.d.). The Changing Role of Librarians in the Digital Age. Retrieved June 23, 2017, from www.codesria.org/IMG/pdf/Obadare_S_O.pdf

15. Prema. (2016). Role of Librarian in Changing Era: Trends and Challenges. In G. Anandhalli (Ed.), Facets of Information Literacy (pp. 238-244). Vijayapur: Siddalingeshwar.

16. Rao, N., & Babu, K. H. (2001). Role of Librarian in Internet and World Wide Web Environment. Information Sciences , 4 (1).

17. Sarasvathy, P., Nambratha, G. R., & Giddaiah, D. (2012). Changing Roles of the Librarians in the Digital / Digital Era. SRELS Journal of Information Management , 49 (5), 495-500.

18. Sharma, P. L. (n.d.). Changing Role of Librarians in Digital Library Era and need of Professional Skills, Efficiency and Competency.

19. Sreenivasulu, V. (2000). The Role of a Digital Librarian in the Management of Digital Information Systems. Electronic Library , 18 (1), 12-20.

20. Thangarasu, K. (2011). The Future Role of Librarians in the Virtual Library Environment. In M. Nagarajan, R. Ponnudurai, & S. Ravi (Ed.), National Seminar on Redefining the Role of Libraries in the Digital Era. Chennai: Department of Library and Information Science.

21. Vishwanath, B. H., & Bhixavarthimath, H. A. (Eds.). (2011). Digital Light. Seminar on Digital Library Managment (p. 255). Harihar: Principal, S.J.V.P.College Autonomous.

22. Wiederhold,Gio (1995). Digital Libraries: Value and Productivity. Communication of the ACM, 38(4).

23. Witten, Ian H etal (2001) Greenstone: Open Source Digital Library Software...... DLib magazine, 7(10).

# 17

# Online and Open Access Resources in the Field of Agriculture Science and Technology

**Dr. Nirendra Kumar Pachauri**
*Librarian, Kendriya Vidyalaya No. 3 Agra (UP), India*
**Dr. P.K. Dixit**
*Assistant Professor, Bisawar, Agra*

## ABSTRACT

India is a country of Agriculture and almost people depends upon Agriculture. India ranks second in agricultural output and India is in top five positions for about 80 percent of products produced from farm. Agriculture, with its allied sectors, is unquestionabl y the largest livelihood provider in India, more so in the vast rural areas. It also contributes a significant figure to the Gross Domestic Product (GDP). The research and development activities are the key to the success of any country and in R&D activit ies literature and resources play a very significant role. Electronic and online Resources are one of the emerging environment in libraries & Information communication in the competitive service.

E-Resources usually consist of e-books, e-Journals, articles, newspaper, thesis, dissertation, databases and CD-ROMs, which are likely to be the alternative to the print media. All updated information is published in these e-resources. The familiarity and use of electronic information resources in the libraries for rapid development is necessary and important. This paper deals with the online Open Access Resources in the field of Agriculture Science and Technology.

**Key works :** Agriculture, e-resources, open access, institutional repositories, e-journal, consortium, OPAC.

## INTRODUCTION

In the world oral communication has been an integral part of people t o people interactions in all ancient civilizations. Now a days the advancement of science and technology, the process of communication has been expanded over the years to cover print and other modelike computer and associated gadgets. The Internet and the Web are constantly influencing the development of new modes of scholarly communication; their potential for delivering goods is quite vast, as they overcome successfully the geographical limitations associated with the print media. Further, the distribution time between product publication and its delivery has been drastically reduced. The Internet can be used for efficient retrieval and meeting information needs. This is very important for university libraries since most of them call for more and more research work. This important fact is convincing many libraries to move towards digital e-resources, which are found to be less expensive and more useful for easy access. This is especially helpful to distant learners who have limited time to access the libraries from outside by dial-up access to commonly available electronic resources, mainly CD-ROM, OPACs and Internet, which are replacing the print media.

## AGRICULTURE IN INDIA

Southern Asia is considered to be the birth place of

agricultural revolution where wild ancestors of wheat and barley and domesticated animals like goat, sheep, pig and cattle are found. The period from 7500-6500 B.C. was the period of discovery of agriculture. The period from 3000-1700 B.C. marked the spread of agricultural revolution to Egypt and subsequently to Indus valley. Mohenjodaro to Harappa territory was the centre of agricultural revolution in Indus valley. Agriculture was very important profession during Vedic age 1500 -1000 B.C. Use of iron implements, particularly iron ploughs became prevalent. Buddhist period 600 BC marks the importance of trees. It can be called as a period of Arboriculture and Horticulture.

In total 70 per cent of India's exports comes from agricultural sector. The increased exports pay for the imported oil, machinery, etc. Advancement of civilization is closely related to agriculture which produces food to satisfy hunger. In the world nearly one billion people are living below poverty line. Libraries are changing and they are collecting and dissemination the online resources.

## ONLINE AND OPEN ACCESS E - RESOURCES

E-Resources are those electronic products that delivers a collection of data, be it text referring to full text basis, e-journals, image collection, other multimedia products andnumerical, graphical or time based, as a commercially available till that has been published with an aim to being marketed. These may be delivered on CDROM, on tap via internet and so on. Some of the common types of e-resources are:

i. E-journals
ii. E-books
iii. Full-text databases
iv. Indexing and abstracting databases
v. Reference databases (like dictionaries, directories, encyclopedias, etc.)

vi. Numeric and statistical databases vii. E-audio/ visual resources

## OPEN ACCESS E-RECOURSES IN AGRICULTURE

In the advancement and rapidly increasing literature of Agriculture science and Technology has developed the big issue of its collection, organization and dissemination of the intellectual work among the research scholars, students and teachers. In India, the major research institute for agricultural research is ICAR - Indian Council of Agricultural Research, New Delhi and global level the organ of United Nation Organization is FAO (food and Agriculture Organization) working in this field. Both FAO and ICAR took initiative to collect, store, organize and distribution of such literature in electronic format. There are various Institutional Repositories, Online Journals, Digital collection and full text database are providing by various agencies and government organization. Some of them are as under :

## DIRECTORY OF OPEN ACCESS JOURNALS - DOAJ

The Directory of Open Access Journals was launched in 2003 at Lund University, Sweden, with 300 open access journals and today contains 9000 open access journals covering all areas of science, technology, Agriculture, medicine, social science and humanities. Directory of Open Access Journals (DOAJ) is a website provides the lists open access journals and is maintained by Infrastructure Services for Open Access. DOAJ is a nonprofit organization managed by Infrastructure Services for Open Access C.I.C. (Community Interest Company) based in the United Kingdom. DOAJ relies entirely on the voluntary donations of its members and on sponsorship monies received. This project defines open access journals as scientific and scholarly journals that meet high quality standards by exercising peer review or editorial quality control and "use a funding model that does not charge readers or their institutions for access".

## AGROVOC

AGROVOC is a controlled vocabulary system. It is covering all areas of interest of the Food and Agriculture Organization (FAO) of the United Nations, including food, nutrition, agriculture, fisheries, forestry, environment etc. It is published by FAO (UN) and edited by a community of experts.

It consists of over 32,000 concepts available in 23 languages: German, Hungarian, Italian, Japanese, Korean, Hindi, Czech, English, French, Lao, Malay, Russian, Slovak, Spanish, Telugu, Thai, Turkish and Ukrainian, Arabic, Chinese, Persian, Polish and Portuguese.

We can use AGROVOC to look up the common name of a plant in a language that you do not master, or to find relations between a commodity and the crop from which it is produced. AGROVOC is used to index its documents, or you can use it from inside your content management system to organize your documents or web site. It is also used as hub to access many other vocabularies available on the web.

No a days, AGROVOC is used by researchers, library scientists and information managers for indexing, retrieving and organizing data in agricultural information systems and Web pages. Currently, AGROVOC is an SKOS-XL concept scheme and linked open data set aligned with 16 other multilingual knowledge organization systems related to agricultural science.

## AGRICOLA (AGRICultural OnLine Access)

It is an online database created and maintained by the US National Agriculture Library of the USA Department Agriculture (USDA). This database serves as the catalog and index for the collections of the United States National Agricultural Library (USA), but it also provides public access to information on agriculture and allied fields.

**PubAg**

It is an Agriculture Science full text database. PubAg was released in 2015 and is focused on the full-text publications from USDA scientists, as well as some of the journal literature. PubAg was designed for a broad range of users, including farmers, scientists, scholars, students, and the general public.

The distinctions between AGRICOLA and PubAg include "AGRICOLA serves as the public catalog of the National Agricultural Library and it contains records for all of the holdings of the library. It also contains citations to articles, much like PubAg. AGRICOLA also contains citations to many items that, while valuable and relevant to the agricultural sciences, are not peer-reviewed journal articles. Also, AGRICOLA has a different interface. So, while there is some overlap between the two resources, they are different in significant ways. There are no plans to eliminate AGRICOLA.

**CORE HISTORICAL LITERATURE OF AGRICULTURE (CHLA)**

The literature of agriculture is replete with information about sustainable agricultural methods, observations, production, and effects. CHLA is a core electronic collection of agricultural texts published between the early 19th century and the middle to late 20th century. It contains Full-text materials cover agricultural economics, forestry, human nutrition, rural sociology, agricultural engineering, animal science, crops and their protection, food science, and soil science. Scholars have selected the titles in this collection for their historical importance.

**AGORA - ACCESS TO GLOBAL ONLINE RESEARCH IN AGRICULTURE**

AGORA - Access to Global Online Research in Agriculture is a programme to provide free or low cost access to major scientific journals in agriculture and related biological, environmental and social sciences to public institutions in developing countries. Launched in October 2003, AGORA provides access to up to 6500 journals from the world's leading academic publishers.

It is an initiative of Food and Agriculture Organization (FAO) of the United Nations. The objective of AGORA is to improve the quality and effectiveness of agricultural research, education and training in low-income countries, and in turn, to improve food security. With the help of AGORA, researchers, educators, students, technical workers policy-makers and extension specialists have access to high-quality, relevant and timely agricultural information via the Internet. **TEEAL (The Essential Electronic Agricultural Library)** and AGORA (Access to Global Online Research in Agriculture) are the pioneer e resources in the field of Agriculture. TEEAL is a program of Cornell University launched in 1999, and AGORA launched in 2003. They offer free or low-cost access to developing world institutions in 116 eligible countries to hundreds of leading scholarly journals in agriculture and related fields. Both TEEAL and AGORA grew out of the development of electronic journals and CD-ROM technology during the 1980s, which suddenly allowed additional ways to obtain journal content at a very low marginal cost. This in turn allowed librarians and publishers to work together in public – private partnerships to meet the challenge of access for the developing world head on, and the agricultural-journal access programs we have today.

## RESEARCH IN AGRICULTURAL AND APPLIED ECONOMICS - AGECON SEARCH

It is a free open access repository of full-text scholarly literature in agricultural and applied economics. It includes working papers, conference papers and journal articles. It is part of the University of Minnesota's Digital Conservancy.

## AGRIS - INTERNATIONAL INFORMATION SYSTEM FOR AGRICULTURE SCIENCE AND TECHNOLOGY

It is an International Information System for Agriculture Science and Technology . In this system database maintained by FAO with more than two million structured bibliographical records that cover many aspects of agriculture, including forestry, animal husbandry, aquatic sciences and fisheries, human nutrition and extension from over 100 participating countries. The bibliographic references contain either links to the full text of the publication or additional information retrieved from related Internet resources. The available material includes unique grey literature such as unpublished scientific and technical reports, theses, conference papers, government publications etc.

## AGRICAT 2.0

The union catalogue Agricat 2.0 developed under eGranth project is a very good contribution to the Agricultural Information system in India. It is an Union Catalog of Library Resources of Indian National Agricultural Research & Education System (NARES). It provides open access to all the catalog of the holdings of NARES libraries so that the sharing of library resources becomes possible. One can easily locate resource availability and the complete details and previews in some cases. Today 38 libraries are part of this activity. The NAIP which objectives to facilitate accelerated and sustainable transformation of Indian Agriculture Science through innovation has supported this development though eGranth sub-project.

## KRISHIKOSH

It is a digital repository of collect knowledge in agriculture and allied sciences, having collection of old and valuable books, back volume of journals, dissertations, thesis, research articles, popular articles, monographs, catalogues, conference proceedings, success stories, case studies, annual reports, newsletters, treatise, pamphlets, brochures, bulletins and other grey literatures spread all over the country in different ICAR Research Institutions and State Agricultural Universities (SAUs). Under the ICAR's Open Access policy, Krishikosh provides ready software platform to implement all aspects of the open access policy, similar to 'Cloud Service' for individual institution's self-managed repository with central integration.

## CONSORTIUM FOR E-RESOURCES IN AGRICULTURE (CERA)

ICAR is having network connectivity across institutes and state agricultural universities, select journals could be made available over the network for the use of scientific community. Accordingly, the Consortium for e-resources in Agriculture (CeRA) was established in November 2007 for facilitating accessibility of scientific journals to all researchers / teachers in the National Agricultural Research System by providing access to information specially to journals online which is crucial for having excellence in research and teaching.

A web-based application was developed for facilitating the online access. All Consortium members are provided the access through respective IP address(es). The main goal of CeRa are :

1. To upscale the existing R & D information resource base of ICAR Institutions/Universities comparable to world's leading institutions organizations.?
2. To subscribe e-journals and create e-access culture among scientists / teachers in ICAR Institutes / Agricultural Universities.
3. To assess the impact of CeRA on the level of research publications measured through NAAS ID and Science Citation Index.

## INDIAN AGRICULTURAL RESEARCH JOURNALS

There are various online journals available by ICAR for research and development in the field of Agriculture Science . It is an online Journal publishing system for Research Journals in Indian Council of Agricultural Research.

## CONCLUSION

Information technology has become very fast, information can be access easily just in a single click through various searching, linking and facility. Users' preference towards electronic resources is rising and their demand for providing electronic information services in the library is increasing. Therefore, academic libraries. in particular are concerned in building and purchasing e-resources. The need for e-resource to users are growing and becoming very essential. The impact of web based e-learning and teaching environment has influenced every facet of academic libraries and providing new opportunities and challenges to the library and library professional for involvement in the knowledge based society including electronic and multimedia publishing, internet based services, global networking, web based digital resources etc. All these electronic resources, e-journals, institutional repositories and e-collection are playing a significant role in the research and development in the field of Agriculture and allied sciences.

## REFERENCES

1. Bell, A. "The Internet": a new opportunity for information specialist. Information outlook. 1, 9; 1997; 33-36.
2. Dixit, P.K., Dubey, J., and Pachauri, NK . LIS Profession in Digital Era: Current Trends, Challenges and Future. Agra : YK, 2017
3. Gupta, Mohit. "Pocket Library and Bundelkhand University." National Conference on Transformaing Libraries : Lucknow :DLIS, BBA, 2017

4. Singh, R.K. Joteen, Madhuri, Th. and Chaudhury, Arup Ray. "Use of internet based e- resources at Manipur University: a survey. Annuals of Library and Information Studies Vol. 56, March 2009; p52-67.
5. *http://cera.iari.res.in/attachments/article/19/cera_leaflet-2012-FINAL.pdf*
6. *http://aims.fao.org/vest-registry/vocabularies/agrovoc-multilingual-agricultural- thesaurus*
7. *https://india.gov.in/topics/agriculture*
8. *http://www.economicsdiscussion.net/essays/india-essays/essay-on-indian- agriculture/21152*
9. *http://chla.library.cornell.edu/*

# 18

# A study on Digital Reference Services in Agricultural Libraries

**_Narendra Kumar Patidar_***
*Research Scholar*
*Dept. of Library & Information Science*
*Mandsaur University, Mandsaur (M.P.)*

**_Dr. Ashwani Yadav_**
*Asst. Professor & Head*
*Dept. of Library & Information Science,*
*Mandsaur University, Mandsaur (M.P.)*

## ABSTRACT

Reference and information services have always been the main component of library services. They implementation individual assistance to library users in accessing adequate information resources to meet their requirements. This paper attempts to describe the paradigm of reference and information services in the digital library environment. This paper highlights the appearing formats and models of digital reference services, including email and web forms, Ask a services, online chat reference, video conferencing, digital robots, and cooperative digital reference. The current chapter of digital reference services in selected Agricultural libraries in Madhya Pradesh.

**Keywords :** Introduction, Agricultural libraries, Reference services, Types of Digital Reference Services, Elements of Digital library Services, Advantages & Disadvantages.

## INTRODUCTION

Agriculture is one of the most essential sectors in India that controls the economy of the country. It supports directly or indirectly about 70 percent of the Indian population for their livelihood. Both the central and state governments are involved in the establishment and application of policies and programs to achieve rapid agricultural development. The country has 329 million hectares of land area; nearly half of it is farmable. Agriculture requires land, sunshine, and rain, which the country has, in abundance. Nature too is generous and India is blessed with varied agro-climatic conditions as illustrated by success of green, white, blue and golden revolutions. Besides agriculture is one of the few divisions in India which enjoys international competitiveness.

Reference and information services have always been the main features of library services. They provide individual support to library users in accessing suitable information resources to meet their requirements. This paper tries to describe the paradigm of reference and information services in the digital library environment. This paper highlights the appearing structure and models of digital reference services, including email and web forms, Ask a services, online chat reference, video conferencing, digital robots, and cooperative digital reference. The current chapter of digital reference services in selected Agricultural libraries in Madhya Pradesh.

## THE ROLE OF AGRICULTURAL LIBRARIES IN MADHYA PRADESH

Agricultural libraries in this paper suggest to libraries attached to universities and colleges, serving the teaching, learning and research needs of students and staff. In Madhya Pradesh, every university has its own main library. Each of the agricultural libraries comes under the jurisdiction of the respective universities. Associated to other types of libraries such as school libraries, special and public libraries in Madhya Pradesh, agricultural libraries hold comparatively hug collections as well as they are better funded and staffed. Additionally, the agricultural population in the country has introduced the establishment and use of the Internet and Web sites. As a result of these developments, agricultural libraries have been in more exclusive position to deliver better and more services to their users.

Reference librarians are differently mentioned to as 'mediators between the user and the information', and 'navigators of information superhighway'. The role of the reference librarian has modified extremely over the last two decades with the appearance of information technology and the huge impression in the librarianship and information provision. The role has grown from that of a collector and preserver of information resources to a professional complicated in very laborious issues of organization, the dissemination of and access to information.

Conventional, the librarian's function was to support in the collection development and acquisition, cataloguing and classification, circulation, provision of reference services, and preservation, conservation and archiving. As the library develops into the digital library, reference librarians have been observing how to adjust reference services to the new environment and new information needs. According to some statistics; for instance, users' enquiries at the reference counter are decreasing. Despite this, however most researchers and practitioners agree that reference service and user education are quite fundamental in the digital library. Today the reference librarian's liabilities have raised by societal expectations for information access through improved electronic capabilities. Reference librarians are the key to the continued success of libraries.

## BACKGROUND OF REFERENCE SERVICES

Reference service is one of the library's primary activities moreover acquisition, classification, cataloguing and physical planning. The title reference services or sometimes referred to as reference and information services can be definite as personal assistance offered by trained personnel to library users seeking information. Bunge and Bopp noted that such personal assistance is the essence of reference services and is the fundamental role of the reference librarian. The goal of the reference librarian is to meet the information needs of the users. How and to what extent this is done changes from library to library and depends on the type of library.

## EVOLUTION OF REFERENCE SERVICES

As a major part of library services, reference services are regularly developing as is the library itself, changing from the traditional, to automated, to hybrid, and eventually to digital.

Historically, libraries have been described as the 'storehouse of knowledge' and been organized along traditional and functional lines of acquisition, cataloguing and loan services.

## NECESSITY OF DIGITAL REFERENCE SERVICES

Digital reference is a service by which a *library* reference service is managed online, and the reference transaction is a *computer-mediated communication.* It is the remote, Next computer-mediated delivery of reference information offered by library professionals to users who cannot access or do not want face-to-face communication. Virtual reference service is most often an extension of a library's present reference service program. The word "*reference*" in this context refers to the task of providing assistance to library users in finding information, answering questions, and otherwise fulfilling users' information needs. Reference work often but not always involves using *reference works*, such as dictionaries, encyclopedias, etc. This form of reference work expands reference services from the physical reference desk to a "virtual" reference desk where the patron (users) could be writing from home, work or a variety of other locations.

## DIGITAL REFERENCE SERVICE

The primary aim of the library is to offer many services to its clientele to meet their specific information meets. Many techniques such as classification, cataloguing, shelving lists, opacs, open access to its readers and similar other types of services are all indirect form of assistance to users to find their document in the library. One of the elementary objectives of every library and information centre is to save the time of the user as well as to offered specific information as soon as possible. The method used for the same involve personal efforts to bring together user and his document. Hence this method of providing personal consideration to readers in terms of meeting their personal needs is given the name. 'Reference Services.

## TYPE OF DIGITAL REFERENCE SERVICE

**1. E-mail Reference Services :** The Electronic-Mail reference transaction involves back-and-forth exchange of information; users would not get any immediate answer. But users can ask a question when they think of it, at any time of the day or night. And they do not have to take time to make a special visit to the library. In other words, the users send e-mail to the library with a reference question, asking whatever information they feel necessary. The library sends reply by e-mail, fax, phone or letter as it finds convenient. In such a case, the controller of all questions at the beginning receives and examines and then routes them to appropriate staff. Technical questions are transferred to technical staff, circulation related questions to the circulation staff, reference questions to the reference librarian, and so on.

**2. Real Time Digital Reference Service :** Real Time Digital Reference Service In real time digital reference service, the replacement of information is live (it takes place in real time) between user and reference librarian. This service is after all on experimental stage in developing countries because it requires advanced computer technology, faster and better communication connectivity, respective audio and video capacity and availability of computers at home and work place. This service is not a replacement of traditional or e-mail reference service but the other part of these services.

**3. Web forms :** Web forms are created for digital reference services in order to help the patron be more productive in asking their questions. It helps the librarian locate exactly what the user is asking for. Creation of web forms requires design concentration.

**4. Chat using marketable applications :** Several applications continue for providing for chat best tool service. Some of these applications are: Virtual reference Toolkit...7 references. Question point. etc. These applications process functionality such as fast (on the spot) messaging, co-browsing, web page and document publishing, customization of per-scripted messages Real-time chat techniques involve how to communication digital reference, as there are no oral suggestions. Since communication is act as middle through software and reference is taking place on the World Wide Web.

**5. Chat using on the spot massaging :** Instant messaging or online chat is one of the most popular forms of computer communication. It is more fast than email if you can type pretty well. For eg. Messaging librarian use messengers like. Yahoo messenger, Google talk. MSN messenger etc.

**6. Video-Base Reference Services :** A video-based Virtual Reference Wit, also called Video Help. A client / server infrastructure was adopted for the Video Help system and time, were used to achieve the video synchronization between the librarians and palm A client/server infrastructure was adopted. On the server side, as session manager, implemented using Java socket video sharing.

## COMPONENTS OF DIGITAL REFERENCE SERVICE

According to Linda Berube, a digital reference service incorporates the following three basic elements:

- The User
- The interface (web form; e- mail; chat; video etc.)
- Electronic resources (including electronic or CD – based resources; web
- Resources; local digitized material etc.) as well as print resources
- The information professional

## ADVANTAGES OF DIGITAL REFERENCE SERVICES

This is a contemporary service in which reference librarian responds immediately in real time. Reference interview is conducted at a faster pace than e-mail. Clarification can be desired online. Reference librarian can demonstrate to the user about how to use reference sources, web sites, expert or whom the user should contact. This allows user to walk through the reference source to find answer. In addition to this, Voice over Internet Protocol (VOIP) allows reference librarian to talk to users and hear them while connected and while locating the sources. This service can be provided at any time, any day (24/7 basis). Reference librarian can chat with several persons together.

## DISADVANTAGES OF DIGITAL REFERENCE SERVICES

The technology is quite at premature stage. It is a labour-intensive service. It makes reference librarian too busy in answering the questions because it involves several back-and-forth message conventions. He may not find time to answer the fastly needed questions. It is stressful for reference librarian as well as user because one is waiting for other's message. For every inquiry? user needs to type questions every time and reference librarian also need to answer in typed form. Typing speed and errors occurring during typing in the text attempt, both reference librarian and user, difficulties in communicating their messages because real time chatting demands fast and accurate typing speed.

## CONCLUSIONS

Digital reference services are being provided by librarians in order to provide personal assistance to local or remote users of the library employing modern Internet technologies. People with special needs, accurately, can be greatly helped by these digital reference services if applied properly with appropriate skills. Visually impair red and low vision people who have on the spot been deprived from getting the right information at the right time find these new types of reference services in the digital environment as a blessing since these enable them to seek information independently. Autistic adults as well as children can be greatly served with the latest developments in mobile technologies. Senior citizens along with children are greatly enriched in getting digital reference services from the libraries and information centres through mobile apps and other similar kind of technologies.

## REFERENCE

1. Janes, J., Carter, D., & Memmott, P. (1999). Digital reference services in academic libraries. Reference & user services quarterly, 145-150.

2. Steinfeld, H., Gerber, P., Wassenaar, T. D., Castel, V., & de Haan, C. (2006). Livestock's long shadow: environmental issues and options. Food & Agriculture Org...

3. Han, L., & Goulding, A. (2003). Information and reference services in the digital library. Information services & use, 23(4), 251-262.

4. Rothstein, S. (1990). The development of reference services through academic traditions, public library practice and special librarianship. The Reference Librarian, 11(25-26), 33-155.

5. Kresh, D. (2005). Going where the users are: We'll get there only if we want to. In Advances in librarianship (pp. 133-158). Emerald Group Publishing Limited.

6. Hernon, P., & Altman, E. (2010). Assessing service quality: Satisfying the expectations of library customers. American Library Association.

7. Shirky, C. (2008). Here comes everybody: The power of organizing without organizations. Penguin.

8. Chandwani, A. (2010). An overview of digital reference services. Modern Practice in Library and Information Servoce, Nagpur.

9. Bhattacharya, U., & Roy, A. (2013). Digital reference services for people with special needs: what, why and how?

# Part IV

# 19

# Library Classification: Need and Purpose

***Balaji A. Kamble***
*Librarian , Hon. Sri. Annsaheb Dange College, Hatkanangale.*

## INTRODUCTION

Books,User and Staff are the main elements of Library. Library is the place which collect all types of information to it's user and a well trained staff is fusion between the books and user for best result of qualitative service..For the qualitative service classification is main activity in the library which can manage all type of information books journals and other reading materials which is collected in the library. It is necessary to know that libraries hold several types of collections like printed books, journals, manuscripts, maps, charts, micro-documents, CD-ROMs, video and audio cassettes,. etc. All these collections should necessarily be arranged systematically. There are three predetermined ways in which a reader may demand library material. They may ask by the name of the author, by the title of the book and third situation is that he may need book(s) on a particular subject. This last one is known as subject approach. In short, subject approach is the means of securing unknown items from the collection, and classification is the means of facilitating it. Library classification yields subject-wise arrangement of library materials in which documents are arranged by subject. The need for classification is all the greater in modern libraries, as they store different types of documents requiring diverse storage media. In other words, documents on the same subject get scattered throughout the collection because of their diverse physical forms. Classification, however, is the means of bringing books on the shelves and their entries in a catalogue or index at one place. Let us, therefore, acquaint ourselves with these different types of documents that modern libraries acquire and store.

## READING MATERIALS

We find in libraries various types of reading materials, viz., manuscripts, printed books, periodicals, pamphlets, reports, photo reproductions, sound records, films, musical scores, microfilms, maps, atlases, charts, illustrations and electronic media items, such as CD-ROMs, through which human thought is communicated and preserved. Proper collection, storage and maximum use of these documents is the prime concern of present day libraries Each material, like an individual, is not only unique but also exhibits relations of considerable complexity with other information sources. Extrinsic features like size, colour, volume, binding, year of publication and intrinsic features like thought content and their arrangement inside the document, or the nature of information, i.e., textual, numeric, bibliographic or graphic, also add to the complexity of the problem of libraries for achieving the objective of maximum utilisation of their collections.

The complexity of thought content and the nature

of relationships between various types of documents must be known and clearly established for their maximum use The maximum use of reading materials can be ensured by:

(i) individual help to readers,

(ii) systematic arrangement, and

(iii) proper display of materials in the library.

If the collection of a library is arranged in a systematic way documents can be located and retrieved easily. A classification scheme is the map or device for the arrangement of books in the library.

## MEANING OF CLASSIFICATION

Systematic grouping of entities (both abstract and concrete) to meet one's requirement is known as classification. Classification lies at the root of all human activities. Our daily life is very much dependent on the process of classification, however, elementary this process may appear. You can surely recall a number of activities around you where classification plays its part. Take, for example, the arrangement of contents in a railway time table, the display of goods in a grocery shop, the arrangement of modules in a departmental store to facilitate the selection of goods by customers, the seating arrangement in a theatre or stadium, the assignment of registration numbers to various motor vehicles by a state transport authority, or the sorting of letters by postmen first by the city, then by the street and lastly by the house numbers for quick delivery of post. These are simple examples of how we use classification in our activities.

S.R. Ranganathan, in his Prolegomena to Library Classification (1967), elaborately discusses the meaning of classification. In the case of physical objects, division and assortment are the two results of classification, According to Ranganathan, while division implies sorting objects into two or more groups, assortment additionally denotes arrangement of these groups in a predetermined sequence. Further, in library classification, the sequence of objects, i.e., documents, is so mechanised by the use of notation that it is reflected in the notation when a document is withdrawn or added.

## DEFINITION OF LIBRARY CLASSIFICATION

1. According to Margaret Mann, classification is "the arranging of things according to likeness and unlikeness. It is the sorting and grouping of things, but in addition, classification of books is a knowledge classification with adjustments made necessary by the physical form of books".
2. According to Ranganathan, "it is the translation of the name of the subject of a book into the preferred artificial language of ordinal numbers, and the individualisation of several books dealing with the same specific subject by means of a further set of ordinal numbers which represent some features of the book other than their thought content". In this definition, we find three important phrases

## NEED OF LIBRARY CLASSIFICATION

According to 5th Law of library science 'library is growing organisation'.It means the physical instument of every library is increase day to day fro example if your library is providing a quaity service automaticaly users are going to increase

(i) The first and foremost purpose of any library classification scheme is to create a helpful sequence of all the subject material acquired by a library so that same could be used by users of library in most convenient way without wasting much time and energy in searching the documents.

(ii) Library Classification helps to accommodate all the newly published literature in an already created order of arrangement in a filiatory sequence. Even a document on its return with the help of classification attains the same position and the same place among the already created sequence of document

(iii) Library Classification helps a great deal in exploiting the information to its optimum by maximizing the use of a library documents

## PURPOSE OF LIBRARY CLASSIFICATION

### Systematic Sequence

Classification helps in organizing the documents in a method most convenient to the users and to the library staff. The documents should be systematically arranged in classes based on the mutual relationship between them which would bring together all closely related classes. The basic idea is to bring the like classes together and separate these from unlike classes. The arrangement should be such that the user should be able to retrieve the required document as aresult it will make a helpful sequence.

### Replacement

Documents whenever taken out from shelf should be replaced in their proper places. It is essential that library classification should enable the correct replacement of documents after they have been returned from use. This would require a mechanized arrangement so that arrangement remains permanent.

### Automated Arrangement

It means to adopt a particular arrangement suitable for the library so that the arrangement remains permanent. The sequence should be determined once for all, so that one does not have to pre-determine the sequence of documents once again when these are returned after being borrowed.

**Addition of New Document :** Library would acquire new documents from time to time therefore library classification should help in finding the most helpful place for each of those among the existing collection of the library. There are two possibilities in this regard. The new books may be or a subject already provided forin the scheme of library classification, or it may be or a newly emerging subject that may not have been provided in the existing scheme.

## WITHDRAWAL OF DOCUMENT FROM STOCK

In this case, the need arises to withdraw a document from the library collection for some reason, and then library classification should facilitate such a withdrawal.

## BOOK DISPLAY

Display is adopted for a special exhibition of books and other materials on a given topic. The term is used to indicate that the collection in an open access library is well presented and guided. Library classification should be helpful in the organization of book displays.

## FACTORS DETERMINING ARRANGEMENT OF DOCUMENTS

Documents can be arranged in various ways in a library,

(a) author,

(b) title, or by,

(c) subject basis such as

(d) size,

(e) language,

(f) colour of binding

(g) any other such criterion.

The needs of the readers may be the criterion one can consider for arrangement of documents in a library.

Mills, in his book 'Modern Outline of Library Classification', lists the following possible characteristics determining the arrangements of documents:

(i) Age of reader.

(ii) Conditions attached to the use of the material.

(iii) Documents of unusual size.

(iv) Documents of unusual gross body.

(v) Thought content of the document (subject matter).

(vi) Language of the document.

(vii) Value of the document.

(viii) Peculiarities of form of presentation.

(ix) Date of printing.

(x) Local history.

(xi) Gift collection:

## ARRANGEMENT OF DOCUMENTS IN LIBRARIES

### (a) Approach of Readers for Documents

As stated earlier, documents can be arranged in libraries on the basis of the colour of the binding, the size, the language, the year of publication, the accession number and so on. But these methods are outdated and unhelpful, as they cannot bring to the notice of the reader the author, the title or the subject matter of a document. There is little or no chance of your finding today a library, which arranges its collection on the basis of colour, size, year of publication or even the name of the publisher. It was possible to use these characteristics for arranging books when the collections were very small in size.

There are a few libraries where the collections are arranged on the basis of accession number or serial number. The other methods by which documents are usually arranged are by title, author or subject. This is because in present-day libraries, the reader's approach for a specific document is by title or author or subject. It is common practice that fiction is arranged by author, periodicals by title and scientific factual literature by subject. In some libraries, you can find that even imaginative literature (belles letters) is arranged first by language, and within each language by form followed by author and, if necessary, by work number.

It has already been explained in Section 2.1 that a reader may demand a document by a particular author or of a particular title or on a particular subject. There are, thus, mainly three approaches to a collection, viz., author, title and subject. To what extent each of these is helpful is explained below.

**(b) Author approach :** Generally readers go to a library to find:

(i) a particular document whose author is known or

(ii) what documents by a particular author are in the library.

But the arrangement of documents on the basis of the author is not always helpful. If you want a particular document, or documents on a particular subject, the author arrangement fails to bring documents having the same specific subject and related subjects at one place. Here is an example:

**(c) Title approach :** Sometimes you may go to a library to get a document whose title you know. If the books in the library are arranged by title, it will meet your requirement. But the method of arranging documents on the basis of title is also not very helpful. There is always a chance of a title being misquoted. Titles sometimes change from one edition to another. The title of the same document would differ when translated from one language to another. Sometimes the same document is published in different countries under different titles, though the language may remain the same.

Title arrangement, like author arrangement, fails to bring together documents having the same specific subject at one place. Because of these limitations; the arrangement of documents on the basis of title is not very helpful. Here is an example:

- Introduction to Botany by Vaishith P.M
- Introduction to Zoology by Harry Lister
- Introduction to Computer science by Stalin Wiliam
- Introduction to Marketing Management by Philip Kotlar

In above example the title are samy but subjects are different when the library used only title for arrangement of document at that time the main theme will be miss place.

**(d) Subject approach :** In a academic library , special library , technical library and research libraries, and to a large extent even in public libraries, you will find that the majority of readers approach documents on the basis of the subject. This subject approach by readers has increased due to the growth in science and technology and also to a large extent in social sciences where the author and the title of a document are important but not adequate. Due to the enormous output of documents in these fields, it is often difficult to recall a specific title or author correctly except in the case of classics. Therefore, one finds that in well organized libraries documents are arranged on the basis of subject matter. This arrangement helps to bring documents embodying the same specific subject together and those on related subjects in their close proximity on the shelves. Subject approach of arrangement will be more useful and quickly helpful in search of information or documents for users, Classification helps bring together on the shelves documents on one and the same subject followed by those of related subjects. Suppose you are looking for a specific document on say, physics, you can find, where subject arrangement exists, documents not only on physics, but also those related to it in close proximity, i.e., chemistry. It may so happen that if a specific title wanted by you is not available, you can find another title on the subject that may very well meet your requirement. Some scholars may need everything available on their topic. You will notice that near the books on chemistry you will also find books on related subjects like mathematics and astronomy on one side and chemistry and biology on the other.

Subject arrangement of documents helps in to know:

(i) Number of documents available on specific subject;

(ii) Duplication of documents on a particular subject

Apart from the subject arrangement means a subject classification is more efficiency in library for easy access of books from shell.

## ARTIFICIAL LANGUAGE

In library classification we use symbols to denote subjects. The names of subjects are in ordinary language understandable to an ordinary person. Therefore, we call it the natural language which comes naturally to the human being living in a society. On the other hand, the symbols that we may use to denote a subject, say B, or 510, or QA for mathematics, are artificial in the sense that the common man will not ordinarily understand the meaning of these symbols. Hence these are artificial and intelligible to a specifically trained class of professionals. Their value is only ordinal, which means that these symbols have no quantitative or qualitative value; they only determine the sequence/order of documents on the shelves. These symbols also maintain/preserve the chosen sequence as the books will be replaced at their proper place after taking them out for reading or lending. These symbols do not indicate anything except the order/ sequence of these documents on the shelves.

## ORDINAL NUMBERS

These are used not for the purpose of counting but ordering and mechanising the arrangement of things.

For example, participants in a conference can be listed in a desired sequence on the basis of some suitable principle and then this sequence can be mechanised with the help of ordinal numbers. Melvil Dewey (1851-1931) , the father of modern library classification, was the first classificationist to use simple Indo-Arabic numerals (0-9) as ordinal numbers for the systematic listing of subjects both broader and narrower, in his Decimal Classification Scheme.

## CLASS NUMBER

Dr.S.R.Rangnathan and Dr.Melvil Dewey are the classifier of library documents they emphasized classification schemes.They used notation for assiegned class number.In their classification scheme they used mixed and pure notations.Dr.Dewey has been used Arabic number for the title .We can more understand by following title

title 'Reserve Bank of India'

Within each class the arrangement is carried out finally and minutely, e.g.,

300 Social sciences

330 Economics

332 Financial economics

332.1 Banks and banking

332.11 Central banks

**331.110 954 Reserve Bank of India**

## CALL NUMBER

The call numbers' for a document consists of three elements, viz.,class number, book number and collection number. The following example will show the presence of these three elements in a call number.

Knowledge economy : the Indian challenge by M.K. Khanijo Unique Publisher, New Delhi,2004.

The call number for this book according to Dewey Decimal Classification is

**658.4038/KNO**

## CONCLUSION

Classification is one such activity which we believe every living being is bestowed inherently by nature and is being used by one and all in every day activity. Classification has always been the backbone of Library services and activities and without it, library is definitely going to suffer in its recourse and to find a particular piece of information from unorganized heap of knowledge is almost impossible. It is very essential that various types of collections in a library should be classified and arranged in a helpful sequence so as to maximize their use. In this Unit, Library classification is the tool for achieving subject arrangement of documents and their catalogue, entries in a library.Dr.Melvil Deway and Dr.S.R.Rangnathan's contribution in the classification context is more valuable. The found DDC and CC classification schemes and still today it is more popular and familiar to overall librarian in the world. Classification is the primary activity of arrange all the documents for better user quality library services to it's user group.

## REFERENCES

1. Bhattacharya G.(1972)General theory of library classification scheme,Delhi:vikas pubishers.
2. Bliss H.E(1992)Organization of knowledge in libraries and subject approach of books,ed.2,New York:W.H.Wilson
3. Dewey Melvil(1996)Dewey Decimal Classification and relative Index (21st Ed.)Albany,New York:Forest Press.
4. Gopinath M.A.(1986)Construction of depth Version of colon Classification : A manual, New Delhi.
5. Khanna J.K.(1986)Colon Classification,New Delhi:Ess Ess.
6. Rangnathan,S.R.(1951)Colon Classification Madras:Sarada Rangnathan.
7. Rangnathan S.R.( 1957) Prolegamana to Library Classification : Madras : Sarada Ranganathan Endowment.

# 20
# Cloud Computing in Libraries

***Uma Rani***
*Asst. Lib. Bhai Gurdas Institute of Engg. & Tech., Sangrur (Punjab)*

## ABSTRACT

In this era cloud computing is most usable service. This service is more productive and has broad network access. It permits to user a flexibility service .it provides a systematic service by offer to user easy run software as a platform on demand discuss here how it work with its source model and gives different types of service to its different user like Saas,Paas, Iaas. It gives facility to library user anywhere and anytime promptly. I focus in this paper cloud computing characteristics, its model and how is useful in library services. However there are barrier of this service like its security and privacy.

**Keywords :** cloud computing, saas, paas, iaas, cloud base library services

## INTRODUCTION

Cloud computing is latest and popular technology based on internet. Computing where we can share computer resource or data with each other on demand.

It is big pool which is managed by third party .it allows to different capability to preserve and allow to user, when he need. Gmail is very big cloud base server we keep our snaps, documents and papers etc. on this without any time limit and storing place. Cloud computing provide their user to get their application promptly with improved method. After 2013 cloud computing exposition is at the peak rate. When we store data on our computer at home or office this type of storing is local networking and limited user can use this data . When we access our data through internet it changed in broad sharing. Uncountable users can use our data through cloud . cloud computing is technology where we can access service anywhere and anytime

## DEFFINATION

Computing is virtual storage application,. It is server of servers that shared via internet. This is simplest term for store data on internet rather then computer hardware "cloud computing is a model for enabling convenient, on demand network access to a shared pool of configuration of computing resource (E.g. Network server, storage application service) that can be rapidly provisioned and released with minimal management effort or service provider interaction.(Tim Grace and Peter Mel )

## CHARACTERISTICS OF CLOUD COMPUTING

1. Broad Network Access As we know this service is depending on internet so, sharing area is broad here. We can share and access our document anywhere .This service is on network and access through standard mechanism which can be use on thick or thin platform like smart phones, computer, tablets etc.
2. On Demand self Service Here user can use service when he need without requirement of human interaction because it is mechanism service and it run automatic for its user

3. Maintenance cloud computing is very easy service because there is no need to install on each device. It can be found anywhere, where internet available. We can use the service while traveling also.
4. Reliable Service This service is hosted by expert companies which make well designed sites that user can use easy way for different departments
5. Performance cloud computing is designed by IT experts Engineers so they monitored their services via easy and effective way ,as a result service performance will automatic good.
6. Productivity many users can work on same time here rather then wait for each other. There is no need to retype when same field work. Here is no need to install/upgrade separate application to user.
7. Multitendency Service for sharing resource with lower investment. Here enterprise no needs to hire separate engineer because it is already monitored by IT experts.
8. Device and location independence This service can be accessed on moving device like smart phones, laptop, tablets etc. So user can use the service through internet from any corner of the world. So, we can say it is location free service

## DEPLOYMENT MODELS

There are four types of cloud deployment model which are discuss following

**Public cloud :** This model is made for general public, here user can use the service but don't know visibility or control on the main server .all user can share resources in same pool with limited configuration

**Private cloud :** It is dedicated to a specific organization. It has control of data security which right has not to public cloud but it is managed by third party.

**Hybrid cloud :** This cloud is mixture of all models(private ,community, private) and made a unique entity but bond to standardized technology

**Community cloud :** This cloud is made for two or three organization and support a specific community for special mission or Security It may managed by one organization or by third party

## SOURCE MODELS OF CLOUD COMPUTING

There are lot of models by web but we discuss here only three main models of cloud computing.

For example if any person lend a palace for party there are three options first he can lend only palace and all arrangement will done and managed by person second he will book palace with decoration, and third one he will book that palace as decorated and with catering same is in cloud computing models where we can rent a readymade software. second we can rent a platform where we will design a software according to our needs , and third is we can rent only infrastructure all arrangement will done by user so following are models of cloud computing :

**SAAS (software as a service)** in this model user can use only software that is on web with cloud. Here user needs not to buy any special software and no worry to install or manage the software. He can only use online software to complete his task as his needs. In this software free and unlimited service by computer with internet

**PAAS (Platform as a service)** in this model a platform of software are managed for user where he can design his application according to his requirements. User has right to run software without managing the hardware and software. Most current Examples of Paas are Amazon provides user in maintain and supporting their IT infrastructure without invest any money

**IAAS (Infrastructures As A Service)** Here user can take wide range feature and help to build a virtual computing. In this model basic infrastructure is provided to user for storage and computing capability as a network server Savvis, Sunand Google base and Amazon web service are example of IAAS.

## CLOUD BASED SERVICES IN LIBRARIES

As we know the library play dramatic role in education field it trains the best brain. By applying this technology libraries have facility to access their service anytime and anywhere There are some possible areas we applied cloud computing service in library

**Searching Data Tool :** OCLC is one of the best services for search data. OCLC world cat is now on cloud based that offer the library various service like cataloging, circulation, acquisition on cloud platform via internet this technology share open and collaborative service each library

**Digital repository :** In this technology era, today non documentary resources are demanded by user so, cloud computing solve this demand within seconds. Now every library build digital library by adopting online software.Dspace and fedora are the best software by duraspace for repository.

**Library Automation :** cloud computing made easy to complete daily task of library operation like circulation, no dues, acquisition and micslenious work of libraries. Many cloud based commercial and open source software are prepared for library automation which are support by Marc21 and Z39.50 and Unicode. Koha is one of the best example cloud based software for automation tool. Koha modified by librarian which is example of private cloud and managed by third party which is example of hybrid cloud.

**File storage :** It is helpful to access any file via

internet. There are some example of cloud based services like dropbox, googledocs, flicker and jungle disk etc.these services provide without limitation of time and place virtual share files LOCKSS and CLOCKSS are popular tool for preserve virtual sharing.

**Web sites hosting :** Many libraries are adopting web host service which is cloud based. Libraries preferring their websites with help of third party. Library makes their Google site so that user can check their account and library resources at their own place.

**Improve community power :** This cloud computing service provides network by using social network for share information for information seeker. Social network are utilize the time and make the person knowledgeable as the interest of user. These social has proper and daily backup. With the help of these network libraries are little relax from maintenance and software updates.

## ADVANTAGES OF CC

**1. Cost effectiveness :** this cloud computing is capable to increase or decrease the consumption of hardware or software resource promptly and automatically.

**2. Adjustable Storage :** In earlier time there was need a large place to keep server. But in cloud computing we can manage this server according our needs in library. So, it is flexible to keep store.

**3. Great reliable and Security :** As we know this cloud computing is managed by expert third party it is full of security with reliable source.

**4. Probability :** this is full fledge web based service so, we can avail this service any corner of world.

**5. Cloud Opac :** Every library has a web Opac, when a library catalogue through cloud, it will give four moons in library service

**6. Scalability :** It provides to user share resource

and hosting a customer on pay as you use basis.

**7. Lower investment :** This cloud computing is capable to immediate the service in proposed hardware and software.

**8.** This service is full of knowledge and experienced. which is given to its user.

## DRAWBACKS OF CC

- If we think about this service we have to purchase costly computer laptop or other electronic device
- It is web based service so we have to take costly net plans for avail this service.
- Every department has their own secrets, as we know it is managed by third party so, much valuable secret information like bank information can tracked by third party.

## CONCLUSION

It is concluded that Cloud computing is most latest and popular technology that act a effective role in every department and organization. Library use of cloud computing service for archiving economy in library function in this digital era. Libraries daily task like circulation, cataloging and acquisition are now possible within seconds. Cloud computing Design software for enterprise or library which is cost effective, adjustable storage ,high scalability, with lower investment. Cloud computing make easy access and retrieve information where internet access within seconds. it is managed by third party so here is lack of privacy .

## REFERENCES


- http//www.tnbs.com/download/cloudcomputing. overviewpdd.
- http//www.webopedia.com/term/ccloudcomputing
- national conference on library information science and technology for education ISBN.1-63102-455-8

- international journal of information dissemination technology ISSn2229-5984Oct-Dec2013Vol.3application of cloud computing in libraries by Anna Kaushik and Ashok Kumar

# 21

# Cloud Computing For Library Management

***Mrs Urmila Rajendra Kadam***
*Librarian, Kamala College, Kolhapur-416008*

## ABSTRACT

Cloud computing is new idea in the time of data edge. It gives different aspects for procuring data from assortment of branches like Amezon.com Yahoo. Goole,& Rediffmail. Storage of data, Retrieval of data, Speed, Accuracy, Eassy availability are the characteristic of cloud computing. So it will be useful to custodians for better servces. Iaas, Paas Saas are the kinds of cloud computing. In preset situation web technology can't satisfy the data seekers. so on the vital platform cloud figuring pattern is created it contains features of various technologies, including utility, Grid computing web 2.0 administrations etc.

**Keywards** : Cloud Computing, Library database, Management, Net working, Storege of knowledge, Net working, Iaas, Paas Saas

## INTRODUCTION

In old time curator and library experts were working manually there was no utilization of machine. But now a day's computerization task put in the field of library.

Through the assistance of changes programming libraries were coming close and close. Because of impact of robotization computerization web intranet different databases and web crawlers, data providing organizations World is coming close. Late idea distributed computing is created for looking information storing &data providing to clients. The quick improvement of ICT ,alongside the huge development of written works in all field of learning, changing clients slant/interest for online assets, contracting library spending plan, advancement of different library systems and consortia and soon have constrained all libraries to create different ICT apparatuses and administrations to cook their clients appropriately. Distributed computing.

## WHAT IS CLOUD COMPUTING

A Cloud computing is portrayed in essentially way that is, information storage, security of information, recovery of data, accurate and extremely enormous amount with the assistance of most recent technology. A term distributed computing is characterized and Described in just manner. Such framework give, put away Maintain, Security of data to its client exact, quick and colossal way. Distributed computing can be characterized as "A model for empowering pervasive, advantageous, on-request arrange access to a mutual pool of configurable processing assets (e.g., systems, servers, stockpiling, applications, and administrations) that can be quickly provisioned and discharged with insignificant administration exertion or specialist organization collaboration." "Distributed computing," essentially, signifies "Web Computing." The Internet is regularly pictured as mists; thus the expression "distributed computing" for calculation done through the Internet. With Cloud Computing clients can get to database assets through the Internet from anyplace, for whatever length of time that they require, without stressing over any upkeep or administration of genuine resources" An rising PC paradigm where information and administrations live in hugely versatile server farms in the cloud and can be gotten to from any associated gadget over the web "Distributed computing is related with another worldview for the arrangement of figuring foundation. This change in perspective the area of this framework to the system to lessen the expenses related with the administration of equipment and programming assets. The Cloud is drawing the consideration from the Information and Communication Technology (ICT) people group

## CHARACTERISTICS OF CLOUD COMPUTING

**1. Self Healing :** Any application or any administration running in a distributed computing condition has the property of self mending. In the event of disappointment of the application, there is dependably a hot reinforcement of the application prepared to assume control without disturbance. There are different duplicates of a similar application - each duplicate refreshing itself routinely so that now and again of disappointment there is no less than one duplicate of the application which can assume control without even the scarcest change in its running state.

**2. Multi-tenancy :** In this framework multi inhabitants can be utilize site and get the required data With distributed computing, any application bolsters multi-occupancy - that is different occupants at a similar moment of time. The framework enables a few clients to share the foundation apportioned to them with no of them monitoring the sharing. This is finished by virtualizing the servers on the accessible machine pool and after that apportioning the servers to various clients. This is done such that the protection of the clients or the security of their information isn't traded off

**3. Linearly Scalable :** Distributed computing administrations are straightly adaptable. The framework can separate the workloads into pieces and administration it over the foundation. A correct thought of direct versatility can be acquired from the way that on the off chance that one server can process say 1000 exchanges for each second, at that point two servers can process 2000 exchanges for every second.

**4. Service Oriented :** Distributed computing frameworks are all administration situated - i.e. the frameworks are to such an extent that they are made out of other discrete administrations. Numerous such discrete administrations which are autonomous of each other are joined together to shape this administration. This permits re-utilization of the distinctive administrations that are accessible and that are being made. Utilizing the administrations that were simply made, other such administrations can be made.

**5. SLA Driven :** Typically organizations have concessions to the measure of services.Scalability and accessibility issues make customers break these assentions. In any case, distributed computing administrations are SLA driven to such an extent that when the framework encounters pinnacles of load, it will consequently alter itself in order to consent to the administration level assentions. The administrations will make extra cases of the applications on more servers with the goal that the heap can be effortlessly overseen.

**6. Virtualized :** The applications in distributed computing are completely decoupled from the hidden equipment. The distributed computing condition is a completely virtualized condition. Framework serves to client that data to be adjusted consequently .

**7. Flexible :** This administration is exceptionally adaptable in setting of client of data which he needs Another element of the distributed computing administrations is that they are flexible.They can be utilized to serve a vast assortment of workload writes -

changing from little heaps of a little shopper application to overwhelming heaps of a business application

## TYPES OF CLOUD COMPUTING

**1. Software as s service (SaaS) :** PC construct service, and consequently put away data in light of his or her record client it self Software bundle, for example, CRM or CAD/CAM can be gotten to under distributed computing plan. Here a client upon enlistment is permitted to utilize programming open through net and utilize it for his or his business procedure. The related information and work might be put away on nearby machines or with the specialist co-ops. SaaS administrations might be accessible on rental premise or on per utilize premise

**2. Platform as a Service (PaaS) :** In highlight there may many cloud seller organizations that offer distributed computing administrations and items. to part client one of the administrations that they give is called PaaS. Under this a figuring stage, for example, working framework is given to a client or end client on a month to month rental premise. A portion of the real distributed computing seller is Amazon, Microsoft, and Google and so on.

**3. Infrastructure as a service (IaaS) :** The distributed computing merchants offer foundation as an administration. One may benefit equipment administrations, for example, processors, memory, systems and so forth on concurred reason for particular length and price. In this framework data isn't on free,user must pay the cost.

## USE CLOUD COMPUTING IN LIBRARY AND INFORMATION SCIENCE

Cloud computing offers many interesting possibilities for libraries that may help to reduce technology cost and increase capacity reliability, and performance for some type of automation activities. Cloud computing has made strong inroads into other commercial sectors and is now beginning to find more application in library science. The cloud computing pushes hardware to more abstract levels. Most of us are acquainted with fast computing power being delivered from systems that we can see and touch.

## ROLE OF CLOUD COMPUTING IN LIBRARIES

Cloud computing is a completely new in technology and it is known as 3rd revolution after PC and Internet. Cloud computing is an enhancement of distributed computing, parallel computing, grid computing and distributed databases. Among these, grid and utility computing are known as predecessors of cloud computing. Cloud computing has large potential for libraries. Libraries may put more and more content into the loud. Using cloud computing user would be able to browse a physical shelf of books, CDs or DVDs or choose to take out an item or scan a bar code into his mobile device. All historical and rare documents would be scanned into a comprehensive, easily searchable database and would be accessible to any researcher. Many libraries already have online catalogues and share bibliographic data with OCLC. More frequent online catalogues are linked to consortium that share resources.

Following companies are providing "Cloud computing" Facility.

1. Akamai
2. Layered Techonology
3. Amazon Cloud
4. Rackspace
5. Areti Internet
6. Enki
7. X Calibre
8. Terremark

9. Joyent
10. Salesforce.com

**Advantages of Cloud computing in libraries**

1. Cost saving
2. Flexibility and innovation
3. User centric
4. Openness
5. Transparency
6. Interoperability
7. Representation
8. Availability anytime anywhere
9. Connect and Converse
10. Create and collaborate

**Disadvantages of Cloud computing in libraries**

1. Controlling agencies may became powerful
2. System required highly technical persons
3. Data may be correputed
4. It may be costly
5. User may need of training for useing

**Examples of Cloud libraries**

1. OCLC
2. Library of Congress ( LC)
3. Exlibris
4. Polaris
5. Scribd
6. Discovery Service
7. Google Docs / Google Scholar
8. Worldcat

## CONCLUSION

Cloud computing is not a completely new concept in the library and information field but it is in a developmental phase. Academic libraries are facing challenges in the information technology era. Libraries are trying to provide their users cloud based services but due to lack of good service providers and technical skills, they are pushing back. But apart from cloud computing and taking advantages of cloud based services specially in building digital libraries. The role of library professionals is make cloud based services as reliable medium to disseminate library services to their users.

## REFERENCES

1. Sampath Kumar, B.T and Biradar,B.S.2010. "Use of ICT in college libraries in Karnataka, India: a survey". Program: electronic library and information systems 44(3):271-282.
2. Khan, S., Khan, S. & Galibeen, S. (2011). Cloud computing an emerging technology: Changing ways of libraries collaboration. International Research: Journal of Library and Information Science, 1(2).
3. Pandya, M. (2012).Cloud computing for libraries: A SWOT analysis. 8th Convention PLANNER-2012 Sikkim University, Gangtok, 387-394
4. Srivastav, K. & Kuma, A. (2011). A new approach of cloud: Computing infrastructure on demand. TRIM, 7(2), 145-153 5. Goyal, S. (2012). A comparative study of cloud computing service providers. International Journal of Advanced Research in Computer Science and Software Engineering, 2(2), 1-5.

# 22

# Cloud Computing: A Recent Trend in Library and Information Science Services

***Jitamoni Bhattacharya***
*MLISc, MPhil, Librarian, Biswanth College, Biswanath Chariali, Biswanath (Assam)*

***Niharika Sharma***
*M.Sc, BLIS, Assistant Librarian, Pandit Deendayal Upadhyaya Adarsha Mahavidyalaya, Behali, Biswanath (Assam)*

In recent years, cloud computing has received much attention and appreciation as a dynamic reliable, oriented, customized and high-quality computing service. Cloud computing mainly refers to the internet-based computing. But as they grow up and become more sophisticated, we will probably see the spread of computer 'utilities' which, like present electric and telephone utilities, will service individual homes and offices across the country." Cloud computing use the technologies of Grid Computing and Virtualization for the delivery of scalable IT services. Information is growing rapidly in everyday life every time. Today, all the information officers as well as librarians should know how to deal with both physical and digital information. Cloud computing is mainly based on the idea of reusability of capacities.

In general, the service rendered by cloud computing is referred to as Software as a Service (SaaS). The main advantage of using this type of software service is that rather than a traditional computer that requires being located in the same location, as that of the data storage, the cloud computing service doesn't need to be present in the same physical location.

## CLOUD COMPUTING MODELS: CHOOSING A PROVIDER

Cloud providers are mainly are of three types that serves a specific function.

1. Software as a Service (SaaS)
2. Platform as a Service (PaaS)
3. Infrastructure as a Service (IaaS)

**SaaS :** This type of provider generally gives access to both resources and application through the internet. One need not to install a particular application, rather can access simply via the internet. One advantage of using this provider is that here, users can have control over the cloud.

**PaaS :** Apart from giving access to the resources and application, this provider provides access to the components also that are required to develop and operate the application. PaaS can be delivered in two ways-

(i) As a public cloud service from a provider.

(ii) As a private service within the firewall.

**IaaS :** This type of computing enables the users to the facility of basic storage and computing capacities. IaaS mainly provides the service of remote delivery of computer infrastructure.

**Cloud Clients**

Web browser, mobile app, thin client, and emulator

**SaaS**

CRM, Email, virtual desktop, communication, games

**PaaS**

Execution, runtime, database, web-server, development tools

**IaaS**

Virtual machines, servers, storage, load balancers, networks

***Source : http://en.wikipedia.org***

Cloud mainly refers to the data centre software as well as hardware. The computers that are connected on this network can communicate among them through a special kind of software known as 'Middleware'.

The whole architecture of cloud computing is mainly divided into two parts -

(a) Front End

(b) Back End

Front End is mainly the client or any application that runs on cloud service whereas; Back End is the main network on which the server runs.

It is to be noted that in this type of computing, the demand for resources is not always same for client to cloud.

## TYPES OF CLOUD COMPUTING

**1. Public Cloud :** This type of cloud can be accessed by any subscriber having access to cloud space.

It is one of the most traditional cloud computing where an organization rents cloud service from cloud providers.

**2. Private Cloud :** This type of cloud providers is generally a restricted type which is maintained within an organization.

Private cloud consists of set of applications or virtual machines in a company's own set of host.

**3. Community Cloud :** Community cloud is that type of cloud computing which is shared by a community.

It seems that though more expensive, this type of computing provides higher degree of privacy and security.

**4. Hybrid Cloud :** It is a combination of minimum two clouds which may be either internal or external. This type of cloud computing mainly utilizes 3rd party Cloud Providers in full or partial manner.

## ADVANTAGES OF USING CLOUD COMPUTING

Cloud Computing is quite an old paradigm, but recent technologies has made it more enthusiastic for the users.

**1. Cost Reduction :** Providing cloud services needs very little investment. Also, the infrastructure does not need to be purchased, thus lowering the cost deployment even more and adding to the demand of this type of service by the user.

**2. Increased Flexibility :** As this type of computing is location independent, it thus increased flexibility and market agility.

**3. Increased Storage :** Cloud Computing offered the users the provision of storage and maintenance of large volume of datasets with its massive infrastructure.

## SOME LIMITATIONS OF USING CLOUD COMPUTING

**1. Data Protection :** Data security is must in any kind of computing service and cloud computing is not exceptional. Service providers are responsible in maintaining data security.

**2. Data Recovery :** Sometimes, the damage o9ccured by a service provided by a cloud provider could be server. This may be the case of data replication, system monitoring, disaster recovery, etc.

**3. Managing Capacities :** Technologies to manage cloud computing are still very less developed and still in its infant stage.

## CLOUD COMPUTING IN EDUCATION

It has been observed in recent years that the education system is highly benefited with the advent of cloud computing. This system has deliberately reduced the cost of buying expensive textbooks as students can now access all the important topics over the internet no matter where they are. Cloud computing in the field of education has not only just lowered the cost and expenditure through introduction of e-textbooks, but also has made the contents up-to-date. Cloud based learning materials can be updated in no time and therefore students can access the most current resources at anytime. Moreover, neither expensive hardware nor expensive software is required to operate the cloud computing service.

## CLOUD COMPUTING IN LIBRARY AND INFORMATION SCIENCE

Library automation has increased the use of digital information through internet and web-tool application meant for library and information science. Introduction of cloud computing in the field of library and information science has been a great help in commercializing the ideas of e-libraries.Today, many libraries are sharing the databases with OCLC, which is one of the best example for sharing library data through cloud computing. Besides this, OCLC is also providing all the essential library services like acquisition, cataloguing, circulation, etc. For storage purposes, libraries are seen to be moulding themselves to the habit of using internet,digital library, library consortia etc. instead of using age old methods like CD-ROMS or floppy disc. Cloud-based computing in libraries has initiated a step forward to the progress of a paperless society. Also, it is worth mentioning that cloud computing is not the only first service in a digitalized platform to be used in the field of library science. At present, several other services, for e.g., Web 2.0, Open source, library websites are running successfully. But, above all, usage of cloud computing in library science will definitely bring a positive change as it has some characteristic advantages over the already existing ones. Some of them are as follows:

(1) The service oriented architecture provided by the cloud made easy access to the resources.

(2) Its portable nature makes this service as the first choice of the users as they can avail it from any part of the world.

(3) Cloud computing platform is very flexible and provides an innovative platform to introduce new technologies.

(4) Storage capacity of cloud computing service can be adjusted according to the needs of the users.

Though cloud computing is still at a very nascent stage in the field of library and information science. But, seeing its popularity and increasing demand, it is very clear that in the coming years, it will be the primary platform satisfying all the requirements at an ease.

## REFERENCES

1. King, R. (2009). Cloud Computing: Small Companies take Flight. *Business Week*. Available at: *http://www.readwriteweb.com/archives/amazonwebservices sucessstories.php*.
2. Gosani, N., Shinde, S. S., Dhakulkiar, B.(2012). Use of Cloud Computing in Library and Information Science Field. *International Journal of Digital Library Service*. Available at: *www.ijodls.in*.
3. Kaushik, A. and Kumar, A. (2013). Application of Cloud Computing Computing in Libraries. *International Journal of Information Dissemination and Technology*. 3(4), 270- 273.
4. Sahu, R. (2014). Cloud Computing: An Innovative Tool For Library Services. *National Conference on Library Information Science and Information Technology for Education*. ISBN 1-63102-455-8.
5. Saini, L., Jyoti, H. (2017). Role of Cloud Computing in Education System. *International Journal of Advanced Research in Computer Science*. Available at: *www.ijarcs.info* ISSN No. 0976.5697, Vol.8, No.4.

# 23

# E-Resource Management in College Library

***Y. B. Koradur***
*M.L.I.Sc., M. Phil., DCM.,D. Pharm Librarian*
*STC Arts and Commerce College,*
*Banhatti. Dist: Bagalakoti*

## INTRODUCTION

The e-Resources available in a library play a prominent role in facilitating access to required information to the users in an easy and expeditious manner. The digital resources available in a library play prominent role in facilitating access to the required information to the user are an expediency manner. Further one need not go to the library to make use of print formats as the digital resources can be made use of by any user through On-line access via networks or authentication methods at any time by comfortably Now. web-based electronic resources have become most popular tools in academic research.

At present the online databases, E-resources facilitate formation of the colleges at resource sharing among the libraries. Library functions a very important role in this fast changing go green of publishing. Their role includes identification of selection of information, its organization of management, storage retrieval and dissemination to right users at the right time at right place at right price and in right format. The goal of any academic libraries is to meet the teaching, research and other information needs of the user.

The aim of this study is to identify how electronic information resources are utilized by academic library users and specific trends that can be seen among faculties and students. Further the study also examine the use pattern, acceptance, perceived importance and satisfaction on electronic resources over print resources.

## COLLEGE LIBRARY

The library is a comfortable place to study, to investigate a topic of interest, or to enjoy reading a current book, periodical, or magazine. Please feel free to ask for assistance in using the library; a reference librarian is available to help you with your research questions.

## CONCEPT OF E-RESOURCE

E-Resources is nothing but electronic resources which is one of the emerging environment in libraries & Information communication in the competitive service. In these days, there are digital resources available in a library play prominent role in facilitating access to the required information to the user are an expediency manner.

E-Resources usually consist of e-books, e-Journals, articles, newspaper, thesis, dissertation, databases and CD-ROMs, which are likely to be the alternative to the print media. All updated information is published in these e-resources.

Some of the most important e-Resources contain the following -

### E-book Collection

This electronic library is a searchable collection of eBooks. Sources include reference books, scholarly monographs, fiction, and non-fiction. Searches can be done within a particular title or performed across hundreds of titles.

### Academic Search Complete

A scholarly, multi-disciplinary full-text database of full-text periodicals, including peer-reviewed journals. In addition to full text, this database offers indexing and abstracts of journals and publications including monographs, reports, conference proceedings, etc.

### Book Index with Reviews

Use this extensive database when looking for trustworthy and reliable book reviews. It contains access to only limited scholarly, peer reviewed book reviews.

### Newspaper Source Plus

This database provides access of full text news papers. This includes television and radio news transcripts.

### Religion and Philosophy Collection

This database is the one to use when researching topics such as eschatology, "world religions, major denominations, biblical studies, religious history, epistemology, political philosophy, philosophy of language, moral philosophy and the history of philosophy."

### e-Library

This broad-based database is comprised of articles from hundreds of popular magazines and scholarly journals, dozens of current newspapers and newswires, thousands of television and radio transcripts, photographs and maps, and numerous reference books.

The database can be searched by subject and all articles may be printed from the computer screen or e-mailed.

## e-Journal

Journals are a vital source of information for the scientific research and development in college Libraries and information centers. Getting access to E-journals involves various modalities viz. identification of journals, corresponding with the publishers/aggregators, signing the agreements etc. Electronic journals offering tremendous possibilities and advantages over print journals; ease of use, "anywhere-any time", accessibility, share ability, hyperlink to related text or multimedia content. E-Journals also offering solution to other major logistic problems faced by libraries such as follow up of missing issues, binding, shelving etc.

## E-RESOURCE MANAGEMENT IN COLLEGE LIBRARY

The-resource management is the rapid growth of electronic resources. Because of this growth libraries are experiencing issues related to time management, staffing, and the time-honored task of deliberating the set-up of logical workflow systems for such resources.

The e-resource management can be considered from the perspectives of planning, policy, and workflow issues experienced by libraries. Many libraries attempt to transfer and incorporate the print workflow onto electronic resource management.

The challenges, methods, and impacts on electronic resource management perceived by libraries are described. The authors suggest methods and ideas to address these topics that may help libraries create a sense of order for electronic resource management.

Following are the important methods used for e-Resource Management in College Library

### ERM System

In recent years, many libraries have created or purchased Electronic Resource Management (ERM) systems to keep track of their online subscriptions and license agreements. The ability to view all information related to a particular resource without having to consult multiple files and spreadsheets is perhaps the greatest benefit of using an ERM system.

### ERM Processes

The steps required for managing e-resources are more complex than those for print resources. A process that consisted of selecting, ordering, cataloging and binding now includes selecting, evaluating, approving, licensing, billing and registering access and is accompanied by a series of technical aspects, such as usability, performance, access technologies, public interfaces, troubleshooting and usage statistics. E-resource management is a time-intensive and iterative process, often requiring more staff with a greater skill set at each stage. As demand for e-resources grew, storing and managing administrative information in spreadsheets, paper files or email folders became increasingly cumbersome, and a more integrated solution was called for.

### Home-grown ERM Systems

At first, several libraries began to develop their own e-resource management systems to integrate such elements as the relationships between packages and their constituent parts, use permissions and constraints, authentication and contact information, as well as workflows for trialing, licensing, ordering, implementing access and notifying relevant staff.

### DLF ERMI Report

It helps to develop common specifications and tools

for managing the license agreements, related administrative information and internal processes associated with collections of licensed electronic resources".

**ERD, Data Element Dictionary, Data Structure**

The entity-relationship diagram (ERD) is a visual representation of the major entities needed for managing electronic resources and the relationships between them. It is the basis for the database structure of an ERM system.

**ERTS**

The electronic resources tracking system (ERTS) to serve as a central repository for administrative metadata such as license restrictions, technical contacts, statistics availability and payment information. The ultimate goal was to merge ERTS and the trials database into a single system that would hold data from the trial phase through purchasing and renewal.

**ERM System Technology**

At the center of any ERM system is a knowledge base, containing bibliographic, URL and holdings information.

**Future Releases of ERM Systems**

In future releases, vendors plan to incorporate overlap analysis and cost per- use analysis into their ERM systems to help with collection development. Integration with content modules, such as e resource registration processes, incident report mechanisms and license descriptions, is also on the agenda. Standardizing usage data collection is a major objective of the ERM industry, as represented by the Standardized

## CONCLUSION

With the help of emerging trends in e-Resources, now the college libraries are more digitally resourceful & also have started collecting information in the electronic modes likely in Online Journals, Online books, CD-ROM, DVD-ROM, e-journals, audio cassettes, video cassettes and internet. Now they have slowly started replacing the importance and usage of print media. And, because of e-resources availability there is easy access to valuable information in an expeditious manner.

## REFERENCES

1. Savage, Anne R. (1999). Assuring quality distance learning programs. The emergence of a new faculty. Higher Education in Europe Vol. XXIV, No.2 pp.209-211.
2. Chutima, Sacchananda (1999). Distance Education in Library and Information Science in Asia and Pacific region. IFLA Journal, Vol. 25, No. 2, pp. 97-100.
3. Rath, P.K. (1999). Quality Assurance in Professional Education through Distance mode with special reference to "Library and Information Science Programmes in India". Quality Assurance in Distance Education, New Delhi, Association of Indian Universities.
4. Samantaray, M. and Rath, P.K. (1998). Library and information Education (LISE) through Distance mode in India. An overview. In, Towards the New Information society of Tomorrow: Innovations, Challenges and Impact. 49th FID conference and Conference volume, Publication No. 719, pp. 136 – 142.
5. Simkins, M.A. (1993). The impact of new Technology on the information profession. Aslib proceedings 25(5) April 82-89. Project Document *http://www.sakshat.ac.in/PDF/Missiondocument.pdf*

# 24

# Academic Plagiarism : A Besetting Sin

***Meenakshi Gupta***
*Department of Library, Eternal University,*
*Baru Sahib (H.P.) India-173101*

## ABSTRACT

According to Alvin Toffler society is suffering from information overload leading to stress.Stress and plagiarism are two buzz words of today society. Plagiarism is "wrongful appropriation" and "stealing and publication" of another's Language, thought, ideas or expression and representing it as "own original work". Though considered theft or stealing plagiarism does not exist in legal sense, but may meet some definition of fraud and is different from copy right. In academia, plagiarism by students, professors or researchers is considered academic dishonesty or academic fraud which leads to academic censure world's differentinstitutions of higher learning defined plagiarism in different senses.According to health informatics Department of university of Illinois (Chicago) there are ten main forms of plagiarism committed by students which is the result of academic procrastination.

**Keywords** : Plagiarism, Information Overload, Wrongful Appropriation, Academia Plagiarism.

In future shock published in 1970, a sociologist and futurologist ALVIN Toffler describes the overwhelming flood of "information and abled it as an information overload". He further argues that society is undergoing on enormous structural change. Man has moved from 'Cave 'to 'Space'. The society marched from agricultural society to industrial society; form industrial society to informational society; from information society to knowledge society.This change will overwhelm people become the accelerated rate of technological and social will leave them disconnected and cause "shattering stress and disorientation-future shock.A term coined by AlvinTofler (1970) means (rapidly increasing amount of published information and its effects) due to growth of data in abundance, managing the information becomes more difficult. It is state of having heavy amount of information to make a decision or remain abreast about the topic).

One other off-shoot of this"information explosion" or "information overload"is plagiarism because information explosion has made plagiarism a besetting sin. Stress and plagiarism are two buzz words of today's society.

Plagiarism is the "Wrongful appropriation" and "Stealing and publication" of another author's "Language, thoughts, ideas or expression" and the representation of them as "once own original work" [1-2].

The idea remains problematic with unclear definitions and unclear rules[3-5]. The modern concept of plagiarism as immoral and originality as an ideal emerged in Europe only in the 18th century, particularlywith romantic movement as per etymological dictionary of the Latin languages it is plagiarism=plagiary(N)-ism; plagiarist, literary thief. Therefore form Latin Plagiarises is "Kidnapper, reducer, plenderes,, one who kidnaps the child or solve of another." Pagiare is "to kidnap according to Frances Edward Jockson "Plagiarism" means the crime of kidnapping. In English the term fast was used byBenjonson in 1601 the word appeared in dictionary in 1755[6-8].

In this knowledge information age and information explosion, copying and cheating is becoming the easy way for many students/research scholars.Theterm plagiarism, its relevance, consequences, and other things related there to become important to be defined.

## DEFINITION OF PLAGIARISM

According to Oxford Dictionary "Plagiarism can be defined as taking someone else's work and pretending it to be your own work" It is in fact more than simply copying someone else's work [2].

## IN MERRIAM-WEBSTER ONLINE DICTIONARY "PLAGARIZE MEANS"

- To steal and pass off (the ideas or words of another) as one's own
- To use (another's production) without crediting the source
- To commit literary theft
- To present as new and original, and idea or product derived from an existing source.

**BelaGripp (2014) opined** that academic plagiarism encompasses "the use of ideas, concepts, words or structures without appropriately acknowledging the source to benefit in a setting where originality is expected[9].

These can be consideration as plagiarism:

- Changing words but copying the sentences, as such. Moreover, without giving credit to the original writer.
- Copying too much from any source is a case of plagiarism whether you admit it or not in your article.

- Never forget to put your sentences borrowed from any source in inverted commas.

**"T Fishman (2009)** is of the opinion that plagiarism occurs when someone:

- Uses words, ideas or work products.
- Attributing the work to the source from it has been obtained
- In a situation when there is legitimate expectation of original authorship.
- In order to gain some benefit, credit or gain which need not be monetary [10].

According to O'Connor (2015), plagiarism is an academic dishonesty and breach of journalistic ethics. It is subject to sanctions like penalties, suspension etc. identified in academia [11].

### From Legal Eyes

Although plagiarism in some context is considered theft or stealing, the concept does not exist in a legal sense, although the use of someone elses works in order to gain academic credit may meet some legal definitions of fraud [12]. "Plagiarism" specially is not mentioned in any current statute, either criminal or civil [13-7]. Some cases may be treated as unfair competition or a violation of the doctrine of moral rights[7]. The increased availability of copyrighted material due to the development of information technology has furthered the debate as to whether copyright offences are criminal. In short, people are asked to use the guideline, "if you did not write it yourself, you must give credit" Gabriel(2010)[14].

Plagiarism is not the same as copyright infringement. While both terms may apply to a particular act, they are different concepts, and false claims of authorship generally constitute plagiarism regardless of whether the material is protected by copyright. Copyright infringement is a violation of the right of a copyright holder, when material whose use is restricted by copyright is used without consent. Plagiarism, in contrast, is credit, that is achieved through false claims of authorship. Thus, plagiarism is considered a moral offense against the plagiarist's audience (for example, a reader, listener, or teacher) (http:/en.wikipedia.09/wiki/plagiarism.)

Plagiarism is also considered a moral offense against anyone who has provided the plagiarist with a benefit in exchange for what is specifically supposed to be original content (for example, the plagiarist's publisher, the plagiarist's or teacher). In such cases, acts of plagiarism may sometimes also form part of a claim for breach of the plagiarist's contract, or, if done knowingly, for a civil wrong.

## TYPES OF PLAGIARISM

The plagiarism can be classified into different types on the basis of characteristic, the basis of the degree to which academic dishonesty has been committed. The main categories are as under [15]:

**Ghost Writers :** In which writer claims another writer's work word-for-word, as his or her own original work as a verbatim copy.

**Photocopy :** It includes copying of significant portion of text straight from a single source, without making any improvement, alternation.

**The Pothiek Paper :** In this type the writer writes in disguise plagiarism by copying from several different sources, altering a few sentences and paragraphs here and there to provide rational continuation in the ideas while retaining most of rational continuation in the ideas while retaining most of original paraphrasing in a clandestine manner.

**The self-stealer :** The writer "borrows" generously from his or her previous publications, violating criterion of expectation of originality embarked by different educational institutions.

**Rogeting :** When students, research scholars, teachers resort to change words in a large number so that anti plagiarism software could not able to check it by substituting synonyms for sufficient words.

The common thread among all types plagiarism cited above is that in all of above the sources of original work is not referenced.

There are some other types of plagiarism where though the sources of original works are cited, yet they are labelled as plagiarised works. These are:

**Forgotton footnote :** In this the author mention author's name for a source, but omit specific information pertaining to the location of the material quoted. This technique if adopted marks other forms of plagiarism by cancelling source location.

**Resourceful citer :** In such writings where the line between compiling and plagiarizing is so thin, difficult to be noticed. The writer here properly quote all sources, paraphrasing and using quotations appropriately but in reality the paper contains almost no original work but it looks like any other well-researched document. Misinformed in such writings, the writer provides wrong information regarding the source, making it impossible for anyone interested in finding them.

## ACCIDENTAL PLAGIARISM

Sometime the author has never read an article or the piece ofwriting, but has unknowingly committed plagiarism. In such cases the author choses to write on the topic on which someone has already written, and conveys the same ideas with a similarity in his/her paper. He/she may be with a similarity in his/her paper. He/she may be accused of plagiarism. Because one could have read accused of plagiarism. Because one could have read a piece of writing and forgotten that he had actually read it. Somewhere if one thought or idea turn out to have been influenced by a source that he/she might read somewhere but failed to acknowledge for any reason, he/ she could be guilty of plagiarism.

## Paraphrasing and Plagiarism

Changing a few words with the help of synonyms from on original writing is not paraphrasing but then plagiarism a combination of first stealing them hiding the references of the original service in paraphrasing the writer is supposed to make significant alterations in the style, texts of the original writing while retaining the ideas conveyed in the original text. But if the original text could be identifiable and has not been fully acknowledged then it lead to plagiarism.

## ACADEMIC PLAGIARISM

Plagiarism is now considered to be an academic sin by universities all over the world. Within academia, plagiarism by students, professors, or researchers is considered academic dishonesty or academic fraud, and offenders are subject to academic censure, up to and including expulsion. Many institutions use plagiarism detection software to uncover potential plagiarism and to deter students with through plagiarizing. Most universities address the issue of academic integrity by providing students with through orientations, required writing courses, and clearly articulated honour codes. Indeed, there is a virtually uniform understanding among college students that plagiarism is wrong. Nevertheless, each year students are brought before their institutions' disciplinary boards on charges that they have misused sources in their school work". LIPSON (2003) [16]

However, the practice of plagiarizing by use of sufficient word substitutions to elude detention software, known as rogeting, has rapidly evolved as students and unethical academics seek to stay ahead of detection.

Grove (2014) [17]Software an extreme form of plagiarism, known as contract cheating involves students paying someone else, such as an essay mill, to do their work for them. (Newton and Lang (2016)[12].

Susan (2010)[18] viewed that predicted upon an expected level of learning/comprehension having been achieved, all associated academic accreditation becomes serious by undermined of plagiarism is allowed to become the norm within academic submissions.

## WORLD'S DIFFERENT INSTITUTIONS OF HIGHER LEARNING DEFINED PLAGIARISM AS UNDER

The boundary between plagiarism and research is often unclear. It ever includes copying from unpublished works plagiarism is usually discovered by students and researchers during the continuance of their research.

- Stanford sees plagiarism as the "use, without giving reasonable and appropriate credit to or acknowledging the author or source, of another person;s original work, whether such work is made up of code, formulas, ideas, language, research, strategies, writing or other form[19].
- Yale views plagiarism as the ".....use of another's work, words, or ideas without attribution, "which includes"......using a source 's language without quoting, using information from a source without attribution, and parapharasing a source in a form that stays too close to the original."[20]
- Princeton perceives plagiarism as the "deliberate" use of" someone else's language, ideas, or other original (not common-knowledge) material without acknowledging its source".[21]
- Oxford college of Emory University characterizes plagiarism as the use of "a writer's ideas or phraseology without giving due credit.
- Brown defines plagiarism as "........ appropriating anotherperson's ideas or words (spoken or written) without attributing those word or ideas to their true source."[22]

## COMMON FORMS OF STUDENT'S PLAGIARISM

According to "The Reality and Solution of College Plagiarism"[23]created by the Health informatics Department of University of Illinois (Chicago) there are 10 main forms of plagiarism that students commit:

- Submitting someone's work as their own work.
- Taking passages form their own previous work without adding citations.
- Re-writing someone's work without properly citing sources.
- Using quotations, but not citing the source.
- Interweaving various sources together in the work without citing.
- Citing some, but not all passages that should be cited.
- Melding together cited and uncited sections of the piece.
- Providing proper citations, but fails to change the structure and wording of the borrowed ideas enough.
- Inaccurately citing the source.
- Relying too heavily on other people's work. Fails to bring original thought into the text.

## FACTORS INFLUENCING STUDENTS DECISION TO PLAGIARIZE

Several studies investigated factors that influence the decision to plagiarize. For example, a panel study with students from German Universities found that academic procrastination predicts the frequency plagiarism conducted within six months followed the measurement of academic procrastination[24]. It has been argued that by plagiarizing students cope with the negative consequences that result from academic procrastination such as poor grades. Another study found that plagiarism is more frequent if students perceive plagiarism as beneficial and if they have the opportunity to plagiarize[25]. When students had expected higher sanctions and when they had internalized social norms that define plagiarism as very objectionable, plagiarism was less likely to occur.

## REFERENCES

1. 1995 Random House Copact Unabridged Dictionary.
2. Djdj
3. U(1959) quotation: (p.40) "The boundaries between permissible and impermissible, imitation, stylistic plagiarism, copy, replica and forgery remain nebulous."
4. Haywood (1987) P.109, QUOTING Arnau
5. Eco (1987) p. 202,quoting Arnau
6. Lynch (2002)
7. Green, Stuart P. (2002). "Plagiarism, Norms, and the Limits of Theft Law: Some observations on the Use of Criminal Sanctions in Enforcing Intellectual Property Rights". Hastings Law Journal. 54 (1). SSRN 315562
8. Valpy, Francis Edward Jackson (2005). Etymological Dictionary of the Latin Language. P.345. "entry for plagium, quotation:"the crime of kidnapping"
9. Gipp, Bela (2014).Citation-based Plagiarism detection Disguised and Cross-language Plagiarism using Citation Pattern Analysis. Springer Vieweg. ISBN 978-3-658-06393-1. P.10.
10. Fishman, Teddi (Sep 28-30, 2009). "We know it when we see it is not good enough: toward a standard definition of plagiarism that transcends theft, fraud, and copyright" (PDF). Proceedings of the 4th Asia Pacific Conference on Educational Integrity. P.5.
11. O'Connor,Z (2015) Extreme_Plagiarism_The_rise_of_the_e-Idiot_2015_)
12. Newton, Philip M.;Lang, Christopher (1 January 2016). Bretag, Tracey, ed. Handbook of Academic Integrity. Springer Singapore. pp. 249-271. Doi:10.1007/978-981-287-098-8_38-via link.springer.com.

13. Landa, Robert (1999) *Plagiarism is no Crime* (http:/ www.theaoi.com/articles/texts/1999/decplagiarism. html)published by the Association of illustrators (aoi), December 1999.Quatation.

14. Gabrel, Trip (1 August 2010). "Plagiarism Lines Blur for Students in Digital Age". The New York Times.

15. http://www.legalserviceindia.com/article/1222-plagiarism.html

16. Lipson, Abigail (2003). "The Responsible Plagiarist". *About Campus*. 8-issue 3:7.

17. Grove, Jack (7 August 2014). "Sinister buttocks? Roget would blush at the crafty cheek Middlesex lecturer gets to the bottom of meaningless phrases found while marking essays". Times Higher Education. Retrieved 15 July 2015.

18. Susan D. Blum, *MY Word!*: Plagiarism and College Culture (2010)

19. "What is Plagiarism" (*http://studentaffairs.stanford.edu/judicialaffairs/integrity/plagiarism*). Stanford University.

20. "What is Plagiarism" (*http://writing*. Yalecollege. Yale.edu/ what –plagiarism). Yale College. 2012-07-27.

21. "Defining and Avoiding Plagiarism: The WPA Statement on Best Practices"(*http://wpacouncil.org/positions/ WPA plagiarism.pdf*). Princeton University. 2012-07-27

22. "Student Honor Code" (*http://oxford.emory.edu/audiences/ current_students/Academic/academic-success/students-honor-code /*). Emory: Oxford College.2010-07-27.

23. The Reality and Solution of College Plagiarism (*http:// healthinformatics.uic.edu/infographics/the-reality-and-solution-of-college-plagiarism/*) University of Illinois at Chicago.

24. Patrzek, J.;Sattler, S.;VanVeen, F.;Grunschel, C.;Fries, S.((2014). "Investigating the Effect of Academic Procrastination on the Frequency and Variety of Academic Misconduct: A Panel Study". *Studies in Higher Education:*1-16.doi:10.1080/03075079.2013.854765.

25. Sebastian Sattler, Peter Graeff, and Sebastian Willen: Explaining the decision to plagiarize: An Empirical Test of the interplay Between Rationality, Norms, and opportunity. In: Deviant Behavior. 34,2013, S 444-463.

# 25

# Document Reproduction (Reprography and Micrography)

***Dr. Bramha Prakash Srivastava***
*Assistant Professor, Library*
*D.S.N.P.G. College, Unnao (U.P.)*

## 1. INTRODUCTION

Document reproduction is the process of creating copies from a source document. Reproduction is an important stage in the preparation of documents for reference, information, engineering, designing and administration. The term reprography was first used in 1954 to denote all types of facsimile reproduction of documents. It signifies a group of mechanical devices whereby one or multiple copies of document can be produced through copying and duplicating process. Copies of any document can be reproduced quickly and economically through reprographic methods. Its advantages became manifest when one thinks that it is no longer possible for any individual or institution to get all the material needed for academic, research and other activities. It is thus applied widely in processing information by making copies of published or unpublished material, rare documents, manuscripts, pages of periodicals, books, newspapers, graphic materials etc. No information centre/ library can function effectively if it is not equipped with requisite document reproduction facilities. Reprography has become an essential part of information storage and retrieval systems and is an important tool for efficient communication and dissemination of information. It comprehended reproduction techniques such as Photostat; microfilming and contact printing by the silver halide process, now it is also includes a wide range of processes which make use of heat-sensitive papers or static electricity for the production of images.

## 2. DEFINITION OF REPROGRAPHY

According to Oxford Dictionary: Reprography is the science and practice of copying, producing document and graphic material.

According to Wikipedia: Reprography is the reproduction of graphics through mechanical or electrical means such as photography, or xerography.

Reprography is commonly used in catalogs and archives as well as in architectural, engineering, and construction industries.

Peter G. Nen defines reprography such as: "photocopying, micro copying, duplicating and in plant printing and it is in general characterized by the small scale of its operations and the non-professional nature of its operatives.

T.P.Saxena writes that reprography signifies all the various activities and techniques associated with the facsimile reproduction of documents. Microfilm, microprint, Photostat, reflex copy, xerography, thermo fax, diazo offset and all other bewildering varieties of processes used for making copies of documents constitute reprography."

## 3. IMPORTANCE OF DOCUMENT PRODUCTION

Reprography facilities access to documents and play an important role in the communication of information such as:-

a. As we know Library is a growing organism and reprography takes valuable space, so it becomes difficult to store this huge collection, particularly of wood-pulp newspapers and periodical holdings. By using microforms, their bulk can be much reduced which save precious space in the library.

b. Rare and out of print documents can be placed at the service of the clientele through microforms .It also helps in the preservation of rare and fragile manuscripts by providing cheap and easily handled copies.

c. This facility also helps to share precious and rare books / documents to users which the libraries do not want to share through inter-library-loan. It also helps in procuring expensive material at low cost by using reprographic techniques. During wars originals cab be kept in safe custody and their facsimile reproduction can be made available without any danger or loss.

d. Now it is possible to copy a document as a whole, a page from originals, a small part of a document containing experimental data, a chart or a diagram in research paper through print out devices, which save the time and energy of the researchers.

e. Many times, one is unable to get hold of documents, even some of the important papers because someone else may be using the originals. So the reprographic techniques help in prompt duplication and reproduction of large mass of textual and graphic material to make it available to those who need of it across the space.

f. By reprographic techniques permanent copies of the originals can be obtained even in the cases where the original document itself is in a poor condition or otherwise physically not durable.

## 4. TYPES OF DOCUMENT REPRODUCTION METHOD

Document reproduction methods can be divided in two categories:

A. Photographic Copying Process

B. Micro-Recording Process

### A. Photographic Copying Process

Photographic process enables librarian to have photocopies of any size enlarged, reduced or full size. This process can be further divided into two groups, i.e. wet process and dry process. Wet processing includes techniques like : Photostat, lithography, reflex copying, direct positive copying and heliographic dyeline methods or diazo printing.

Dry processing includes such techniques as xerography, copyflo, thermo fax and copy cat diazothern.

The latest technological advancements have added new dimensions to the usefulness of copies. The telecommunication, computing and reproduction technology have been integrated for transmission of information across the world. Copiers with greater speeds and capacities for making 3-dimensional copies are making their way in the market. A few of them are Stereoscopic copier, Column-on-colour copier, Digital copier, Three –in- one, Bubble Jet copier etc.

### B. Micro-Recording Processes or Micrography or Microform

Micro-recording processes consists of microfilm, micro-opaques, microfiche, filmstrip, COM (Computer Output Microfilm) and CD-ROM.

Microform is a generic term used to refer to all records of human readable documents which require magnification devices for reading and reviewing, micro format, micromedia, micro image, optical storage and micrographics are the alternative terms. Microforms offer a method of storage retrieval and display of images recorded on microfilm or any other magnetic media.

The application of micrography in documentation of scientific material especially in the form of microfilm, micro card, microfiche, ultra fiche, film strips and computer stored media are fairly in use particularly in western countries.

The Indian Copyright Act 1954, amended in 1956 permits exclusive right over his work to the author during his life time and 50 years after his death. But under the heading of "fair dealing and copying by libraries documentation and information centres under specified conditions" making of photocopies and micro recording of documents for the research and private study does not tantamount to be an infringement of the copyright act.

## CONCLUSION

A wide variety of reprographic techniques are available which has its own advantages and disadvantages. It is also important to know that every method is not appropriate for every kind of reproductory work. This technique offers a very good opportunity for academic, special and technical libraries not only for maintaining a systematic and classified record of scientific knowledge, but also providing the whole or any required portion of a book, periodicals or diagram to Academicians/ Scientists/Users promptly at lower cost.

Today reprography plays a very important role in the transmission of knowledge within library resources and services. The reprography service also helps library to preserve rare and special material and collections from being stolen or mishandled and then maintain availability of the resources. So it is clear that reprographic copies are not for sale, except at cost price. Any library/ information centre cannot work effectively without document reproduction facilities. To save valuable storage space, and to protect rare, out of print and irreplaceable materials from the ravages of war, fire, vermins or theft, the micrography has assumed great importance.

## REFERENCES

1. Khanna, J.K. "Information technology for librarians, information manager & information scientists", Agra : Y.K. Publishers, 2012, pp. 162-185.
2. *https://study.com/academy/lesson/document/reproduction.definition.methods.html.*
3. *https://en.m.wikipedia.org>wiki>repro...*

# Author Index

1. Mr. Anil Kumar Jharotia
   Librarian, Tecnia Institute of Advanced Studies
   Rohini, Delhi
   *Email : aniljharotia@yahoo.com*

2. Dr. Arul Pragasam
   Librarian, Seva Sadan's College of Education
   Ulhas Nagar, Mumbai (Maharashtra)
   *Email : arulunr@gmail.com*

3. Dr. Ashwani Yadav
   Librarian & HOD Library and Information Science
   Mandsaur University, Mandsaur (M.P.)

4. Balaji Abhimanyu Kamble
   Librarian, Hon. Shri Annasaheb Dange
   Art, Commerce & Science College
   Hatkananagle, Kolhapur (Maharashtra)
   *Email : bkamble33@gmail.com*

5. Dr. Bramha Prakash Srivastava
   Assistant Professor, Library & Information Science
   DSNPG College, Unnao (U.P.)
   *Email : bramhaprakash1969@gmail.com*

6. Mrs. Dhanwanti Sunil Bamne
   Librarian, Jaisingpur Collge,
   Jaisingpur (Maharashtra)
   *Email : dhanwantibamne@yahoo.in*

7. Jeetamoni Bhattacharya
Librarian, Biswanath College, Biswanath
Chariali, Biswanath (Assam)
*Email : jitamoni096@gmail.com*

8. Dr. Jitenedra Kumar Dubey
Librarian, Hindustan College of Science & Technology
Farah, Mathura (U.P.)
*Email : drjkdubey5@gmail.com*

9. Dr. Jayaprakash P. Hugar
Librarian, Dhyanprassarak Mandal's
College & Research Centre
Assagao, Bardez, Goa
*Email : dmclibrarian@rediffmail.com*

10. Dr. Kunwar Surendra Bhadur
Regional Director UPRTOU Allahabad
147, A Civil Line, Near Circuit House
Opp-Allahabad Bank, Bareilly
*Email : ksbuprtou@gmail.com*

11. LD Nagda
Assistant Librarian
Department of Physiotherapy
Janardhan Rai Nagar, Rajasthan
Vidyapeeth University, Udaipur, Rajasthan
*Email : ldnagda@gmail.com*

12. Meenakshi Gupta
Librarian, Deptt. Of Library & Information Science
Eternal University, Baru Sahib – (H.P.)
*Email : mgmeenakshigupta76@gmail.com*

13. Dr. Mehtab Alam Ansari
Associate Professor in
Deptt. Of Library & Information Science
At Aligarh Muslim University, Aligarh
*Email : mehtaba@rediffmail.com*

14. Mr. Mohd. Shikoh
Research Scholar
Dept. of Library & Information Science
Aligarh Muslim University, Aligarh
*Email : shikohmohd@gmail.com*

15. Mr. Mohd. Imarn Khan

16. Dr. Narendra K. Pachauri
Librarian, Kendriya Vidhyalya No-3
Agra (U.P.)
*Email : nkpagra@gmail.com*

17. Mr. Narendra K. Patidar
Research Scholar
Mandsaur University, Mandsaur (M.P.)
*Email : narendrapatidar.1067@rediffmail.com*

18. Mrs. Naurin Ashraf
Librarian, Urdu Academy
Malerkotla Distt. Sangrur
Punjab
*Email : nauash1@gmail.com*

19. Miss. Niharika Sharma
Assistant Librarian
Pandit Deendayal Upadhyaya Adarsha Mahavidyalaya
Behali, Biswanath (Assam)
*Email : niharika77900@gmail.com*

20. Mrs. Nibedita Chaudhary
Librarian, Nowgong Polytechnic College
Nagaon-Assam
*Email : nibetditachaudhary@gmail.com*

21. Nisha
Research Scholar
Baba Mastnath University
Rohtak (Haryana)
*Email : nishabalambia@gmail.com*

22. Mrs. Pankaj K. Bhardwaj
Librarian, R.D.S. Public Girls College
Rewari (Haryana)
*Email : pankajkbhardwaj9@gmail.com*

23. Dr. Pankaj Kumar Singh
Asst. Prof. Library & Info. Science
DSN PG College Unnao (UP)
*Email : dr.p.k.singh@gmail.com*

24. Dr. P.K. Dixit
Assistant Professor
SBJ Degree College, Bisawar Agra (U.P.)
*Email : pkdixitagra@gmail.com*

25. Mr. Pradeep Kumar Gupta
Research Scholar
Mandsaur University, Mandsaur (M.P.)
*Email : pradeep.madhu2007@gmail.com*

26. Reena Anand
Assistant Librarian
The IIS University, Jaipur
*Email : riyareena.84@gmail.com*

27. Dr. S.M. Abbas
Documentation Officer ( Sr. Scale)
MMAJ-Academy of International Studies
Jamia Millia Islamia, New Delhi
*Email : drabbasam@gmail.com*

28. Uma Rani
Assistant Librarian
Bhai Gurdas Institute of Engineering & Technology
Sangrur Patiyala (Punjab)
*Email : umasharma762@gmail.com*

29. Urmila Rajendra Kadam
Librarian, Kamala College,
Kolhapur (Maharashtra)
*Email : kadamurmila76@yahoo.co.in*

30. Sh. Y.B. Koradur
Librarian, STC Art and Commerce College
Banhatti Distt-Bagalakoti (Karnatka)
*Email : koradur.yallapa779@gmail.com*